Wittgenstein's City

MATHEMATICS

TRACTATUS

DREAMS

SENSATION

COLOR

PAIN

EMOTION

EXPECTATION

GESTURE

Wittgenstein's City

Wittgenstein's

C I T Y

Robert John Ackermann

The University of Massachusetts Press

Amherst

Copyright © 1988 by The University of Massachusetts Press

All rights reserved

Printed in the United States of America

LC 87–10895

ISBN 0–87023–589–3 (cloth); 590–7 (paper)

Set in Linotron Trump at Rainsford Type

Printed by Cushing-Malloy and bound by John Dekker & Sons

Library of Congress Cataloging-in-Publication Data

Ackermann, Robert John, 1933–
    Wittgenstein's city.

    Bibliography: p.

    Includes index.

    1. Wittgenstein, Ludwig, 1889–1951. I. Title.

B3376.W564A64   1988   192   87–10895

ISBN 0–87023–589–3 (alk. paper)

ISBN 0–87023–590–7 (pbk. alk. paper)

British Library Cataloging in Publication Data are available

Augustine, we might say, does describe a system of communication; only not everything that we call language is this system.

INVESTIGATIONS, 3

And to say that a proposition is whatever can be true or false amounts to saying: we call something a proposition when in our language *we apply the calculus of truth functions to it.*

INVESTIGATIONS, 136

CONTENTS

PREFACE

I T IS OBVIOUS that Ludwig Wittgenstein always strove for clarity. This compulsion is illustrated in his life as well as in his philosophy. Wittgensteinian clarity differs from Cartesian clarity or phenomenological clarity in Wittgenstein's recognition that there is no transcendental point of view from which clarity can be achieved. Clarity is reached through correct forms of expression in the language that we already use, not through the discovery of supposed clarifying philosophical doctrines. We cannot get outside the interweave of language and life; all distinctions must be drawn within it, and clarity is simply a level of interpretation at which we can stop, at which a particular use of language makes sense.

Losing touch with clear ordinary usage can be easily caricatured. A woman and a man walk down a street and decide to have a donut and coffee. Their talk of donuts is restricted at first to the donuts available in the coffee shop and is under perfect control. But if the pleasure of the moment causes the participants in this scene to wonder whether the universe could also be a donut and, if so, whether it would be glazed, sentences that sound like English are being produced, but clear sense has been lost. Philosophy appears in a similar manner when illicit generalizations are made in all seriousness from ordinary sentences, even those of science and mathematics.

Philosophy is not a necessary aspect of human life. Wittgenstein was impressed with the fact that people had, at certain times and places, gotten on quite well without philosophy. If they lapsed into a few generalizations by playing with their language, it seems not to have caused much harm. Rather than adopting philosophical skepticism, Wittgenstein rejected generating philosophical doctrine. Philosophical problems can legitimately arise only as real and concrete puzzles for particular human beings, puzzles that will disappear once one considers carefully the clear use of language. Puzzles are often to be laid aside as having no solution but as resulting from linguistic confusion. Much of traditional philosophy is a peculiar chronic disease of language that refuses to recognize the inherent confusions in many questions, and Wittgenstein thought that he had found a cure.

If Wittgenstein wanted to eliminate traditional philosophy and if the excitement of reading him stems from the impulse to eliminate rubbish and leave clarity in its place, the *critical* Wittgenstein has been identified, neutralized, and eliminated. Wittgenstein's interpreters have worked at the hermeneutics of his texts, turning him relentlessly back into a philosopher with precise and complicated philosophical doctrines that are deployed against other philosophical doctrines. In a curious way, this development is a confirmation of the insight that the reader typically supplies much of the content of the text to be interpreted: philosophers have read Wittgenstein, and they have discovered him to be a philosopher. Wittgenstein's defenders have stressed the subtlety of his views, at times aping the behavioral characteristics of the master but always suggesting that others are the boors at the feast of philosophy, picking up the wrong forks and turning the wrong edge of their spoons to the soup.

Wittgenstein is liberating but flawed. To circumvent the philosophical polemics and the interpretations that have dominated the first generation of Wittgenstein scholarship, it is time to take a fresh look at Wittgenstein's texts without the hermeneutical coercion of those who trace their authority of interpretation to personal acquaintance. Recent work by David Bloor, Jaakko Hintikka, and Merrill Hintikka shows that new readings are possible that recover the excitement of Wittgenstein without the necessity of defending everything. My view is that the philosophical Wittgenstein is a product of the early interpretations of the *Tractatus* and the *Investigations* as separate, clashing texts. The clash, which Wittgenstein was well aware of, has been misinterpreted as a clash of philosophical doctrines.

I argue instead that Wittgenstein's later philosophical work restricts the domain of validity of the *Tractatus*, retaining its analysis of certain kinds of factual assertion, and rejects only its pretension to have offered a complete analysis of clear meaning and language. The same basic ideas for finding clarity run throughout Wittgenstein's work, and in a sense the later view of language is immanent in the early view, although it took Wittgenstein time to see that point. A more unified Wittgenstein can remain an antiphilosopher. The unified, critical Wittgenstein that I see would rightly strike down most of the literature interpreting his work as nonsense. This account is intended for the uncommitted. I appeal to them to contrast this account of Wittgenstein's development against standard interpretations, and to do so against the full range of texts.

This study is a caricature of Wittgenstein's development, a caricature forced by a desire to survey his development on a scale allowing for a comprehensible orientation. Some legitimation for this approach can be snatched from the fact that Wittgenstein himself was not afraid of caricature. Caricature, as he noted, can enable us to notice features and resemblances that might otherwise be lost in complexity. This study must also disconnect Wittgenstein's doctrine from Wittgenstein's life, doing a disservice to the Wittgenstein who insisted that legitimate philosophy had to be done by individuals in the service of untangling their own anxieties and confusions. On Wittgenstein's view, however, we speak a common language, so that we should encounter the same intrinsic reference points in any survey of language undertaken to resolve philosophical confusions. This is a book about the salient points of Wittgenstein's survey of the terrain of language, and not a book about Wittgenstein's philosophy. Wittgenstein's philosophy was interwoven with a life that is largely inaccessible to us.

Wittgenstein's survey of language and his philosophy are not ultimately separable, hence what comes must be caricature, an attempt to transmit what may be communicable to others (for use in their own philosophical investigations). The immanent approach to language involved in Wittgenstein's philosophy, and measured in the small scale by the fragments of which his writings were always composed, threatened constantly to lapse into private language, a prospect that produced a terrible anxiety in Wittgenstein. His contrary impulse was to assemble these fragments into the kind of book about language that could win him justified fame, such as the book on philosophical grammar that he once contemplated writing. This book would have had chapter headings such as "Color," "Tone," "Number," etc.; but Wittgenstein never completed the relevant grammatical investigations. These contrary impulses are both coded into the contrast between local puzzles and horizons of meaning that are involved with the conception of Wittgenstein's one-step hermeneutics to be developed below. Wittgenstein must have hated himself when he gave way to the impulse to arrange his fragments into books, since by his own lights this threatened a lapse into the incoherent generalizations of philosophy. No effort is made here to reproduce Wittgenstein's torments, but only to give an account of Wittgenstein's temptation to the book, a temptation that yields Wittgenstein's transmittable legacy to later philosophers. It is only the doctrines of the book's manuscripts, reflected into our own philosophical anxieties and puzzles, that can ultimately reveal why Wittgenstein's struggle for clarity was so different from Russell's.

Wittgenstein could never have completed his investigations in the sense that Russell kept on completing his investigations. In the caricature that follows, Wittgenstein's investigations are "completed," but only for a special purpose, and in complete admiration for the integrity of the thought that this caricature preys upon.

Wittgenstein's City

One

PANORAMA

T HE LIFE of Wittgenstein was quite different from the lives of most of those who later extolled him as perhaps the major philosopher of the twentieth century. He was born into the large family of a wealthy Austrian industrialist in 1889 and was educated at home until he was a teenager. Music was an important means of expression in the Wittgenstein family, in whose circle Brahms was a familiar acquaintance. Wittgenstein himself could whistle entire concertos and played the clarinet as a release from other pressures. His brother Paul, in spite of losing one arm, became a renowned concert pianist, for whom much of the contemporary repertoire for one hand at the piano was written. Three other brothers committed suicide, perhaps a comment on the expectations generated in this familial setting, and there were also three sisters, for one of whom Wittgenstein later designed and built a house. Wittgenstein began a serious study of science, which led him to the study of aeronautical engineering in England and to a patent application in 1910 for hollowed propellers for aircraft engines. The hollowed nature of the propellers permitted them to function as intake manifolds and combustion chambers for the aircraft engine itself.[1] His engineering study seems to have interested him in the nature of mathematics, which led him somehow to Frege and Russell, who were at that time engaged in philosophical studies of the foundations of mathematics.

Wittgenstein studied at Cambridge with Russell, and then, after working alone in Norway on logic, he returned to Austria during

3

the First World War as a volunteer in the artillery, where he earned citations for bravery as an observer. These years show two prominent features of Wittgenstein's life. The decision to volunteer represented a commitment to coercive values for which Wittgenstein thought no discursive justification could be given. At the same time, Wittgenstein worked almost daily at recording notes on philosophical problems into a series of notebooks. This method of developing his thoughts became his habit. These early notes were later organized and edited into the manuscript of the *Tractatus*, a manuscript that he had with him in prison camp at the end of the war.

Considering that his *Tractatus* had solved the problems of philosophy, Wittgenstein turned to the life of a village schoolteacher. This step again represented important values, but the compulsion of the values ran into the realities of the situation in such a way that Wittgenstein, who was constantly in difficulty with local parents, wrestled with the possibility of his own suicide. He had given away a rather large inheritance early in this period and now returned in 1926 to work as a monastery gardener. Invited to work on the construction of his sister's house in Vienna, Wittgenstein moved there and gradually began to discuss philosophy and his views in the already-famous *Tractatus* with Schlick, Waismann, Carnap, Feigl, and other members of the Vienna Circle. Dissatisfied now with some of the views of the *Tractatus*, he decided to return to Cambridge to work on philosophy, where he was ultimately granted a Ph.D. on the basis of the authorities' considering the *Tractatus* retrospectively as a dissertation.

In following years, Wittgenstein alternated between Vienna and Cambridge, giving a series of lectures in Cambridge during the early 1930s. The notes associated with these lectures and Wittgenstein's ongoing collections of remarks developed into the manuscripts from which ultimately the *Investigations* was assembled. After a visit to the Soviet Union and then another stay in Norway, Wittgenstein returned to Cambridge and became a British citizen. During the Second World War, Wittgenstein again served as a volunteer, this time as a medical orderly in London and Newcastle upon Tyne. He returned to his duties as professor of philosophy at Cambridge, where he was Moore's successor, but found the formal teaching of philosophy to be a living death and an exercise in artificiality. A visit to the local movie house was always more salutary for him than reading a journal of philosophy. True once again to the forces and values that drove him, he left academic life and settled in Ireland, until his health disintegrated under the ravages of cancer. He died in Cambridge in 1951.[2]

This biography reveals an apparent academic outsider who may have written—in German—the two most influential books for English-speaking philosophers of the twentieth century. As an outsider at Cambridge, he appeared awkward and tormented, and his English was not fluent. He often lectured in English by producing bursts of a few sentences that were bracketed by tortured silences. And yet this outsider became an insider and a living legend, a fact that is not to be explained by the argumentative weight of his two masterworks, for they seem to the uninitiated to be unintelligible—and they seem to professional philosophers to require serious efforts at interpretation to yield any sense at all.

It is essential to know something of the atmosphere surrounding Wittgenstein at Cambridge, the gossamer network of reputation and fashion, in order to grasp the nature of the interest centered on Ludwig Wittgenstein. Russell's brilliance was already established, and although he seems not to have understood Wittgenstein (and no doubt, vice versa), Russell's admiration and protection appear to have been crucial. If Wittgenstein became interested in philosophy through working at Russell's calculi, perhaps believing at the time that they held the key to his own problems, Russell may have thought that Wittgenstein's insights were essential to the philosophical application of his calculi to ordinary language. It might have been crucial that neither was, by wider European standards, terribly cultivated. They both seem to have read only sporadically and somewhat superficially in literature and philosophy, a fact that allowed them to meet in the plane of mathematics, Russell with overwhelming technical brilliance, and Wittgenstein with a sobering and cautious concern for its ultimate meaning. His early fame assured by his connection with Russell and kept alive by his reputation for genius, Wittgenstein's *Investigations* appeared in prepared soil. The legend of Wittgenstein was already formed. The *Tractatus* and the *Investigations* simply had to be interpreted.

The reception of Wittgenstein has largely taken the following lines. Scholars have paid the most attention to his two classics, published roughly thirty years apart. They have noted Wittgenstein's observation that the second work was the product of dissatisfaction—even disgust—with the first work. Early supporters of Wittgenstein accepted the incompatibility of the *Tractatus* and the *Investigations.* Either they chose the *Tractatus* as the rigorous early classic, regarding the *Investigations* as marking the deterioration of a great mind, or they chose the *Investigations* as the definitive correction of the repudiated errors in the earlier *Tractatus* and as the statement of an ultimately defensible philosophy.[3]

Wittgenstein's early supporters, no matter which of the classics they preferred, found it hard to believe that he could be correctly understood and criticized. The novelty of Wittgenstein's approach and his cultic status produced intense conviction. Now that the influence of Wittgenstein's personality is fading, however, the question of interpreting Wittgenstein's texts can be approached in new ways. One might suggest the overtly Wittgensteinian move of introducing complexity into the scene whose major features are still the *Tractatus*, the *Investigations*, and their alleged incompatibility. With some brief exceptions, Wittgenstein seems to have worked daily at a very steady rate of production of philosophical observations and remarks for about forty years, producing a complex panorama in which related topics recycle and develop over time. Concentration on the *Tractatus* and the *Investigations* may seem justified because these works were published over Wittgenstein's name (the latter posthumously), but Wittgenstein's method of working suggests that the meaning and significance of these works is not independent of the context from which they are assembled.

The *Tractatus* and the *Investigations* are most appropriately seen as two assemblages from this vast collage of material, not as two conflicting books for which some rigid relationship of comparative worth is to be found. With this more complex context in place, Wittgenstein's supporters and those who find his work a clutch of unsupported and unsupportable opinions can shift the black and white of controversy into a more detached observation of heterogeneous detail. Wittgenstein's corpus then appears quite differently.[4] In the following study, I indicate how a detailed reading of Wittgenstein can be developed that avoids the judgmental choices that seem forced by the extensive body of interpretation based primarily on settled judgments concerning the *Tractatus* and the *Investigations*.

The coherence of Wittgenstein's critical and therapeutic project and his own bitter and halting adjustments to perceived errors disappear when he is studied only through a comparison of the twin towers, the *Tractatus* and the *Investigations*. Differences between these two works, especially as they have been historically reflected and magnified in positivism and ordinary-language philosophy, force an interpretation of Wittgenstein as having undergone something like a religious conversion at some point between the construction of the two major works.

Scholarship based primarily on the *Tractatus* and the *Investigations* has produced detailed philosophical interpretations of these two works that have fixed certain parameters for the exploration of the other texts as they have become available. This scholarship is enormous, and it is not simply incorrect, since in some sense it fits the texts that it is concerned with. It has produced a Wittgenstein, however, who cannot allegedly be understood apart from an enormous critical literature that is accessible only to specialists. Philosophical scholarship asserts that Wittgenstein is always saying more than he seems to be saying in any local context, so that attempts to summarize penetrating local insights in Wittgenstein are countered by a protective layer of extenuating sophistication, claiming that anything short of a feeling for Wittgenstein's entire corpus as the context of interpretation will undoubtedly distort the meaning of any isolated passage. This scholarship then protects itself further by reference to the enormous difficulty that Wittgenstein found in arranging his own remarks. In short, the extensive literature available has produced readings of the *Tractatus* and the *Investigations* as fixed sets of ideas that contradict one another, and the larger corpus is then interpreted as charting the voyage of Wittgenstein's thought from the *Tractatus* to the *Investigations*. The complexity of this voyage is thought to preclude any reasonably clear overview of Wittgenstein's path, an overview that would in any case conflict with Wittgenstein's cautions about generalization.

It is time to challenge this conception of the complexity of Wittgenstein's voyage with another orientation, one that can do justice to Wittgenstein's intentions without a commitment his being infallible. Here I claim that Wittgenstein always operated with an immanent understanding of language, according to which, when we have a puzzle that seems to call for philosophical treatment, some localized language usage is recognized as perfectly clear, and other language usage as obscure. To solve philosophical puzzlement, we can use our present ability to recognize these crude distinctions in order to resolve what is obscure by a study of what is relatively clear.

Wittgenstein was not a philosopher with doctrine but a thinker who viewed philosophy as the project of resolving unclarity in thought by close attention to linguistic detail. The basis for the philosophical task of removing unclarity is always already available to us, if we take care in observing it. Philosophy uses language to repair itself, just as a book written in English about better writing can help one to write better by a self-imposed discipline of identifying some clear simple cases of generally agreed upon usage and by carefully building up complicated structures in terms of these clear basic cases. Wittgenstein's philosophical survey invokes no special terms, no special worlds, and no special doctrines but proceeds as though we already have the tools of analysis that we need to resolve linguistic and conceptual puzzlements. Wittgenstein's key to philosophical analysis was to discover a network of clear horizons of understanding that are implicit in our language but that are typically not respected when language becomes confused. These horizons are not easy to discern in our confusion, but they are already there to be traced out, after which our confusions should disappear when we are able to orient ourselves to the relevant horizons.

Before Wittgenstein, philosophical systems assumed that ordinary language, or ordinary expression, was ordinary in the sense that it was too crude to deal with the rarified, subtle, and complex questions of philosophy. Philosophical systems then impose a supposedly clarified structure on ordinary language, coining new language in the process, as though language could be circumvented and the structure of reality observed directly. Wittgenstein notes that all such projects remain within language and must be communicated in language, even though philosophers may deceive themselves into believing that they can survey the inadequacies of language only from a neutral standpoint. Ordinary language is not to be condemned as an instrument that is too crude for philosophical purposes. All language use, including philosophical and scientific usage, is merely an exploitation of the potentialities that are already inherent within ordinary language. If we cannot vault ourselves outside language, we need to make distinctions within it and recognize when language is being misused, or where language is obscure, by utilizing our linguistic intuitions with respect to the clear use of language. What may seem clear can turn obscure and vice versa, but this historical and personally observed fact must not tempt us into trying for certainty in a system, since our observations of clear usage will remain the only basis, no matter how shifting, for the removal of puzzlement.

Sometimes in our linguistic usage experience, behavior, and language seem completely coordinated, and we can say only one thing, aware that it is true (or false) and could not be otherwise. Because language and experience are interwoven in these locutions, perhaps as the result of something like linguistic natural selection, we cannot imagine that different behavior or experience could follow if we were to change the syntax of our language arbitrarily. Sentences at these hinge points seem to expose the structure of reality directly, but other sentences that are developed with implicit reference to these points will typically not be certain, even if their meaning, when clear, can be traced to such hinge points. The sentences at the hinge points appear on the horizons of language; we can find them when we note where meaning seems to break down, but we cannot explain why they are as they are. Wittgenstein works to achieve clarity where there is unclear usage by surveying to find the relevant hinge points within language, by surveying to note carefully where language seems to turn into nonsense in a peculiar grammatical way. When the relevant hinge points are found, the philosopher should stop and use the results of the survey to resolve the problematic obscurities that initiated the survey. At any given time, the task is to survey language sufficiently to remove local problematic usages.

Wittgenstein did not think that all of language could be surveyed, for there could be no extralinguistic perspective from which the result of such a survey could be stated. An effort to explain hinge points themselves, rather than merely locating them in language, leads inevitably into the philosophical nonsense that characterizes the vast metaphysical systems. For Wittgenstein, there is no clarity other than the clarity of settled linguistic usage, and therefore his resolution of perplexity stops when clear usage yields the horizons that allow specific puzzles to be resolved. Any attempt to do more than note the clear usage and the horizons marked by hinge points to resolve puzzlement is self-defeating and slips away into philosophical explanations and philosophical nonsense.

The first horizon that Wittgenstein discovered was the true/false structure of factual assertion. Any clear factual assertion can be broken down into a truth function of elementary factual assertions whose truth or falsity is perfectly clear on observation. Obscure, puzzling factual assertions are simply those for which the truth function and the constituent elementary factual assertions are not clearly specified. In our general language use, the clear use of language moves within implicit horizons of meaning that yield only to philosophical investigation. Such investigation ultimately establishes the fact that unclear usage is usually associated with movement that is uncertain with respect to these horizons.

The tracing of the first horizon took years of exhausting intellectual labor, culminating in Proposition 6 of the *Tractatus.* Horizons thus are not obvious to inspection and are given only implicitly in the language that we speak. They have to be found by delicately probing the limits of what we can say. We can speak correctly in our native language without being able to cite or explain its grammatical structure. Grammatical structures and all of the limits on what we can say yield only to explicit investigation. Having found these structures, we can use them to straighten out puzzlements about obscure or complicated expression. Wittgenstein uses this technique for all language usage, not just for the question of correct syntax. Horizons must be carefully traced by noting where clear language develops into nonsense on its own terms or where it turns into nonsense in some special way. The first horizon, that of factual assertion, is given by sentences that are apparently nonsensical and do not say anything because they are always true or always false. The tracing of this horizon in the *Tractatus* seems to have solved the problems Wittgenstein confronted at the time, and he stopped doing philosophy; that is, he stopped stretching language to the limits of intelligibility in deliberate philosophical analysis because the *Tractatus* had ended his puzzlement. He later returned to philosophy because he began to suspect that the single horizon of the *Tractatus* had to be replaced by a complicated network of horizons and language games, the latter having associated local horizons.

Language is conceived by Wittgenstein as divided up into areas within which clear expression and usage are possible. Language games provide local horizons that can sometimes be completely spelled out, using the resources of the language that we already speak. These horizons will be interwoven with human activities, and although they permit clear usage within their boundaries, their limits will be marked by sentences that are not clear and that represent the limits of clarity of some kind. Philosophers can find these horizons by putting pressure on clear usage, noticing where it gives way systematically to nonsense of a special kind. All of the sentences on the horizon of the *Tractatus* can be characterized in this way, marking the point at which ordinary clear factual meaning gives way to a puzzling, if not nonsensical, form of pseudoassertion.

In the later philosophy, the horizons are those of language games. Mathematics is described as a grouping of related language games. The language games of mathematics resemble one another in that surveyable proofs determine whether a mathematical sentence or its negation can be asserted in a game, but they differ in the details of their domains and in the details of the allowable proofs. Because mathematics uses language differently than does factual assertion, mathematics will have a kind of mathematical grammar in each language game. Specific language games, which can at times be completely analyzed, provide the horizons for philosophical analysis. The independence of the elementary sentences of the *Tractatus* is taken over into the independence of language games. One language game can be changed without affecting (necessarily) another language game. If their horizons are disjoint, they are completely independent. In addition to the specific nonsense, marking the limits of clear language usage (literally, the possible limits of sense), there can also be another kind of nonsense produced by linguistic confusion, a cobbling together of language that does not fit within appropriate horizons.

Wittgenstein's later view is captured in a remarkable image: "Our language can be seen as an ancient city: a maze of little streets and squares, of old and new houses, and of houses with additions from various periods; and this surrounded by a multitude of new boroughs with straight regular streets and uniform houses."[5] Wittgenstein had first surveyed the City while standing in a borough or suburb, the severely regular Levittown of the *Tractatus*, in which the total plan could be easily grasped. The later image locates the center of the City somewhere else and recognizes that the *Tractatus* explores only one borough of language. Every language game has roots in everyday life and everyday understanding but, in a sense, replaces and refines cruder but significant action with the potentially more sophisticated articulation of language. The different areas of the City need not be isolated; they can overlap, and clearly words may have layers of use traceable to different origins in time and related to different horizons. But then some areas of the City can have sharp boundaries, especially when they correspond to the horizons of clear language games.

One of the problems in sorting out all the complexity is that some of the areas of the City—languages of mathematics, science, emotions, and so forth—are seemingly polyglot, embracing a motley of language games whose relationship is obscure. We cannot assume that areas of the City are always clearly marked out by horizons or that ordinary-language categories will coincide with the horizons that are marked out in philosophical surveys. In the case of advanced mathematics and scientific theorizing, relevant language games can be construed as built above the common level of understanding and in danger of losing touch with it. Some apparent assertions in these areas are not really assertions but are the means of generating specific factual assertions. The sense of these generating sentences must be derived from the assertions that they generate. Except for common origins in action and in mutually recognizable behavior, the language of the City is not constructed to fit a single plan. Philosophers survey the City. They do not improve discourse, although they show how confusions can be resolved, and they cannot, as philosophers, add a special technical philosophical discourse to the life of the City. When the language games are laid down by the survey, their grammars lay out the space of possible clear assertion.

When he was a schoolteacher, Wittgenstein published a spelling list for his students, reducing problems with orthography to a matter of consulting a fixed list of correct spellings.[6] This concern illustrates the way in which language becomes interwoven with received action and usage. Questions of orthography can be settled. Wherever language seems to become mysterious or controversial, Wittgenstein analogously calls for a return to clear cases. Because we can lay down rules that articulate syntax and survey usage, questions of language lie within our control and within the resources of language as interwoven with life, allowing us the clear anticipations of meaning that are required to use language coherently. Language that cannot at all be used coherently in the light of an appropriate horizon is counterfeit. Wittgenstein's philosophical assertions show where language becomes nonsensical, thus marking a boundary. These assertions are minimally clear assertions of ordinary language, and they are not the precise assertions of a superior philosophical insight.

What is the crude, large-scale map of Wittgenstein's City? First of all, no section of the City represents logic, grammar, or philosophy. Philosophy is the process of surveying the City, constructing its map, using the fixed spaces of logic and grammar as the reference points for the survey. Logic and grammar, as well as the philosophical assertions marking their horizons, appear everywhere on City boundaries. Language is not a section of the City; language is simply spoken everywhere. The borders of language are the borders of the City. Within the City, however, recognizably distinct areas separated by boundaries correspond to distinct uses of language. One major area of the City is that of clear factual assertion, the original area surveyed by the *Tractatus.*

The first major areas that were next closely explored and found to be different in their detailed grammars from each other and from the logic of factual assertion are the areas of color and mathematics. These two areas, which were already troublesome in the *Tractatus* (although the trouble was repressed there), were found to require special survey techniques when Wittgenstein returned to a study of the notion of an elementary sentence in the late 1920s. Still in the grasp of his earlier views, he began to think that elementary sentences would have to contain numbers in addition to other symbols for names and logical constants, thus laying aside his earlier logicist tendencies, and he began to believe that one could draw inferences about the relationships of pure colors that could not be modeled in logic.[7] The most complete surveys here are to be found in Wittgenstein's *Remarks on Colour* and *Remarks on the Foundations of Mathematics.*[8] All of this activity, however, articulates the resources for the description of the physical world, in effect extending and refining the *Tractatus* project.

The great fracture in the survey came with the recognition that coherent language about the self had intruded and that the *Tractatus* had simply ignored vast tracts of controllable assertion regarding personal experience. At this point a portion of the self that had been extruded from clear language in the *Tractatus* begins to speak coherently. The self cannot ultimately be ignored, even with respect to color phenomena, since close investigation of these phenomena encounters both a physics of color and the experience of color, the latter being highly context dependent and not reducible to known laws of physics. We can note these changes occurring in the *Blue Book*.[9] At the start of that book, Wittgenstein observes that meaning can be given by verbal or ostensive means. Mathematical meaning begins as an extension of verbal resources, and color begins as an extension of ostensive resources. Later in the *Blue Book*, Wittgenstein observes that there are two worlds, a world of physical description and a world of personal experience.[10] At this point, the major areas of the City have been laid out for detailed grammatical survey.

Wittgenstein came closest to closure of the survey in the case of mathematics, and he collected his mathematical remarks separately, for the most part, from the material on philosophical psychology and general considerations of the language-game method that appears in the *Investigations*. His remarks on psychological grammar never reached the same level of secure expression as his remarks on mathematics. A number of complex topics open up in psychological grammar: seeing and seeing as, intention and expectation, feelings as represented in sensations and emotions, and pain as an important bridging concept between sensations and emotions. Philosophical psychology is a jumbled and complicated terrain whose crisscrossing horizons are most difficult to survey. *Philosophical Remarks, Philosophical Grammar, Remarks on the Philosophy of Psychology*, and large swatches of the *Investigations* are devoted to this material and its difficult reworking.[11]

It may seem that Wittgenstein's project is not so unusual, but of course part of that suspicion would occur now in a context that has been influenced by Wittgenstein, since such movements as conceptual analysis and various forms of linguistic semantics have been heavily influenced by Wittgenstein's work. Although immanent analysis of language can be traced to philosophers before Wittgenstein, it is usually more piecemeal and usually in the service of a propaedeutic for some philosophical system. Formal linguistics and various kinds of scientific linguistics need not conflict with Wittgenstein's method, but Wittgenstein would be the relentless critic of any pretension that linguistic theory can provide an analysis of language from an exterior point of view. Whatever might be clarified and formulated in linguistic theory must have roots in our prior understanding and usage of language, according to Wittgenstein, and hence can provide explanation of only limited linguistic phenomena from an assumed base in clear usage. Wittgenstein would surely find modern formal linguistics to be so severely abstracted from usage that it could be only of limited use in the philosophical understanding of language. Perhaps Wittgenstein's original claims would seem most threatened by confusion with the hermeneutical tradition, which has always assumed a base in already understood language usage, yet even here Wittgenstein seems to have marked out his own turf, an observation that perhaps requires a brief excursus.

Let us consider the intuitively recognized grammatical sentence. Some hermeneuticists and philosophers have taken the clear sentence to be the unit of linguistic meaning, regarding the meaning of sentence units as built up in turn from the meanings of constituent words. The general idea involves the notion that clear sentences can always be completely understood in isolation as a function of the references assigned by semantic theory to constituent naming expressions. The *Tractatus* may seem to present such a theory, but naming expressions in the *Tractatus* cannot be assigned independent objects as references, as will be seen below in detail, although this limitation is already implicit in the fact that Wittgenstein can find no standpoint outside language of the kind that such a semantic theory must assume.

Another theory of sentential meaning is associated with hermeneutical theories that assert that the meaning of sentences can be understood only in wider linguistic contexts. The possible meanings of a particular sentence are allowed to play against the wider contexts in which it is embedded, the sentence modifying understanding of these contexts, and vice versa, until (where it is possible) a clear meaning is attained.[12] Isolated sentences are ambiguous without the provision of a wider, and suitable, context. The *Investigations* may seem to present such a theory, but the hermeneutical circle is terminated with the discovery of the meaning of a sentence when an appropriate horizon is found, and Wittgenstein has a hermeneutics that is not threatened by the endless cycles of interpretation engendered by the hermeneutical circle.

The sentence is always the unit of meaning for Wittgenstein. Even when he speaks of "moves in a language game" or develops primitive language games whose units are not articulate in the way our sentences exhibit an analyzable syntax, the discussion of meaning is always in the context of understanding sentences. To understand a sentence, one has to have a relevant context, in partial agreement with hermeneutical theory. For assertions, in the *Tractatus*, the context is logical space, and the meaning of a sentence is equivalent to its position in logical space. In the *Investigations*, relevant contexts are always given in terms of horizons or the horizons of specific language games, which can be seen as a generalization from the limited hermeneutics of the *Tractatus*. The meaning of a sentence, if it is a meaningful sentence, can be completely determined by reference to some appropriate fixed horizon of meaning, and the oscillations of hermeneutical theory are then short-circuited. The meaning is given directly because the relevant horizon is immanent in the language that we already speak. Once the appropriate horizon for the sentence is located, the precise meaning is also known. If we are still learning a new language or are being trained in one, this situation does not yet apply, because the horizons are not yet available. Wittgenstein examines only languages that we already speak, those whose horizons are immanent in our already-given use of language. The horizons block the cycles of hermeneutical theory from extending potentially into all of language. When the appropriate horizon for a sentence is located (or the appropriate set of horizons that constitutes the horizon when the sentence lies within several different horizons), its meaning can be determined completely.

This position is an original one-step hermeneutics, and it always underlies Wittgenstein's notions of dependence and independence in language. What happens outside the horizon of a sentence cannot affect the meaning of sentences within that horizon. If our color language changes, for example, it need not affect mathematics, so Wittgenstein rejects linguistic holism, but yet language does not fall apart into separate domains because horizons overlap in many cases, producing complicated interwoven horizons for certain sentences. The notion of language as a family of language games, to be described below, expresses this structural fact. Wittgenstein's use of horizons avoids the referential problems of linguistic atomism (which require links between language and the world that can be neutrally described) and the problems of hermeneutical holism (which cannot guarantee that the hermeneutical circle can ever be satisfactorily closed). Without recognition of this hermeneutical scheme, Wittgenstein's total remarks on linguistic understanding and our ability to control language cannot fit together without revealing serious breaks and strains.

The fact that we already speak a language allows the horizons of language games to come into view. Philosophy does not explain this fact; it notices it, and it uses this fact to unmask mystification and pursue the process of clarification. Many philosophical problems are caused by our considering sentences without noticing the correct horizon. Wittgenstein's generalizations about language can now be related to this conception. The same horizons may appear repeatedly over time as particular problems are addressed. For this reason we can allude to the available horizons as a way of finding a crude map of our language, even if no total description of the complexity of language is available to us.

One refinement of this stark picture rests on the fact that the meaning of a single sentence can seem to shift from occasion to occasion. It looks as if the meaning of a sentence may be determined by its immediate context, but this conclusion would conflict with the hermeneutics just suggested as central to Wittgenstein. The context of a particular sentential utterance can include what has just happened, what is happening, and what is expected to happen. The moves in a language game are interwoven into a temporal pattern of activities and intentions. The movements in the language game that are interwoven with life help to determine which horizon is right for a sentence on a particular occasion of utterance. Context helps us to find the appropriate horizon, provided that an assertion makes sense, after which one-step hermeneutics delivers the meaning.

This account clarifies several otherwise puzzling features of Wittgenstein's remarks about language. He shares with many versions of positivism an emphasis on the sentence as the bearer of meaning. But a sentence is not intelligible by itself, so that Wittgenstein always avoided the crudest forms of positivist semantics. Wittgenstein uses the possibility of different horizons to escape problems with the idea that a sentence must, if it is an assertion, *say only one thing*.[13] When Wittgenstein says that each phenomenon of mental life throws light on all, he does not refer to inferences between sentences about our mental life that cannot be modeled in standard logic. This fact indicates that mental life is associated with assertions whose horizons show a peculiarly complicated tangle of overlapping horizons, difficult to expose and survey. A solution to the problem of expositing Wittgenstein without reproducing the full complexity of detail of his actual discussions, but yet avoiding nonsensical abstraction and generalization, would be to attempt to stay at the level of these horizons, tracing out what Wittgenstein thought was settled about their location.

Except for some remarks about logic, mathematics, and science, which require specialized language games even for discussion, it is a remarkable fact that Wittgenstein never lapses from ordinary language into specially coined philosophical jargon.[14] Other philosophers (for example, Nietzsche) have attempted to use aphorisms to break the bounds of significance of ordinary language, but Wittgenstein held that everything relevant to resolving philosophical puzzlement lies open to view in our language as it exists, if we will but carefully look. His aphorisms serve a descriptive, elucidating purpose within ordinary language, including its legitimate technical extensions. They never become organized into a system of privileged axioms and derived theorems. In his most systematic work, the *Tractatus,* there are equally privileged major claims, with paths traced through adjoining elucidations, so that its apparent system is closer to that of the *Investigations* than that of *Principia Mathematica.* Wittgenstein appropriately called his aphorisms *remarks,* indicating that they are reminders and hints to be applied to puzzles, not bold new conjectures or dazzling novelties of technical insight.[15]

Wittgenstein looks for horizons by squeezing ordinary language into odd structures whose meaning literally disappears in its usual sense. All of his philosophical explorations are expressed in ordinary language, but ordinary language that is nearly meaningless because it has no clear horizon. It lies *on* a horizon or just adjacent to one. When Wittgenstein repeats remarks but places them in new contexts, he is not necessarily revising their tenuous meanings, as is required by the hypothesis that he was constantly changing his mind. Perhaps, since their meaning is tenuous, he is trying to show the meanings in a pattern or context that will allow the associated horizon to show itself most clearly. The problem is not necessarily the meaning but one of allowing the meaning to become manifest. The arrangement of remarks would be perfect if it mirrored the topography of the City, but that survey project was never completed. Instead, the remarks locate points in the City of language, major landmarks as well as smaller features, by literally bordering on nonsense, showing in this way what it is that we cannot say. When we return to these locations after having traveled different paths through the City, we become more familiar with landmarks, but their location does not change. In the same way, becoming more familiar with the meaning of particular sentences does not change their meanings. The objective meanings are determined by the relationships between particular sentences and the appropriate horizons, and these meanings can be explored over time. The network of horizons provides the fixed points of Wittgenstein's survey of the City, and these fixed points prevent any slide into an unmanageable relativism.

The panoramic view of Wittgenstein's work presented here suggests that Wittgenstein's City, viewed at a glance, should look like greater New York or London, not simply like the World Trade Center, with its twin towers and a framing low-level plaza. Many scholars can accept Wittgenstein's City metaphor. The question is whether the *Tractatus* and the *Investigations* or just one of them should dominate the cityscape or whether Wittgenstein intended that these two skyscrapers would be joined by other major works on mathematics, color, and philosophical psychology as part of his

City planning. Do we look at what Wittgenstein built, or at what he would have built if his career had not been suddenly terminated? Are the plans for additional projects to be found in the incomplete works? Did Wittgenstein repudiate what he did not publish, or did he believe simply that, while the basic structure of new construction was laid down in what we have, he had not been able to draw up detailed plans?

As we know from his work on his sister's house, Wittgenstein was a very careful architect and craftsman who did not work from sloppy blueprints. In a biography, the twin towers can stand, but not in an attempt to assess the philosophical achievement. If Wittgenstein fully repudiated the *Tractatus,* then he meant to tear it down and to replace it with the *Investigations.* The twin towers stand as published work, and if they conflict, a considered philosophical assessment must craft a revised Wittgensteinian utopian blueprint dependent on but one of these structures dominating the skyline. Is it possible that Wittgenstein's repudiation of the *Tractatus* amounted to repudiating only the original City plan, in which it alone was to dominate? Is it possible that the *Tractatus,* with a facelift, has a place in Wittgenstein's City along with the *Investigations,* and even with other skyscrapers whose plans were only beginning to be realized? We must settle this obvious problem before reasonably beginning a survey of the City.

Two

THICKETS

SEVERAL KINDS of intellectual biographies have been used to organize the intellectual development of major philosophers. In one kind, an early philosophical inspiration is developed into a systematic elaboration whose parts remain relatively consistent with one another, while the scope of the system is gradually enlarged. Plato, Aristotle, Descartes, Hume, Kant, Hegel, and many other philosophers, have been portrayed as developing early central insights into systematic presentations of this kind, even if their developments cause some strain between their early texts and their later texts that require interpretive adjustments.

In another kind of intellectual biography that has recently become popular, intellectual development can be marked by a sharp break or rupture between early and late ideas. On this scheme, early influences and style of thought culminate in a sudden leap to new insights of astonishing originality and autonomous brilliance, as the thinker manages to escape from the constraints of early influence to a truly unique style of theorizing. The intellectual developments of Nietzsche, Marx, Freud, and Wittgenstein have been portrayed in this way. Marx, for example, is said by some to have vaulted from an early Hegelian humanism to a new and original economic science. Wittgenstein, for his part, is supposed to have left behind an early version of logical positivism for an originating version of linguistic phenomenology or ordinary-language conceptual analysis. In these cases, it may seem that the bodies of thought lying on either side of the ruptures are incompatible with each other, so that the break marks an objective divide between incompatible systems of thought. In Wittgenstein's case, these two systems do seem incompatible if only the *Tractatus* (interpreted as a central classic of positivism) and the *Investigations* (interpreted as a central classic of ordinary-language philosophy) confront one another, since positivism and ordinary-language philosophy are incompatible systems of thought. In order to work toward an alternative interpretation of Wittgenstein's entire corpus that does less damage to either of these classics, such associations must be decisively broken.

Readings of the *Tractatus* as a central document of positivism overlook Wittgenstein's clearly stated aversion to positivism, his insistence that the important aspect of the *Tractatus* concerned the topics that it did not articulate and could not articulate clearly in terms of its own analysis of language, and they overlook also his insistence in the *Tractatus* that ordinary language is perfectly in order as it is, subject to analysis only for the purpose of determining precisely what its factual assertions mean, a target for analysis that derives from an impulse that can itself be expressed in ordinary language.[1] An appropriate point of concentration here is the insistence of positivism that ordinary language is confused and inaccurate and must be *replaced* by a suitable, precise, and formally controllable technical language for the purposes of developing science and mathematics. Wittgenstein, by contrast, never produces a technical language. He writes in ordinary language to analyze the limits of clear assertion in ordinary language, and his symbolism is produced to analyze one ordinary-language factual assertion at a time, not to articulate a superior and precise language designed to replace ordinary language for philosophical or scientific purposes. The notion that the *Tractatus* is struggling toward a replacement formal language for philosophical purposes is an overinterpretation. Formalism can appear in connection with discussions of science and mathematics because it does so in the daily practice of these domains. Wittgenstein describes clear factual assertion in the *Tractatus;* he does not legislate a new language.

Except for the technical terms that Wittgenstein necessarily refers to in discussing the views of other philosophers and except for his occasional descriptive precision in characterizing clear factual assertion, Wittgenstein arguably uses no technical vocabulary whatsoever. Most of the *Tractatus,* and nearly all of the *Investigations,* is written in very ordinary language—a simple and clear German. For commentary to insist that the German terms Wittgenstein uses (*Gegenstand, abbilden,* etc.) are technical terms is a crude, defensive projection designed to make Wittgenstein a soulmate of positivism and to convert his self-acknowledged near nonsense into deep and tricky philosophical doctrine. Wittgenstein's German terms are no more technical than are the English terms normally used to translate them. Except for the logical symbols used in the early work to discuss the ideas of Russell and others, literally every word used by Wittgenstein appears in everyday usage and and appears in any small and serviceable dictionary. Terms such as *language game* in the *Investigations* are, in German, concatenations of ordinary terms, concatenation being a normal device in German for producing new terms that immediately connote their intended meanings. Wittgenstein does not use opaque terms that necessitate definitions to provide them with meaning. Of course, Wittgenstein could be using at least some of his terms in some special philosophical sense, as many philosophers use ordinary terms with a special philosophical meaning, but such usage would be at odds with his explicit awareness that his philosophical assertions have an imprecise and dubious status, not a clear and precise philosophical status that could be learned by mastering a technical vocabulary.

Wittgenstein uses ordinary vocabulary without ever asserting that he is defining technical terms, although admittedly many of his assertions (in the *Tractatus*, especially) can be read as if they were implicit definitions if Wittgenstein's warning about the status of his philosophical remarks is ignored. The temptation to look for technical meanings relieves the anxiety associated with the difficulty of thinking through what Wittgenstein might mean if he is speaking, as he says he is, in ordinary language. When Wittgenstein later criticizes the *Tractatus* (for example, in the sustained criticism at the beginning of the *Investigations*), he considers failures of earlier reasoning and obscurities due to the constant brushing up of philosophy against nonsense and he especially considers the fact that the *Tractatus* was written to excessively demanding and implicit philosophical expectations, but he does not propose new technical definitions, nor does he ever criticize his older work for proposing wrong or inadequate definitions. I do not deny that he later finds error in the *Tractatus* but note only that error is not later corrected by replacing technical language either with ordinary language or with better technical language. Error is corrected by interpreting the errors of the *Tractatus* as though its assertions were read against the wrong horizon of meaning, without an awareness of the existence of alternative horizons. Wittgenstein never criticizes the vocabulary of the *Tractatus*, only its demands for clarity, its idea of analysis, and its too rigid notion of simplicity.

At times, the later Wittgenstein is puzzled by what the earlier Wittgenstein could have meant, quite consistently with his position of always viewing his older propositions as bordering on nonsense. The numbering of the older propositions confirms the idea that they did not make clear sense and did not have a structure of relative importance that would follow from clear meaning and definition, since the numbering itself is the imposition of a weighting of importance that could not be teased out of cloudy meanings by analyzing the sentences themselves. Making the *Tractatus* a document of positivism is simply the expression of an entrenched prejudice quite at odds with Wittgenstein's use of language and his lifelong insistence that he was criticizing the systematic pretensions of philosophers. If Wittgenstein was a philosopher in spite of himself, as this hermeneutical strategy insists, he was guilty of a massive self-deception.

Similar problems arise when the *Investigations* is made a document of ordinary-language philosophy or speech-act theory or is used to ground a form of philosophical relativism in which the meaning of assertions can always be relativized to language games. Speech-act theory, one of these cases, starts with Wittgenstein's comments on the rich diversity of human linguistic practice and with his observations concerning specific instances of that practice. The impulse of speech-act theorists is simply to catalog that diversity systematically. In the hands of philosophers such as Austin, Searle, and Grice, this impulse has led to a complete typology of English usage couched in a technical and scientistic jargon.[2] The Wittgensteinian impulse embedded in this project is to connect linguistic practice with real-life situations and to observe the vast variety of usages to which languages can be put. The aspect that is not Wittgensteinian is that we cannot have language totally explained to us by a theory, since the theory's meaning must itself be derived from the possibilities immanent in the language we already speak. An abstract theory of language can have clarifying value only for special purposes and in a context in which the clarity of some usage is taken for granted. We can already speak and write, and within that context we seek practical advice and experience for finding the right expression on specific occasions.

Wittgenstein's position is that we should be able to recognize and treat particular forms of linguistic illness and confusion by noting comparisons with clear linguistic health. Healthy linguistic usage is so completely interwoven with the rest of life that any effort to focus on particular instances of it can be accomplished only from a perspective in which at least some features of clear usage are assumed as fixed points for guidance. Some of our linguistic practice must be assumed as the focusing instrument, and this assumed practice cannot be brought explicitly into the discussion. We can focus on a bad case, comparing it with a healthy one or with a group of acceptable and clear cases, proceeding until we discover the root of the problem in some difference or similarity. We repair faulty language by using a fixed and accepted part of it as a basis for the repair in a context that falls far short of a complete theory of language, since we can never articulate a standpoint outside language that would permit the formulation of such a theory. The sure symptom of trouble in speech-act theories is that they require a burgeoning and complex technical language in order to develop their schemata from a viewpoint that has the illusory aspect of seeming to survey language as a whole.

Wittgenstein discussed many specific language games and their interweaving with life, and he said that language itself can be viewed as an assemblage of such games. Language-game relativism catalogs these language games as their range and number expand under analysis. When people seem to be contradicting one another, the contradiction can often be resolved by relativizing apparently clashing assertions to different meanings associated with different language games. Relativism is too sanguine about postulating a language game whenever there is verbal agreement and too sanguine about postulating different language games in order to resolve conflict between different speakers. If this kind of relativism is reached as a general philosophical position, Wittgenstein has been left behind.[3]

There are many different language games, but Wittgenstein thought that they must all be rooted in a common human understanding. Consistent language games can be invented, which are not necessarily anthropological conjectures; they are descriptions rooted in the possibilities of the language that we already speak. Their possibility may show only that the language we actually speak has certain characteristics. When a group of people agree on what to say on certain occasions, they do not thereby participate in a Wittgensteinian language game. When people disagree, we cannot conclude that they are participating in different language games. Language games and their horizons must be interwoven into the fabric of an entire way of life that will typically involve at least some clear factual assertions with any area of language usage.[4] Not everything that is collectively intonated or written makes sense, because of the requirement that it interweave with a way of life.

Language-game analysis should not lead to unbridled relativism. Quite the contrary, it can convince us that a collective practice is nonsense. Wittgenstein is descriptive of usage, not prescriptive. What is found to be nonsense already was nonsense, even if it was not recognized as such. In its systematic form, philosophy, for example, (which is not a language game, because it itself lacks a surveyable horizon and is not appropriately interwoven with clear everyday practice), is shown to be nonsense by Wittgenstein's critique. After learning this fact, we should simply stop trying to speak philosophy, although it remains a viable activity to stress language in the survey of language games that is undertaken in the philosophical spirit of surveying for nonsense.

Both speech-act theory and language-game relativism allow philosophy to go on in the same old way (or perhaps in the same new way), aping science and being only slightly chastened. Both start down a path that Wittgenstein travels, noting some of his particular examples and making a few observations at a modest level of generality, but they finally arrive at a place that Wittgenstein could not reach, at least not consistently with his own method of language-game analysis in the *Investigations*, no matter that the *Investigations* informs both of these later movements.

If interpretation starts with the concession that the *Tractatus* and the *Investigations* are Wittgenstein's major works and notes that Wittgenstein later repudiated the *Tractatus*, the obvious danger is that of taking the *Tractatus* and the *Investigations* as philosophical works in the ordinary sense, that is, as works arguing for philosophical propositions. Such a view construes repudiation as the replacement of earlier philosophical propositions by later, incompatible philosophical propositions, the incompatibility defining the rupture or break in Wittgenstein's development. But if Wittgenstein's works are freed from the task of representing philosophical propositions, another option for describing his development presents itself. As more and more of Wittgenstein's corpus has become available to scholars, it indicates that there was not a sudden rupture in his opinions but years of intense effort, fits and starts of insight, an increasing awareness of the complexity of horizons of meaning, and a desire to let nonsense show itself in the excesses of philosophy. These features are common to all his years of effort.

The *Notebooks*, written before the *Tractatus*, themselves show this picture of Wittgenstein's thought. Their open and exploratory nature raises issues that seem suppressed in the relatively rigid structure of the *Tractatus* but that reappear as the foci of philosophical struggles for clarity after the *Tractatus* loses its grip. As we will see below in connection with specific topics, Wittgenstein kept returning to the same themes, picking up from where he had left them and reworking the same insights throughout his career. The views attributed to Wittgenstein in this study are therefore freely taken from throughout his work, a justifiable procedure because the hypothesis to be illustrated is that Wittgenstein's major views and interests do not change much over time. Quotations from different periods can thus be interpreted against one another within the same general hermeneutical framework. On developmental views that argue for a radical change in Wittgenstein's opinions, this procedure should break down completely, as quotations from different periods should be incompatible. The fact that the breakdown is not obvious when quotations from various periods are juxtaposed is a sign that the postulation of the break may rest on a philosophical prejudice.

There is no doubt that Wittgenstein later found the *Tractatus* inadequate. A famous story traces this realization to an incident involving the economist Sraffa, who showed Wittgenstein an Italian gesture of disapproval and observed that its clear meaning could not be analyzed in terms of the *Tractatus* account. Wittgenstein describes himself as feeling afterward like a tree whose branches had been cut off. As Drury has cogently observed, this image is highly significant.[5] The roots and trunk of this tree, Wittgenstein's fundamental doctrines of one-step hermeneutical clarity and of the inexpressibility of such important matters as ethical values, remained intact. What happened is that the tree grew new foliage in a more luxuriant fashion after this episode. As Wittgenstein reports, one who is used to consider only the description of physical objects will at first consider other uses of language rather strange.[6] Once their possibility became manifest, the newer language games appeared in profusion. Wittgenstein's monochromatic palette rather suddenly was filled with a wide range of colors. Wittgenstein had said that we make pictures to ourselves, and this doctrine remains intact. His view changes in that we make different kinds of pictures to ourselves in order to explore various aspects of reality.[7]

If we look at the *Blue Book* and the *Brown Book*, important works in the landscape between the *Tractatus* and the *Investigations* we see that Wittgenstein introduces the complexity of multiple language games and then begins to trace out the horizons of some of the games that will concern him in his later career. In the world, the meaningful sentences licensed by grammars are confirmed or rejected in appropriate experiences, but often in a way that we cannot anticipate. The world otherwise has no intrinsic structure that is accessible to us. An expectation is a picture of a fulfilling event, but it does not have to be fulfilled, and it is not when the expectation is disappointed. Its two poles are fulfillment and nonfulfillment, so a formal analogy is evident with clear factual assertions and their two poles of truth and falsity, but in the case of expectation we are playing a different language game.[8]

The crucial question for an interpretation of Wittgenstein's development that would retain both the *Tractatus* and the *Investigations* as central works is the question of Wittgenstein's repudiation of the *Tractatus*. If he did not repudiate it because its assertions were false or mostly false, what did he repudiate? He repudiated the pretension of the *Tractatus* to have provided a *complete* analysis of linguistic meaning. The *Tractatus* had provided an analysis only of factual sentences and had mistaken that project for drawing the horizon of all clear language usage. With this extravagant claim removed and with the recognition that its analysis of color and mathematical assertions was inadequate, most of the *Tractatus* analysis could be retained in its detail for the continued analysis of factual assertion in science and much of everyday life. From Wittgenstein's later point of view, the *Tractatus* had located only one horizon.

In the later work, the philosophical assertions made in the *Tractatus* about its scope had to be ignored, and the possibility of the additional language games allowed the philosophical pretensions of the *Tractatus* to be easily recognized. Furthermore, in the context of the later work, the metaphysical claim in the *Tractatus* that there was a single analysis of all factual assertions into one set of elementary propositions also had to give way. An analysis of a factual assertion into its truth-functional structure could depend on context, so that the total domain of factual assertion could be seen as containing various language games, allowing a more flexible approach to the analysis of factual assertions. Clear factual assertion, however, is still analyzed into simpler factual assertions, and truth functions of them, thus not repudiating the *Tractatus* analysis, but factual assertion in the *Tractatus* sense is downgraded into a map of but one area of the City. This downgrading is the linchpin of Wittgenstein's development as it will be explored below.

Wittgenstein's repudiation of the *Tractatus* is a repudiation of the extravagant generalizations about all of language that it contains. In searching for clarity, Wittgenstein had been seduced into a hasty philosophical formalism, thus realizing his own greatest fears. He must have looked back at the *Tractatus* with revulsion, not because it was completely false, but because its truths were too quickly inflated into philosophical nonsense. Mortification must have followed the realization that the role of color and mathematics in elementary propositions had escaped him, in spite of his earlier feeling that all philosophical problems had been solved. Once again in history, the *feeling* of certainty had been a delusion. One standard critique of the *Tractatus* is that its own propositions are not clear assertions and thus fall afoul of its own standards. Wittgenstein knew that the *Tractatus* itself was not written in clear factual assertions. The ladder imagery at the end and the subsequent years of philosophical silence are sufficient to show that Wittgenstein recognized the problems with elucidating his views. And Wittgenstein did not think that his sentences could intimate anything at all to readers who had not struggled with the same problems. The *Notebooks* and the *Tractatus* show a sensitive intelligence grappling with the meaning of new symbolisms and new philosophies that promised, finally, complete clarity and then briefly succumbing to that vision in its own terms.

In failing to be, in retrospect, clear about everything, Wittgenstein had failed to be clear about anything, at least in terms of his own high standards. The crucial problem of the *Tractatus* is the problem of how clarity can recognize itself. If the *Tractatus* failed, do the reflections of the *Investigations* succeed? In not finishing the *Investigations*, Wittgenstein precluded the same failure from occurring a second time. The analysis of individual language games in the later work achieves the goal of clarity locally, and the horizon of the language game contains the result within circumscribed areas. Language games may be cumulatively investigated, and certain results may be tied down within the context of a specific language game, while the investigation remains permanently open to the discovery and elucidation of new language games. Wittgenstein did not repeat the error of asserting that complete clarity about language in general had been achieved with the delicate descriptive apparatus of the *Investigations*.

One obvious objection to the interpretive strategy proposed here is that there is no reason to suppose that Wittgenstein was at all satisfied with the work intervening between the *Tractatus* and the *Investigations*, since he made no effort to publish this work. At the same time, Wittgenstein worked at collecting his remarks on mathematics, on color, and on various topics in the philosophy of psychology. Why would Wittgenstein collect his remarks on mathematics, for example, but choose not to publish them with the newer remarks on philosophical psychology in the *Investigations*? Either he thought they were deeply flawed, or he thought that he had found the essential key to sense in mathematical assertion, the notion of mathematical proof, and he set these remarks aside to receive a fine tuning and an organized account after the completion of the *Investigations* manuscript, with its introduction to the method of language-game analysis and its concentration on topics in philosophical psychology. It is not possible to know what Wittgenstein would have done after completing the *Investigations*. This book makes the assumption that Wittgenstein would have returned to his unpublished collections of writings in order to complete their respective grammars.

Wittgenstein touched on all parts of the City throughout his writings, at times taking only a brief look, at times stopping for detailed surveys and mappings. At all times, he seems to have grasped the extent of the City and was constantly making his understanding more personal and familiar. He talked little of science and mathematics in the *Investigations*, which plausibly suggests that Wittgenstein thought that he had equivalent exhaustive analyses of these parts of the City already developed elsewhere. It is impossible in the order of exposition to focus simultaneously on all elements of this interpretation. The record of citations from all periods of his writing in the following chapters should make it clear that Wittgenstein's general concerns, his constant targets, are always in some sense in his field of vision. In the end, as at the beginning, Wittgenstein sees human language as a large terrain of usage, perfectly in order, whose surveyor is the philosopher.

The strategy adopted here for reinterpretation of Wittgenstein's development is to summarize the large-scale features of Wittgenstein's City and to propose reading Wittgenstein more and interpreting him less, achieving consistency between the major works by refusing the detailed philosophical interpretations that bring them into conflict. There is a development in Wittgenstein, but it is not a development in which old views are refuted and replaced by logically incompatible new views, nor a development signaled by shifts in technical vocabulary, as much as the more usual developmental pattern of genius in which early insights are retained but are turned into an increasingly subtle configuration until the mutual support of their developed forms creates a resourceful philosophical strategy.[9]

It is often claimed that Wittgenstein held a picture theory of meaning in the *Tractatus* and that he abandoned it in the *Investigations*. Wittgenstein rejects, however not the picture theory but the picture theory of the *Tractatus*, the theory that each clear factual assertion can be pictured as a logical function of elementary propositions, each directly revealing reality, and that this view of picturing is sufficient to explain clear meaning in factual assertion as it appears in the guise of ordinary language. A picture does not have significance by itself, it has significance in application. We come to understand things by forming pictures and then using them to interpret reality. Explicit grammar can be regarded as a picture of language, and philosophy provides picture of language in use when it employs language games in analysis. A language game itself is a picture, and the horizon is its frame. Far from disappearing, the picture itself is constantly refined as Wittgenstein surveys other areas of the City. A reading of relevant passages of the *Investigations* will adequately support this observation.[10]

Wittgenstein's later desire to have the *Tractatus* published along with the text of the *Investigations* shows that he had not completely dismissed the former.[11] Whereas he had wanted his early *Notebooks* destroyed, he was willing to preserve the *Tractatus* as a record of errors, a decision that indicates a certain ambiguity in his attitudes. It is noteworthy that he does not later return to all of the themes discussed in the *Tractatus*. The basic ontology of the *Tractatus* and its position on clear factual assertion in everyday life and science is not reworked. Given the obvious criticism of the *Tractatus* in the *Investigations*, one reading of the wish to reprint his first work is that Wittgenstein wanted to show just how completely wrong he had been earlier. Wittgenstein's personality, however, suggests that, if he had intended to repudiate the *Tractatus* outright, he would have wanted to destroy all of the available copies, not deliberately increase their number. The presence of the *Tractatus* would be a reminder of the delusive clarity of the earlier work.

If Wittgenstein, however, wanted to contrast his earlier position with the complex network of horizons in the *Investigations*, he also must have thought it nearly obvious that the *Tractatus* analysis of factual assertion as truth-function construction from elementary propositions could remain in place, provided that an appropriate level of elementary assertion was reached in individual contexts of analysis by reference to a relevant language game. Furthermore, the implicitly adjusted *Tractatus* account would be the perfect foil for the complexity of the psychological assertions discussed in the *Investigations*. This account would explain why Wittgenstein does not attempt a new analysis of clear factual assertion in his later writings and does not return to any sustained discussion of the question of science in clear scientific assertion. Above all, the image of Wittgenstein's City is mirrored by the pattern of development suggested here, taking scientific languages to be among the more orderly and easily traveled sections of the City.

The *Tractatus* defines a boundary for clear assertion by means of what it considers logic. In the context of the later philosophy, this boundary can be seen as the limit of the development of a single extensive language game of true/false assertions. Later, the complexity of use gradually adds other horizons and other language games to the repertoire of the philosopher. All of the horizons later traced out are, in fact, latent in the *Tractatus*. Color, mathematics, and psychology, for example, all make an appearance in the *Tractatus*, but the parts of discourse in these areas not consistent with the scheme of assertion are not noticed and are written off as nonsense. As these language games are carefully articulated later, their grammars allow meaningful sentences to be formed that have two experimental poles against the relevant horizon, one pole of which can be decisively chosen by experience.

There is no independent point from which the adequacy of grammar can be raised. Language is always in order. But ordinary language becomes subtler and requires more articulation than is dreamed of in the original scheme of the general assertoric proposition. If logic describes the order in the *Tractatus*, a set of grammars does so later, but the one-step hermeneutics remains in place. What had seemed to be a second and deeper system, the logic of truth functions, becomes immanent in ordinary language and transmuted into a set of horizons with associated grammars. The earlier error corrected was to have seen too much uniformity, as though each word were much like any other word in its function, an opinion that can perhaps be traced to the uniform appearance of words as sequences of letters on a printed page. In the *Tractatus*, the assumed uniformity of the use of names, the essential words of assertion, had been caused by a philosophical illusion, and the *Investigations* makes much of the diversity of uses of words.[12] In moving from a unitary logic based on naming to a pluralistic logic embracing many usages, there is no need to deny that naming is an important usage that is to be retained in a more complete understanding of language.

In *Investigations*, 1, Wittgenstein introduces a slip of paper marked "five red apples" to show his new awareness of the quite different uses of the three words on the slip, uses that are colorful and wildly divergent in terms of the monochromatic analysis of the *Tractatus*. This slip introduces color terms and mathematical terms, terms belonging to two of the most important quarters of Wittgenstein's City. Where would such heterogeneous expressions fit into the City when they are embodied in full sentences? Clearly the different kinds of sentences in Wittgenstein's later philosophy have complex relationships within intersecting horizons, and if Wittgenstein expends exhausting energies on tracing the respective horizons of divergent forms of discourse, he never says much about exactly how the relationship of the horizons is to be traced, especially when they overlap. Clearly, a hybrid sentence containing words with divergent usages must respect all of the horizons associated with these usages, but there is a problem in that simple color and mathematical words used in quite ordinary contexts do not seem to invoke the precise horizons that Wittgenstein later traces out for such words.

In the *Tractatus*, Wittgenstein gives almost no examples of the kinds of propositions he is talking about, and he gives precious few even later, making it difficult to speak to his intuitions about specific cases. It is certain, however, that statements such as "There are five red apples on the table" need not take us outside the extended domain of clear factual assertion that is retained in the *Investigations*. Neither the full range of mathematical proof nor the full intricacies of the color solid need to be invoked, since we can imagine, as Wittgenstein does in *Investigations*, 1, that an appropriate supply of samples is included in the resources of ordinary language. For ordinary purposes, a memorized sequence of cardinal numbers may do for simple counting, a kernel of mathematics that is retained but transcended in the range of pure mathematical expression. Again, the ability to recognize commonly used colors, backed by a few color samples, is quite sufficient for ascribing color, although more sophisticated treatment of colors requires the notion of the full color solid and the results of color mixing. Wittgenstein says little about transitions from simple everyday usage to more complex theorizing, although both ends of such transitions are carefully anchored in his fully developed conception of language.

A specific theoretical assertion could lie within the surveyed horizons of color assertions, mathematical assertions, and some language game of factual assertion, requiring an awareness of all three horizons to explicate its precise meaning in some controversy. Paragraph 1 in *Investigations* is an announcement that such diverse horizons must be traced, but it cannot settle the question when a particular usage must invoke all of these horizons to settle puzzlement. Perhaps Wittgenstein was suggesting that we move to more analytically difficult horizons only when required for the resolution of specific problems. This understanding of Wittgenstein supports the notion that the later diversity of language games grows out of a *Tractatus* account that is oversimplified, rather than false, and proceeds by locating the horizons that were implicit, but unnoticed, in the original analysis. Where complexity and confusion threaten after this simplicity is noticed, philosophical analysis proceeds by a careful survey of the terrain until the appropriate horizon, which may include elements of several grammars, is located. Unless a precise horizon of meaning can be located, a puzzling sentence cannot be satisfactorily unraveled.

In arguing against a rupture in Wittgenstein's development, one must inevitably turn to detailed refutations of the interpretive claims in the existing literature. It would not be possible to confront the entire literature directly, offering alternative readings of all of the relevant passages that have been discussed in Wittgenstein's corpus as a form of refutation, nor is such an approach likely to encourage acceptance of the view advanced here of Wittgenstein's development. A nomadic strategy is often as effective as a prolonged siege in conquering a fortress, and only two quick arrows will be launched. One obvious location to test differing developmental hypotheses is the opening reflections of the *Investigations*, where Wittgenstein seems to many commentators to be repudiating the *Tractatus* most clearly. Two quotations from *Investigation* paragraphs 3 and 136, taken as mottoes above, will be the focal points for illustrating the differences in reading that are claimed for the approach taken here.

Investigations, 1, opens with a contrast between an Augustinian view of language, in which sentences are interpreted as concatenations of names, and a different conception of language, in which the remarkable different usages of words are noted and in which color terms, mathematical terms, and common nouns are seen to have different uses. It is carefully noted that Augustine does not speak of there being differences between kinds of words. Clearly, Augustine's account of language is to be contrasted with the newer view of language in which diverse usage is stressed, the latter obviously anticipating the account of language to be developed in the *Investigations*. One question is whether Augustine's view really goes proxy here for the account of language that had been presented in the *Tractatus*. Another question is whether Augustine's account, and possibly that in the *Tractatus* are simply repudiated or whether such accounts are granted some form of limited validity.

Augustine's account is like the *Tractatus* account in many respects. Both hold that meaningful sentences are combinations of names, which means, of course, that the *Tractatus* analysis of language is being compared with Augustine's account, since the *Tractatus* analysis holds that sentences that make sense are combinations of names (logical signs do not count as names in the inventory of a meaningful sentence). In the culmination of the discussion of Augustine's account in *Investigations*, 48–49, meaningful sentences are explicitly presented as combinations of names, and they are therefore presented precisely as elementary propositions (the simplest meaningful sentences on the *Tractatus* account) would have to be presented. In *Investigations*, 46, Wittgenstein explicitly connects the ongoing discussion of Augustine's account of language to his own, given in the *Tractatus*. When he considers names in *Investigations*, 1, Wittgenstein explicitly notes that words *stand for* objects, a locution that captures the internal relationship between name and object in the *Tractatus* more accurately than would any mention that words *refer to* objects, a locution suggesting that objects can be known independently of language, thus breaking with the immanent view of language developed in the *Tractatus* and the *Investigations*. These considerations are perhaps sufficient to indicate that Augustine's view can be viewed as a very sophisticated, short summary of the views of the *Tractatus*.

What is Wittgenstein's attitude toward the view of language in Augustine (or the *Tractatus*)? The quotation from Augustine in *Investigations*, 1, is very interesting in that, while it is said to contain the view of language as consisting of sentences that are in turn combinations of names, it also contains a reference to bodily movements as the natural language of all peoples, an idea that Wittgenstein will exploit in the *Investigations*. This reference is, however, not exploited in the Augustinian view explicitly developed in the next few paragraphs. Such a view, which states that sentences are combinations of names, is explicitly said to fit most clearly sentences involving common nouns such *table, chair, bread*, and people's names, from which it might be supposed that other kinds of words could be explained easily by extension. In other words, Augustine's attitude permits an analysis of simple factual assertion that one might see as satisfactory and that one might suppose could be easily extended to the remaining cases (or kinds) of clear assertion. This position describes almost exactly Wittgenstein's later attitude toward his earlier work as it has been characterized here: the *Tractatus* was a satisfactory analysis of certain kinds of simple factual assertion that one might have supposed could be extended to all assertion, a supposition Wittgenstein now attacks with the diversity of usage contained in the simple sequence "five red apples." Wittgenstein is not rejecting the *Tractatus*; he is limiting its scope.

In *Investigations*, 2, we learn that the Augustinian account has a horizon. It can be conceived as a complete account of language, but of a language more primitive than ours. This primitive language can appear *within* our more sophisticated language as a complete language game. The quotation now appears at the start of *Investigations*, 3, and in this context it explicitly notes that Augustine provides a description of a system of communication. Augustine's description of this system is not inaccurate; it is just a description of part of language. The last sentence of this paragraph suggests that Augustine's description is correct if it is restricted to the part of language that it describes. If Augustine's account goes proxy for the *Tractatus* account, then the first three paragraphs of the *Investi-*

gations express the developmental hypothesis argued for here, and they are not compatible with the hypothesis of a rupture or of Wittgenstein's having later rejected the description of the *Tractatus* (rather than merely limiting its scope to a quarter of the City).

It cannot be argued that Wittgenstein is completely fair in exposition of the *Tractatus* at the start of the *Investigations* nor that he decisively refutes *Tractatus* doctrine. By the time he writes the opening paragraphs of the *Investigations,* intervening thought has made the *Tractatus* look completely different. Its rigid description of factual assertion has given way to a view of language as an assemblage of language games, each of which has its own grammar. Even within the horizon of factual assertion, the *Tractatus* account may have to be adapted to fit local language games of factual assertion. In *Investigations,* 39, he alludes to the *Tractatus* notion that names could have a single ultimate analysis as referring to simples, and by *Investigations,* 49, he has indicated that there are no simples in this sense and hence that there is no description of names, except relative to a particular use of language. The claim of the *Tractatus* to have analyzed language fully is rejected as a theoretical pretension, but *Investigations,* 48, suggests several *Tractatus*-style analyses of factual assertions concerning colored squares on a surface, any of which might be adequate for particular purposes in connection with a particular language game.

The usual interpretation of the quotation from *Investigations,* 136, is that it repudiates, rather than restricts, the *Tractatus* conception of a proposition. (No distinction between a sentence and a proposition is made in this study, as the German word *Satz,* used by Wittgenstein, does not mark one side of such a technical distinction.) In *Investigations,* 134, Wittgenstein apparently refers back to his characterization of a proposition in the *Tractatus* and points out that this characterization itself was a proposition because it was taken from ordinary language. The insistence on this origin cuts against the idea that technical philosophical vocabulary was central to the *Tractatus*. Wittgenstein points out that the *Tractatus* proposition characterizing propositions could itself be employed as a propositional variable and that it is ordinarily used in this way and also notes that its *sounding like a proposition* is a feature of propositions (Wittgenstein shifts here to the present tense, suggesting that he still believes that it is so) and that there is no independent check on its relationship to reality. In *Investigations*, 135, the fact that we know what a proposition sounds like is taken to show that we already have a concept of a proposition and that we can illustrate that concept with examples, even if, as we learn later, we cannot give a precise general border for the concept, as the *Tractatus* had assumed. One example explicitly noted is *inductively defined series of propositions*, seemingly a fairly precise way of referring to the scheme that generates true/false assertions in the *Tractatus*. Here the *Tractatus* scheme is explicitly retained as one central example of what propositions are (it should be noted that Wittgenstein is still using the present tense).

Wittgenstein develops this line of thought in *Investigations*, 136. Asked what propositions are (continuing the question of *Investigations*, 135), we can explain by giving the example of factual assertions generated as truth functions of elementary propositions. (The English translation uses *definition* to gloss the German word *Erklärung*, rather than *explanation*, blurring the development of paragraph 136 from paragraph 135. Where Wittgenstein means *definition* in the usual technical sense, he uses *Definition*, rather than *Erklärung*, as a study of the word index establishes.) Wittgenstein is *not* saying that something is a proposition if and only if it is true or false; indeed he could not do so without introducing a technical sense of *proposition*. He gives one obvious example of what we mean by a proposition (or sentence), and he is preparing for the fact that other examples will also be coming into view. Far from repudiating the *Tractatus* account, Wittgenstein here retains it as a central and clear example of what a proposition is and how we operate with propositions (or sentences). Referring back to *Investigations*, 134, Wittgenstein then elaborates that we do not have an independent conception of what *true* and *false* mean that we could use to carve out the borders of even this central example. *True* and *false* thus are not technical expressions; they are the familiar concepts caught up in our ordinary use of propositions.

Paragraph 137 of *Investigations* completes this sequence of thought by suggesting that a child could be *taught* to recognize propositions among expressions, either by thinking whether expressions attributing truth or falsity could be suffixed to the expressions or by asking whether the *Tractatus* formula could be applied. But the context of teaching reminds us that this definition is not a technical one but a workable basis for coming to see clearly what we already understand. The explicit retention of the *Tractatus* conceptions as providing a central characterization of the family concept of *proposition* in the *Investigations* fits the developmental hypothesis argued for here better than the standard interpretation of this passage as a departure from the *Tractatus*. It is time now to leave the thickets of controversy for the work of surveying the major features of Wittgenstein's City.

Three

LANGUAGE

U NLIKE philosophers who are concerned to use various for-
malisms to explicate the relatively precise languages of science and
mathematics, Wittgenstein is concerned to investigate all linguistic
phenomena, insofar as our inescapable involvement with language
allows. Wittgenstein's relentless claim that we necessarily think
and perceive in linguistically coded units is distinctive. In Neurath's
Wittgensteinian image, philosophical analysis of language is like
repairing a ship that is constantly at sea. There are no dry-dock
facilities in which we can leave the vessel and examine it from
outside. Wittgenstein was particularly concerned that formal languages be recognized to have meanings grounded in our common
linguistic understanding and in ordinary needs and practices. At
times, Wittgenstein sounds like a college student initially confronting the bewilderment of formal logic, but his purpose is sustained
and serious. He argued that, unless a clear grasp of formal systems
can be won in terms that we can understand from everyday practice,
formal systems cannot clarify anything, no matter how expertly and
uniformly we can learn to manipulate the symbols. This warning
does not preclude the development of extensions of everyday language for special scientific or mathematical purposes. A precise domain of discussion can be coupled with a precise language, but
ordinary language is the flexible tool that allows us entry into these
specialized discourses.

The grounding of Wittgenstein's discussion in clear everyday language means that there can be no *theory* of language, logic, thought, grammar, or inference that is anything but an organized description of the possibilities inherent in our language. That language is interwoven with action and gesture and often replaces or refines a relatively inarticulate natural expression will not evade this point, since the relevant gestures and actions will have a structure that is comprehensible only in language. Flower arranging, dancing, and musical performance are not necessarily associated with written signs, especially where these activities are undertaken in cultures in which the activities are traditional and passed on by apprenticeship, but they have an implicit grammar whose structure can be grasped and even turned into a linguistic representation. Human communication is always ultimately linguistic in structure. No correspondence between language and the world can be observed by humans; language reaches right out to shape the incoming world of experience. Description and theorizing are two parts of language, but neither gives an independent point of view from which to assess the adequacy of our language. We talk and act. Our talking affects our acting, and our acting affects our talking. When talking and acting do not fit together, we work at making them fit, mutually adjusting them to achieve a comfortable relationship whose consequences are easy to anticipate.

Over a long period of time, successful action is the strongest evidence we could have that our language has some relationship with reality. We act successfully, and in successful action, the world seems to be just as we describe it. Wittgenstein's transcendental observation is that there is an *internal* relationship between language and the world, a shared structure, one in which the multiplicity of language is internally related to the multiplicity of features of the world. Only a direct internal connection allows the certainty with which we speak and act on many occasions.[1] This insight is constant in Wittgenstein. In the *Tractatus*, linguistic structure becomes a logical function of concatenations of names, but the names are related to the world by feelers that reach directly to the world.[2] Except for the names and the transcendental judgment of shared logical structure, we cannot know anything of the world, a fact expressed by saying that the objects to which the feelers attach are otherwise without properties.

In the *Investigations*, linguistic structure is internally related to the world in language games; an internal grammatical interweave with the world exists for each language game. Language games assume such a shared structure as had the analysis of assertion in the *Tractatus*, but sentences are analyzed in more complicated ways in the *Investigations* and not always as concatenations of names. Where there are names, the simples they expose may be given by the language game of which the names are a part. The horizon for one-step hermeneutics is provided by logical structure in the *Tractatus*, and by the grammatical structures of the language games in the *Investigations*. As the map of Wittgenstein's City becomes more complex, the single system of logic gives way to a complicated lot of grammars, but the individual clear sentence, internally related to the world, is always given meaning inside a fixed hermeneutical horizon.

Both logic and grammar must be given completely in advance, or the horizons of one-step hermeneutics would not already exist in order to fix clear meaning. Meaning is determinate because it is created by such structures and not by exploration of the world, Wittgenstein's only transcendental presupposition for the possibility of attaining philosophical clarity. We can foresee what we ourselves construct. In the *Tractatus*, after logic is revealed, the general form of any proposition enables us to work out the meaning of any clear factual assertion. In the *Investigations*, after the grammar of a language game is revealed, we can resolve puzzlement about sentences involved in the game.[3] Within the boundaries of the clear use of language, boundaries marked by logic or grammar, there is a structure in language that can be known in advance that provides the possibility of completely clear expression.[4] Otherwise, meaning might not be determinate when it is analyzed and might ultimately depend on personal decisions or on private feelings.

Sentences, rather than the words that compose them, are the foci of meaning analysis for Wittgenstein. If words had designation relationships to objects in the world and if we could examine these relationships outside of language by correlating words and objects, we would still have to explain the linguistic relationships that combined words into meaningful sentences. On Wittgenstein's view, logic and grammar, which can be given by a survey of the language that we already speak, can set the bounds of meaning. The meaning of words, which is not given by a designative relationship to the world outside of language, is determined by the possibilities of the occurrence of words in meaningful sentences, including the use of sentences on particular occasions. A word in a sentence, like a spot of color in a painting, has no absolute designation and may not designate at all. It has a meaning in a proposition when it is appropriately hooked up with other words, and this meaning depends on a contrast with other similar propositions.

In the *Tractatus*, the logical words help to determine the truth conditions, and hence the meaning, of the sentences in which they appear, but they do not function like names. Some words in ordinary language would disappear under logical analysis, serving only to mark the pictorial form that codes the relevant truth function of a sentence.[5] The constituent names of a clarified sentence seem to reach out to the world in the sense that they stand for objects, but they can do so because of the clarity of their analyzed position. In the *Investigations*, the significance of particular words may bear quite complicated relationships to the use of sentences. The older a word, the more complicated this pattern may be, and the significance of a word in a particular sentence may be dependent on the relevant language-game horizon, from which no conclusions regarding other uses can legitimately be drawn. A word is like a face that may take on a different character in different situations, and a sentence is like a group portrait, in which the faces each make some contribution and in which each face has a particular character because of the group association.

A sentence tells us how things are in some context; it is what we can compare with the world to see if it is true or false, satisfied or dissatisfied, appropriate or inappropriate. The sentence has enough structure to show a structure in the world. Wittgenstein compares sentences to pictures because a picture of something can be seen to be true or false in its representation of reality. A picture or a sentence may contain parts that also picture reality, but simple words cannot. Any blue portion of the world may be represented by the word *blue* or by a small blue portion of a painting, so that neither contains the resources, by itself, to stand for a particular blue portion of the world. In order to connect a word with a portion of reality, additional linguistic context must be invoked. Otherwise, part of the world must become part of language, in that part of the world is accepted as a sample within language or in that a special symbol is defined, connected to the world in a special discourse. The simplest sentences are the simplest structures that can assert something in a language as articulate as our own. Within an appropriate horizon, sentences can say something without alluding to additional semantic explanations. These suggestions will be developed in the next few chapters, but they begin to show how Wittgenstein's observations can flow from acceptance of ordinary usages of language.

When the horizons of logic or grammar have been noted, meaning is seen to be a feature of sentences shown by the structures laid down in the appropriate logic or grammar. Humans can collectively change language over time, but at a given time, structures of meaning transcend immediate desires. This part of Wittgenstein's conception is quite consistent with other theories of linguistics. The meaning of a sentence is not determined by what someone now wants it to mean, nor is its satisfaction a matter of subjective feelings about whether it has been satisfied. The logic or grammar determining the appropriate horizon settles questions of meaning, along with the objective comparison of the sentence's possibilities with reality that logic or grammar permits. As noted earlier, the sentence, properly understood, has a meaning only in such a definite context. A sentence is like a key whose indentations move the levers of a mechanism in a particular way when it is used.[6] The postulation of logic or grammar creates this mechanism.

In another striking image, Wittgenstein suggests that an object on Mars having a physical structure identical with that of a railroad station on earth might have, in its context, a totally different meaning. For this reason it is so hard to say one thing and to mean something completely arbitrary by it.[7] The structure of language and its normal usages have a powerful constraint on how language can be used in particular circumstances. This point may seem trivial, but Wittgenstein is leading up to his view that the interweaving of language and life precludes any significance for the view that meaning is a private mental intention that may be communicated through linguistic means.

The existing world and its practices provide a developed and useful language in which we can speak of colors, numbers, and many other things. We cannot really ask how this situation came to be; in the present situation, the internal fit of language and the world is simply given in successful cases of communication. Our color language allows us to describe the paints we need, the clothes we want, and so on. Are there colors that we have never noticed? Postulating new primary colors could be tried, but it does not seem to lead to new experiences. Our difficulty in imagining it suggests that we are at the limits of current grammar. Our number language allows us to weigh and count in commerce, to diet, to grade examinations, and so forth. Are there numbers that we have never noticed? Postulating new numbers can be tried, but it need not lead to new practices or discoveries. The postulation of new concepts, new logics, or new grammars is completely trivial unless it can be woven into a new form of human practice.

Wittgenstein has, in fact, little to say about this process, although once it has occurred, his techniques can be used to discuss the fit of grammar with the world. In fact, Wittgenstein accepts what may seem a kind of Kantian starting point: our categories are given with the language that we already speak.[8] We already have successful linguistic practices and cases of clear and natural understanding of that practice. Wittgenstein will use that fact to explore the full range of contemporary usage. He can acknowledge that language has a history and a future, but he is not concerned to explain the past nor to predict the future. He *is* concerned to map current clear usage and to recognize fatuous philosophical generalization when it arises within current practice.

It is important to realize that Wittgenstein believes that he can describe a level of language on which theory and philosophizing do not appear. Simple reporting and interacting lie below the level of appearance and reality, where what seems to be the case may be corrected by further investigation. First, we learn what is red, and then what merely seems to be red because of special circumstances.[9] Crude assertion as an entry point is fine-tuned by later linguistic development. Many of the sentences we speak, write, or read are recognizably factual assertions. Frequently such assertions can be said to be definitely true or false, but the *possibility* that they are true or false is given with the appropriate horizon. Without the agreement produced by common action and assertion, language would cease to make sense. The confusions of language are not to be found at this basic level. Language arises not from thought but from a primitive level that does not necessarily involve conscious reasoning.[10] We can restrict the survey of language to this level of ordinary language not marred by the confusions of philosophical abstraction and generalization.

Intellectuals and philosophers tend to overlook plain assertion in ordinary language because they are always trying to escape it. They are likely to be amazed that peasants can build complicated structures while speaking an incomprehensible dialect.[11] Yet primarily ordinary language should be called *language,* the more exotic language games being language only by analogy, extension, or comparison with this level of bedrock. We could even live without a spoken ordinary language, but language must be involved in building, coordinated hunting, or any activity requiring the integration of a group's activities over time.[12] Wittgenstein's builders in *Investigations,* 2, illustrate this point quite nicely, and Wittgenstein's City plainly maps ordinary language. Ordinary language contains clear concepts, but not necessarily explicit rules or theories of those concepts. We speak of what we see, but we do not have a relevant theory of seeing.[13] Doctors can handle diseases, and their language is not hopelessly vague, even though it lacks strict rules. Because ordinary language is interwoven with how we live, its meaning is public and open to view, so that no unclarities need arise. We see people in situations who are angry, who are happy, or who are in pain, and we have no doubt about how they feel. Doubt arises for philosophers who look for general criteria and pathologically worry about specific borderline cases and possible pretense. To understand what ordinary language means, we should look at how meanings are learned, bringing the problem down to earth.[14] There is a foundation for ordinary language in action and gesture, but also dangerous extensions of ordinary language into theory, myth, and philosophy. We will consider ordinary language below with respect to both of these boundaries. It should be explicitly noted that Wittgenstein accepted scientific generalizations, controlled by factual data, as a legitimate extension of ordinary language, but one that was conceptually distinct from philosophical generalizations that lose a grounding in agreed factual behavior.

Wittgenstein seemed to think that our ordinary-language concepts could always be taught to humans who did not have them.[15] This universality is grounded in a common human behavior; Wittgenstein seemed to imagine that human communities could exist without articulate speech or writing, organized solely by gestures and prelinguistic understanding.[16] At times, he also assumed that animals might think or feel in a prelinguistic mode, an unimportant idea, since Wittgenstein found the human form of life he actually surveyed to contain a unique level of articulated human language.[17] The point of grounding human language in human activity and human gesture is really felt at the other boundary of language. If language articulates what is at first a crude level of behavior and gesture, its meaning cannot depend on the expression of internal, private states. The basic meanings of many expressions will be given in situations and behavior that lie open to public view and that do not require the postulation of internal states on the part of the speaker or writer. Postulation of inner states moves philosophy away from the clarity of description and mutual understanding and into the murky and indirect realm of theorizing, but without a solid grounding in fact, thus offering only the pretense of a scientific advance of understanding.

Let us consider a language of gestures. We can imagine pointing gestures leading to naming, nods and shakes of the head leading to assertions and denial, offering objects clutched in the hands leading to choosing among alternatives, gestures or facial expressions leading to aesthetic, ethical, and emotional language, reactive movements leading to verbal expressions of pain or desire, and so forth.

Such prelinguistic behavior is treated by Wittgenstein as primitive, meaning that language, or more properly language games, can be based on such behavior, extending and refining it, until it has a coherent linguistic structure. At a more elaborate level, our ability to walk over difficult terrain, sail across lakes, and build primitive supports and structures leads in symbolic language to the sophisticated assertions of politics, work, and other aspects of our daily lives. In the beginning the deed; then language comes to describe and discuss.[18]

Many of the points that Wittgenstein develops using the relationship of gesture and ordinary language can be illustrated in terms of his conception of music. If music is represented in a score, an understanding of music is shown, not by theoretical explanation, but ultimately by how the score is played, a process that does not require the accompaniment of conscious inner states. Musical themes are analogous to sentences. They are not jumbles of notes, and yet the fitting of the notes together into a theme cannot itself be represented completely. Melodic themes are shown in the sequence of notes and are heard as related notes by a comprehending listener. Music typically does not refer to anything other than itself, and what is conveyed in music depends solely on a place in a system of harmonic and melodic resources.[19] Correct musical expression can be guided by notation, but it is not precisely determined by rules for reading notation. That the notes are indicated to become louder in a crescendo does not determine exactly how such a crescendo is to be played; a musician supplies detailed expression within constraints that are given by context and by experience. In music, the dangers of theoretical abstraction can also threaten clear understanding. If a given theme has a different character when played in major and minor modes, it invites confusion to ask for a general discursive characterization of the difference in sound between the two modes.[20] Certain interpretations of music in a given cultural setting force themselves upon us, and we often play within the constraints of a natural interpretive compulsion. A given tune can sound completely different at other tempi, in other rhythms, or with different harmonies, voicings, and arrangements, just as a spot of color will be sensitive to the context in which it appears.[21]

Understanding a musical phrase bears many analogies to understanding a sentence. Music is not a matter of a few rigid notes and rhythms; its interpretation has an analogous complexity to the total subtleties of linguistic interpretation. If we met humans with only mechanical instruments, their music would not be like ours, with its complicated musical parallel to subtle and gradate human bodily movements, emotional expressions, and displays of feeling.[22] In improving variations on a theme, problems of the use of musical grammar present themselves similar to those that are involved when we want to express something complicated with the language that we speak. The score is a picture of what is to be played, but its application is not given with it as an additional statement; it is interwoven with musical culture.

Musical notation has evolved into a system that works fairly well within our cultural setting, where it is interpreted within a performance tradition. It would be easy to change notation, but Wittgenstein is always aware of the dynamic tension between perspicacity and the demands of ordinary usage. To make ordinary language or a musical score more explicit, to further analyze its articulation, is useful on occasion to resolve puzzlement, but if we everywhere used the fully analyzed form, language usage would still contain ambiguities—and the increased articulation does not guarantee a gain in immediate comprehension. We have no basis for saying whether linguistic usage or musical notation is incomplete against the full set of possibilities, because our linguistic descriptions are our only access to the full set of possibilities. We can expand possibilities *within* our language in order to explore reality, especially when we need to resolve confusion. Musical scores that contained too much explicit performance information would become unreadable, just as it could hardly work to advance explicit truth functions only as assertions. Wittgenstein's philosophical approach is always therapeutic. We survey and analyze when the normally efficient use of language that invokes an implicit horizon has, for some reason, apparently broken down. This observation is quite analogous to analyzing and practicing specific musical passages in order to iron out performance problems.

Perhaps the most interesting way to relate music to Wittgenstein's City is to note that it has origins in humming, singing, dancing, and other activities but that its cultural extensions turn more and more into linguistic forms. Speech with and without thought can be compared with playing music with and without thought. Thoughtful performance is not thinking while performing; it is a manner of performance. Verbal language contains a strong musical element that helps us to decide whether a speaker is thinking. Sighs, modulations of tones, and rhythm are the gestures of speech. We cannot say things one way and mean something sufficiently unusual. How we say something and the occasion on which we say it determine its horizon and hence what it can mean.[23] This fact is sufficient to place the interpretation of language in public, where it can be openly discussed. Sentences can sometimes be understood at the right tempo but not understood if uttered too quickly or too slowly. A laugh and a cry are full of meaning, and much can be gathered from them in the right setting. Such observations are designed to indicate, by analogy to music, that there is no necessity to ground meaning in intention or inner imagery. Meanings and intention can lie open to view in the way in which something is said. Wittgenstein denies not that language can be used to communicate our inner feelings but that the meaning of language is determined by our inner feelings. Wittgenstein grounds language in public gesture in order to establish the point that language does not exist for the sole purpose of bringing the hidden to light.

Wittgenstein grounds language in gesture to avoid the idealist insistence that thought is independent of language and that language exists to express thought in the public realm. Meaningful gestures show that idealism cannot trace a line establishing the autonomy of language at one boundary of language, and at the other boundary of language, Wittgenstein notes that meaningful ordinary language can provide an effective critique of loose abstract thought and the ultimately incoherent language that would seem to express it in the public realm. Ordinary language is in order as it is, for the purposes for which it is employed. It is complicated, like the human organism, and cannot be understood apart from its normal functioning. Ordinary language disguises its own logical and grammatical structure, turning quite different propositions into superficially similar forms.[24] This fact causes no difficulty in ordinary practice, since context provides the means of locating the appropriate horizons for linguistic meaning. When horizons are ignored, as in philosophical practice that attempts general theories, syntax can be extended that loses touch with clear ordinary meaning and that produces incoherent thought and incoherent syntax.

Consider this simple example: "red is higher than green." In terms of our normal employment of language, this sentence is nonsense. Sense can be recovered only by providing a special context, something that usually cannot be done for the zany abstractions produced in logic, ethics, metaphysics, and epistemology. We are not prepared to survey the complete usage of a word such as *think*, which can appear in a myriad of specific language games. We can normally get around in our language, which does not mean that we can profitably theorize about our success. When we try, we may be permanently set on the wrong rails by overhasty generalization. For example, "Jim has a gold tooth" and "Jim has a toothache" seem grammatically similar, based on a superficial glance at ordinary syntax, but if we express that fact in similar subject/predicate structures in analysis, we have made an insidious error. They are both obviously grammatical sentences, but philosophical grammar puts them into different contexts of utterance in order to show an important difference in meaning. The external, empirical, verifiable relationship reported in the first sentence is quite different from the structure of the second sentence, where grammar seems to privilege Jim's report that he feels toothache, without making his report the only possible verification of the claim. Philosophical analysis needs to fight the bewitchment and hasty generalizations that threaten when we attempt to survey the whole of our ordinary language and, in making such a survey, to abstract from the concrete occasions of use of ordinary language. To avoid language that merely idles and has no connection to clear usage, we need constantly to study the interweave of language with common behavior and common understanding.

Wittgenstein was tremendously excited by the work of Frege and Russell in clarifying mathematical language through the use of logical symbolism but also was somewhat puzzled by their failure to push their insights throughout the domain of language. When Wittgenstein first attempted to complete the program of Frege and Russell for all of language, he himself was a victim of the notion that all of language could be logically analyzed, a notion that he quickly came to reject explicitly. His initial success came from assuming that the limits of clear language are the limits of clear factual assertion, and in pursuing the limits of clear factual assertion, he did locate one of the crucial horizons of meaning for his philosophy.

Wittgenstein's early analysis depended on the hypothetical idea that one could analyze a language such as German or English with the tools of logic so as to expose the maximum amount of logical articulation in factual assertions. If this analysis were undertaken, Wittgenstein conjectured, one would probably have an enormous number of elementary sentences or propositions within which no significant further logical structure could be discerned, and one would be able to consider more complicated factual propositions to be logical constructions from these elementary propositions. Elementary propositions would be those propositions without any additional internal logical structure. Wittgenstein conceived of the elementary propositions as configurations or concatenations of names that stood directly for objects in the world. The meaning of an elementary proposition involves a notion of logical multiplicity, the notion of how many names it contains, but this multiplicity is shown in the number of names, rather than expressed with logical symbolism. Elementary propositions, which lack logical structure, are conceived of as pairwise logically independent—the truth or falsity of any of them is logically independent of the truth or falsity of any of the others.

Let us imagine that some such program has been carried out. In completing the program, one might have to utilize intuition quite freely, ignoring some sentences as meaningless and paraphrasing others according to an intuitive grasp of content in order to expose concealed logical structure. This use of intuition would be a delicate matter, and perhaps only a philosophical genius could make the right intuitive decisions. Now let us examine the hypothetical result. There would be something unsatisfactory about what would be obtained. There would be a logical space of symbols and directions for moving about in the space, but there would still be no explanation of how language manages to *say* anything, only an articulation of what we already understood it to say. At this point metaphysics is actually required, even if an attempt to express the metaphysics is nonsensical. Briefly, Wittgenstein's metaphysical idea is that such an analysis would be correct if each elementary proposition discovered in such an analysis is a *picture* of a possible state of affairs in the world.

The logical space of a language (and of the world that it describes) is given by such an analysis. It is not the case, however, that every elementary proposition revealed in the analysis will show that it is a picture. We have to see that it is a picture, and to know whether it is true we have to determine whether what it pictures obtains in reality. Language works because the elementary propositions given by such an analysis can be seen as pictures and can be combined into complex propositions. For various reasons—for example, to facilitate ordinary-language communication in ordinary contexts—it is not necessary that complex propositions be analyzed and that each elementary proposition be spelled out as a picture.

We have noted that each elementary proposition of a language reached in such an analysis pictures a possible state of affairs. The converse proposition, that each possible state of affairs be pictured in an elementary proposition of language, is clearly not required by the analysis. There would be no way for us to know that that analysis had been completed is such a way that all possible states of affairs were pictured in language, since we can know only of those states of affairs whose existence is pictured in the language being analyzed.

That there must be states of affairs consisting of objects in various configurations is a discovery ultimately made in the metaphysical analysis of language. The exact nature of states of affairs and the objects that occur in them, and hence knowledge of which elementary propositions are true, is dependent on observation and scientific discovery and cannot be obtained as a result of mere philosophical reflection. Summarizing to this point, then, the *Tractatus* analysis of meaningful language reveals a logical space consisting of elementary propositions and various complex propositions obtained from them by logical composition. The elementary propositions (and hence the whole of language) will ultimately have meaning because the elementary propositions are pictures of states of affairs and hence are ultimately true or false.

Wittgenstein's first analysis of language in the *Tractatus* is really a sketch of the assertion game of truth and falsity that fits passive observers who confront the world around them. It thus fits both ordinary assertions of fact and the extension of these assertions into scientific theories. It excludes sentences that will not fit into this analysis as meaningless, including illicit philosophical generalizations. The horizon of clear meaning is given from inside the language game in that the analysis reveals the limits of the game (that is, its logical horizon) by starting with clearly meaningful language and finding its structure by breaking it up into smaller meaningful units until both the atoms of meaning and the nonsense of logic are exposed. Wittgenstein had achieved clarity with respect to the assertion game, and he excised a certain kind of philosophical nonsense in doing so. He did not feel that it was necessary to carry out the actual analysis, except for single cases of puzzlement. Elementary propositions would make assertion determinate; the possibility of the analysis was sufficient to fix a horizon for the language game of clear factual assertion.

But the analysis could not escape the taint of the metaphysics involved in the picture theory. The names located by this analysis turned out to be less uniform than Wittgenstein had thought, and there were also patterns of inference that the *Tractatus* could not accommodate. The *Tractatus* was still philosophy and contained philosophical nonsense, although Wittgenstein presented this single analysis as though it were adequate for drawing the total boundary of clear linguistic assertion.

When Wittgenstein returned to philosophy, he quickly augmented the scheme of the *Tractatus*. At first, he was influenced by the concerns of the emerging positivists and taken up with their problems concerning scientific epistemology. He seems for a time to have treated language as a calculus determined by rules, a scheme integral to positivistic attempts to clarify science, but this picture was simply at odds with the deeper insights of his immanent hermeneutical scheme. The facts that humans create mathematical proofs and interact with the world in responding to color phenomena and to expectations of the future spelled the end of the spectator of the *Tractatus* as the privileged model of a language user. As Wittgenstein begins to move toward a more complex account of language usage, he retains the view that the sense of a clearly used sentence is determinate, but he gives up the idea that determinateness of sense must be traced everywhere to a fixed set of elementary propositions and truth functions of such propositions. Determinacy of sense becomes a feature of particular language games that are found as a motley of particular uses of language, and the horizons of particular language games appear to provide the new fixed points for the determination of meaning.

As he did earlier with assertion, Wittgenstein now recognizes that we already use language, at least in primitive ways, in conformity with a variety of language games. The language game of clear factual assertion, the language game of the *Tractatus*, had consisted of a fixed and a variable logical space. Logic provides the fixed horizon within which elementary propositions are contingently true or false. An analogue of this structure appears in the later language games. Grammar provides the fixed horizon of language games, within which the simplest grammatical sentences are contingently appropriate or not appropriate, given the way we see that things are. From the later point of view, logic can be viewed as providing the grammar of factual assertions. The structure of logic, which had been fixed by the work of Frege and Russell, was suitable to many aspects of factual assertion, but it could not be easily modified to handle the differences in the various language games, each of which seems to have its own intrinsic structure. When Wittgenstein speaks of the grammar of language games, he is using the word *grammar* in an ordinary sense. He is interested not just in the syntax of language games but in the semantic and pragmatic constraints provided by the interconnection of language with life. The activities that ground meaning in his later philosophy take the place of the "feelers" that allow a name to stand in for reality in the *Tractatus* notion of assertion. When grammar is discussed in connection with the later language games, it locates the barriers and fault lines of different kinds of assertion.

Language games are independent, in the sense that each has a horizon that can be noticed from inside the game, a horizon that determines the meaning of the sentences that lie within it. If not a great deal can be said about language as a whole, much can be said about particular language games. If we view the *Tractatus* as presenting an analysis of one language game, and if we overlook its false claims to generality, we can retain its analysis and can use it for studying clear factual assertion in a variety of contexts. New language games can be studied individually in terms of their associated grammars, a piecemeal style of analysis that is consistent with one-step hermeneutics and hence with Wittgenstein's practice in the *Tractatus*. In the *Tractatus*, we start with the fact that we do make clear factual assertions, that we can recognize pictures of reality, and we work out the logic that allows us to grasp the limits of such assertibility. In the later language games, we start with such facts as our ability to count and use numbers or to mix primary colors and match given color samples, and we work out the limits of mathematical and color assertion that can appear in philosophical grammar.

Simpler language games than those we actually play can be imagined in order to show by implicit contrast the complexities of our actual language usage. The concepts of others, even imagined others, can cut across ours, dividing up our concepts, but more complex language games will elude us until they are interwoven with more complicated forms of human behavior.[25] In these imagined primitive grammars and associated language games, we can see clearly the different kinds of words that are involved and their exact relationships to practice. These limited settings are more useful than our own everyday usage, which is often too complex to allow easy survey.[26] The manageable simplicity of primitive language games, even when they are imagined, allows us to see the complexity and even the limits of our actual practice. These games, however, are developed within our language as a simplification, so that the immanence of Wittgenstein's style of analysis is preserved. Wittgenstein employs thought experiments here, but he is not presenting philosophical arguments. The relationships between language games and the relationships between our language and specific language games often cannot be stated. We can recognize them only as internal points of comparison that show themselves in the associated practices. Still, although this account may be sufficient to suggest that Wittgenstein develops the language-game techniques from the early analysis of one language game in the *Tractatus*, we are moving at a level of suspiciously high abstraction. Given this analysis of Wittgenstein's development, we must now look at specific language games and trace the order of their development.

Four

LOGIC AND GRAMMAR

WE MAY PLAY a musical instrument without being conscious of our movements but being conscious only of the music produced. A teacher may cause us to focus on the movements associated with making music in order to correct flawed performance, a focus that can be forgotten again when the playing is corrected. Wittgenstein's conception of clear language usage includes a similar temporary focus that may be necessary to correct flawed linguistic performance. The music teacher may call attention to problems by playing more slowly and commenting on this slower performance. Correct performance is thus *illustrated* by the teacher in a special way. Wittgenstein's philosopher will attempt a similar strategy, speaking clearly and distinctly in ways that will illuminate more general problems when linguistic nonsense appears. The realm of language is not left behind or transcended; it is simply surveyed in a special manner, with an eye to locating relevant horizons of sense.

Logic or grammar can be shown to us in a kind of picture we get from finding the immanent constraints on the language that we speak. Such a picture will show the points at which language ceases to say anything. Assertions designed to express logic or grammar will always seem close to nonsensical. Consider this assertion: " 'red' is the name of the color red." How could it plausibly be used? Only in very peculiar circumstances, for normally anyone who could understand it would find the whole sentence something already known.

When the philosopher holds logical or grammatical structures open to our view, we are startled because we do not normally directly look at them. It is like looking at a familiar part of our body, say a portion of our skin, under high magnification. Or it is like noticing that our nose normally appears in our field of vision. The structures of logic and grammar are hidden and open to view at the same time— hidden because we do not usually notice them, but open to view if we concentrate on them. We find them by deliberately removing content from a coherent part of language until only grammatical structure remains visible, defining the limits of what we can say. Beyond the horizons composed by these limit points lies inexpressibility. At the horizon, the fixed limits of structure are shown by the fact that attempts to describe them are either unclear or nonsensical.

Throughout his work Wittgenstein made a crucial distinction between saying and showing. When we *say* something, what we say lies inside a horizon, but the horizon is an immanent part of linguistic structure. Philosophy illustrates this distinction in its survey of language. It cannot *state* the distinction between showing and saying, because what it necessarily shows cannot be stated. Saying involves showing, but something can be shown without anything being said. If Wittgenstein was right in this distinction, commentaries that attempt to state the difference between showing and saying must themselves fall into incoherence.[1]

In the *Tractatus* system, the distinction between saying and showing is stark. There is only one horizon of logic for factual assertion, a horizon that can be clearly and completely shown in advance. The truth or falsity of sentence is simply a matter of seeing whether the state of affairs it alleges to hold in reality actually does so. The truth or falsity of complex sentences is reduced to the truth or falsity of their simplest constituent sentences and a logical calculation. Logic determines the truth or falsity of a complex sentence from the truth or falsity of its constituent simple sentences by means of a mechanical procedure. One cannot move beyond this horizon and still advance sentences that are true or false.

One of Wittgenstein's oldest assertions from the *Notebooks* is that logic must take care of itself, a remark suggesting that it must be able to be laid out without invoking nonlogical notions. Because the language of assertion is already spoken, the horizon of logic is given immanently as a structure that can be shown in this language independently of the truth or falsity of particular factual assertions. Since ordinary language conceals its logic, the philosopher must make a deliberate survey of logic. In the *Tractatus*, Wittgenstein thought that he had given a picture of logic purged of all empirical aspects, one that showed only the hard limits of clear factual assertion. This picture has become identified with propositional or sentential logic.[2] Logical constants are sharply separated in this picture from the names required to express a state of affairs in the concatenation of an elementary proposition. Logical constants show only logical structure. In a philosophically perspicuous symbolism designed to show the structure of clear factual assertion, assertions would consist only of logical signs and the concatenations of names required to express elementary propositions.

Wittgenstein's technical presentation of truth-functional logic in the *Tractatus* is of considerable historical interest. To begin with, he invented a way of representing the truth possibilities of complex assertions in a manner equivalent to that of the modern truth table, a considerable technical achievement. The advantage of Wittgenstein's approach, from his point of view, was that it permitted the analysis of any particular assertion that seemed troubling, without invoking an entire logical system. The horizon of logic is marked by tautologies and contradictions, in other words, those statements necessarily true or necessarily false no matter what the truth values of their simplest constituent sentences. Systems of logic, such as those developed by Frege and Russell, generated tautologies by rules of inference from a selected set of tautologies taken as axioms. Wittgenstein's philosophical objection was that the distinction between an axiom tautology and a derived theorem tautology was a philosophical obfuscation. Later, the completeness proof for propositional logic showed that the tautologies generated in the (consistent and complete) systems were identical to the tautologies established by the truth-table method, but this result directs attention away from the philosophical bite of the *Tractatus.* The local properties of the truth-table method are ideal for Wittgenstein's one-step hermeneutics, assisting analysis in locating the logical structure of an assertion that is causing a puzzle.

Wittgenstein thought that the philosophical superiority of his conception was decisively shown by the fact that the interpretive problems of Russellian systems generated such bizarre concepts as the axiom of infinity and the theory of types.[3] We may represent Wittgenstein's attitude as follows. Logic is restricted to propositional or sentential logic, a logic that can be given in advance, autonomously, thus creating a clear horizon for the interpretation of factual assertions. Quantificational logic, which appears to refer directly to objects as the values of variables, might or might not be able to function as logic in the analysis of specific assertions. Where the quantifiers could be completely understood because the objects constituting their values could be completely listed, quantificational logic is equivalent to propositional logic.[4] Where the quantifiers could not be controlled because they were taken to range over speculative domains whose objects could not be listed, assertions analyzed as containing such quantifiers were not factual assertions but were akin to abstract scientific hypotheses. The use of quantification theory thus divides into cases in such a manner that it cannot provide a uniform clear horizon for factual assertions. Scientific laws requiring uncontrolled quantifiers for their formal expression are not clear factual assertions, although they can be used to suggest specific factual assertions.

On Wittgenstein's analysis of science, we use these derived assertions to guess at the future, but then we must wait to see what happens. From Wittgenstein's point of view, this analysis captures the distinction between the notion of a settled statement of scientific or mathematical fact and a hypothesis, law, or theory, which can never be established as true. If a hypothesis, law, or theory generates specific assertions that are false, it will be either given up or restricted to a domain in which it seems to generate only true specific assertions of fact. Wittgenstein's desire for complete clarity left him with a philosophical basis consisting of simple factual assertions in ordinary language that we already understand and with a simple, clear, and robust logical basis for elaborating on that basis. His aversion to quantification theory as introducing possible nonsense, an aversion that may seem strange in view of the later sophisticated development of quantification theory, is actually required by his philosophical purposes in analyzing language.

At the time of the *Tractatus*, Wittgenstein accepted the logicist approach to mathematics in that he thought that mathematics could be represented in a kind of logical notation that could be brought into a satisfactory relationship with the analysis of assertions in the *Tractatus*. A growing awareness of the fact that the total range of mathematics makes this relationship problematic, as well as an awareness of the difficulties in interpreting various mathematical proofs, moved Wittgenstein toward the idea that mathematics has an indigenous grammar related to an autonomous notion of mathematical proof that does not simply link one factual assertion to another. Mathematics is a motley, and Wittgenstein's final conception of mathematics as a distinct quarter of his City is incommensurate with the tidy logical horizon of factual assertion.

A more or less simultaneous breakdown of the *Tractatus* came in the case of color. The fact that a point in visual space has red associated with it excludes other colors from that point. If it is red, it cannot be blue, and yet the inference from its being red to its not being blue is not an inference that is licensed by propositional or sentential logic without some auxiliary facts about color relationships. An assertion assigning both red and blue to the same point cannot even be immanently analyzed, with the resources of logic, as a contradiction. Wittgenstein recognized this problem in the *Tractatus* but supposed at the time that the structure of color relationships could be exposed in logical structure after the level of elementary propositions related to color phenomena had been found by analysis. Another color problem mentioned, but not discussed, in the *Tractatus* is given by the analysis of assertions referring to lighter and darker shades of the same color.[5] In 1929, Wittgenstein conceded that mathematics might be necessary to analyze this situation, not simply logic and elementary propositions, as he had once thought.[6]

I have suggested here that, by keeping the concept of logic restricted and by becoming increasingly sensitive to the issues of the analysis of color phenomena and mathematical proofs, Wittgenstein may have been forced to find grammars as immanent constraints in the subject matter of various kinds of sentences. Color statements and mathematical statements are the first quarters of the City to be recognized as distinct from the language game of factual assertion. It should be noted that Wittgenstein did not make the transition from logic to grammar as smoothly as he is described as doing in this reconstruction. We can see him struggling with the problem in the paper on logical form as well as in the *Philosophical Remarks*, where it is not clear what could and could not be shown in the relevant symbolism.[7] As early as the *Notebooks*, the powerful hold of the new symbolic logic shows clearly in assertions that the subject/predicate form is central to logic and that relations should be representable in logical notation. But the *Notebooks* also state, not in the spirit of the *Tractatus*, that "the book is lying on the table" has a perfectly clear sense, even if a spatial object has infinitely many points, not all of which can explicitly appear in an analysis.[8] Impulses similar to this second observation are held in check in the *Tractatus*—suppressed, so to speak, and allowed to assume full weight again only after the clarity of the *Tractatus* proved to be an illusion.

Wittgenstein began to suspect that logic contained more conventions and physics than he had realized and that its intrinsic notion that individuals bear properties is fixed on a single image, something like a lump of clay that could be shaped in various ways over a period of time.[9] The idea that there is a single, fundamental level of elementary propositions determining the horizon of all clear assertion gives way to many language games, each used for different purposes.[10] New methods of projection are possible that then result in sharp agreement or nonagreement with reality, depending on the details of the projection. Perhaps we simply calculate the way that we do, and there is no deeper explanation of the validity of calculation, only its success or failure, so that grammar should restrict itself to a description of what we do. "$(\exists x)(Fx)$" seems always a consequence of "Fa," even if "$(\exists x)(Fx)$" is not necessarily a truth function of "Fa," that is, a disguised disjunction with "Fa" as one of its disjuncts.[11] Logic does not capture this fact, but we can describe it. If a stick is white, then if we raise the question whether the middle third is white, the answer will be that it must be, even though the associated inference was not anticipated if the stick was described as white.[12] We do not anticipate all of the inferences that we might later want to make in logical representation. Only if the middle third of the stick has a special use in a game or some other activity will the question of its color seem relevant to our practice.

Wittgenstein is now poised between two worlds. There are clear assertions that seem to burst the bounds of the *Tractatus* analysis. Inferences are discovered piecemeal, and they are not always given in advance in logic. If a bullet hits a target, it does not typically hit a preexistent spot. It marks the spot where it hits, which we can now discuss, although we could not have singled it out earlier.[13] The fixed analysis of assertions about the target in terms of truth functions of elementary propositions is being transformed into an analysis that depends on the relevant use of the target. When a target is used for shooting practice and for marking scores, not all of its points can be given beforehand in a *Tractatus* kind of analysis. What is kept from the *Tractatus* is its one-step hermeneutics: the sense of a proposition is still determined from its analysis within a fixed horizon of usage. If we allowed the sense of propositions to change as we made contextual discoveries about their significance, logic and everyday grammar would become unsettled and mysterious. For this reason one-step hermeneutics must remain in place.

During the process traced here, generality becomes related to individual sentences in particular contexts in such a variety of ways that its uniform representation in predicate logic becomes impossible. It is not often enough noticed that logical representation is hardly used explicitly in the *Investigations,* partly because its appearance of uniformity conceals such a complicated diversity that it is misleading and confusing to employ it. The later philosophy explicitly studies what will *not* fit into a uniform analysis. To talk about an arbitrary circle in a square can be perfectly precise in a context.[14] If the word *arbitrary* is taken seriously, we must think of a circle and square on some elastic medium, so that movement or change of size in either produces an equivalent representation. This concept of an elastic representation will not work in other cases, as when a random selection is to be made from finite cases, but flexibility in representations is crucial for perspicuous mathematical proof. Wittgenstein is opposing moving too quickly from puzzles to representations of puzzles.

In the *Philosophical Remarks*, Wittgenstein is busy articulating the new concept of grammar and relating it to the older concept of logic. Logic (which will become grammar) must include intention, that is, temporal spread, at least in its applications to commands, to intentions, and to knowing what I am going to do, as language unwinds in time. These reflections initiate the topics that will lead to some of the subject matter of the *Investigations,* and they take a different direction from the investigation of the relatively atemporal grammars of color and mathematics. The grammars involving temporality are also given immediately. In stating that I do not have a stomachache, an entire grammatical space involving stomachache is already immanent.[15] Truth-functional logic is not denied its relevance, but the logic of truth functions is but part of the grammar of truth and falsity. If one proposition among various possibilities is selected by experience, other possibilities are excluded, but these inferences are not always to be captured in truth-functional logic. Clearly, the *Tractatus* is not being repudiated; it is being treated here as though correct within its domain but as too crude an instrument to capture everything that needs to be said about language.

Names, the fixed windows on reality in the *Tractatus,* present a variety of appearances. The names of colors, shapes, positions, surfaces, and so forth differ in use and cannot all be appropriately considered to fulfill the same grammatical function.[16] Logic (or grammar) must be tailored to the details of specific situations. Cases of rigid bodies, frictionless surfaces, and talk of infinity cannot be compared with the spaces of experience. Theoretical cases belong to extended linguistic constructions, in which we are free to set appropriate conventions. If one says that space is infinitely divisible, one is not talking about physical space. What is said in the infinite case is a construction which one can use to generate specific assertions with definite truth values, but there are no rules for formulating such constructions. Facts are always finite, as are the assertions of the *Tractatus.* Infinite possibilities can lie only in lan-

guage.[17] For sense to occur, the signs need only have a relationship
to reality that immediate experience can verify. A relevant experience can completely verify a factual proposition, as a look at a chair
can verify its existence, even if we see only one side of it. In this
case, the law of excluded middle says not that there are *only* two
possibilities but that there *are* two, one of which will be confirmed
by appropriate experience.[18] We could arbitrarily legislate more than
two possibilities, because logic cannot say how the world must be.
If we look for a third possibility here, however, we become confused.
Is not a chair to be found *somewhere*? Additional linguistic cases
must be interwoven with relevant experience. One can see that the
Tractatus account of assertion continues to constrain thought, even
though alternative language games are beginning to come into view.

Wittgenstein begins to doubt the inevitability of the *Tractatus*
system. He begins to suspect that contradictions can have a use in
ordinary life. "This is beautiful and it is not beautiful," carelessly
considered, would seem necessarily false. But it can signal a certain
kind of aesthetic contemplation or uncertainty and hence have a
use in a context that would be concealed if one considered only its
truth-functional structure.[19] The meaning of ordinary-language sentences is not always captured in their most obvious logical analysis.
Logic is becoming an autonomous tool of analysis rather than the
necessary immanent structure of all assertion. The *Tractatus* account was too simple: it generalized too rapidly from everyday examples of factual assertion.[20] Wittgenstein's City had not been
noticed in its idiosyncratic concreteness.

Logic had seemed sublime; it had seemed to deal with everything
at once.[21] The inexorability of logic was not the result of immanent
analysis but was a decision to apply logic everywhere.[22] Wittgenstein
turns this understanding around. Our description of what we are
saying must allow us to determine whether logic is useful on any
occasion.[23] "Not" means something different in "$2 \times 2 \neq 5$" than

it does in "iron does not melt at a hundred degrees centigrade."[24] This difference could not be decided by introspection or mechanical analysis; it is a matter of their function. The former is a stipulation; it could not be false in the intended mathematical language game. The latter is an empirical observation; it would not be invalidated by a single observation of iron melting at one hundred degrees centigrade, since we would suspect that we had made a mistake in reading the results. It could be invalidated by repeated experimentation. We cannot appropriately analyze both cases in the same way. A similar difference can be observed between the "is" of "2 × 2 = 4" and that of "this rose is red." Only the former can be expressed by the precise and rigid " = " of mathematical symbolism.[25] Wittgenstein suggests that these differing contrasts indicate differences in meaning, but true to his immanent method, he could not produce a neutral transcendental point of view from which this difference might be asserted or proven. It is shown in a sensitive understanding of different occasions of utterance that intimate different horizons of meaning.

A distinction can be drawn between empirical logic and conventional logic. If a machine's actions seem to be in it from the start, so that it *must* work a certain way, we are ignoring the possibility of physical breakdown and are making conventional or grammatical assumptions.[26] When an apparent empirical regularity is made necessarily true, we are making grammar, or conventional logic, out of empirical logic. The limit of the empirical is the formation of a concept; this limit however, must be as carefully marked as the limit of tautology and contradiction in the *Tractatus*.[27] Logic derives from nonlogical inference. If a wheelbarrow becomes hard to push, perhaps it needs grease. I infer the need from the resistance, but this thinking is not yet modus tollens.[28] Empirical logic is seen to be grounded in common experience, and it may appear as part of the grammar of language games. In the domain of articulate factual assertion, logic is an immanent but precisely surveyable horizon. In the domain of convention, as in certain areas of mathematics, it is an imposed requirement. What has slipped away is not the horizon of logic in the *Tractatus* but the conception that logic can be given a completely a priori justification. Logic is also interwoven with life, and the logic of the *Tractatus* is simply a specially clear license for certain inferences about facts.

The grammars that ultimately replace the notion of logic in the *Tractatus* are intimately associated with language games in Wittgenstein's later work. If assertion was the activity that gave the *Tractatus* its horizon of logic, the new grammars are tied to activities defining the limits of sense in newly recognized quarters of the City. An activity to which linguistic usage is sufficiently closely tied to give rise to a horizon, to clear sense within it, and to a grammar that can be used to show the horizon and the places within it gives rise to a language game. The language game is both the linguistic horizon and the activity with which it is interwoven.

It took Wittgenstein some time to recognize that this interweaving of language and life was essential and that it had already been overlooked in the language game of assertion. For a time, especially when he was discussing his early work, Wittgenstein flirted with the idea that language could be conceived as a calculus and compared to games such as chess.[29] Even in the *Investigations*, this comparison plays an important negative function, when simple rule-governed language games are laid alongside our more complicated language games in order to show differences. The chess game analogy had the virtue of suggesting that the chess pieces, like words in language, did not have to refer to a reality beyond themselves. Their meaning was given implicitly as the set of licensed moves within the syntax of the game of chess. This model could be read back into the logical space of the *Tractatus*, and it seemed to offer hopes for an analysis of mathematics that could avoid the problems with formalism and with Platonism. But the comparison was ultimately unsatisfactory. A game cannot interpret itself; to study its syntax in abstraction from its function in life is to abstract one feature of a game mistakenly and to overlook the fact that not even games can be completely circumscribed by self-interpreting rules.

The calculus image contains the same abstractive generality associated with logic in the *Tractatus*. A game, detached from life, does not have the internal relationship between statement and reality required for clear assertive sense, and chess is a misleading example of a game in this respect. Wittgenstein solved his problems of mathematical assertion with the development of a satisfactory notion of a surveyable proof, and the calculus model of language was left to one side. The concept of a game—circumscribed, surveyable, and linked to a definite activity—survived, but Wittgenstein's concern was now to find the rules of language-game dialects by a series of immanent analyses of particular examples of successful human practice and the language usage associated with them. Unlike checkers and chess, the grammatical rules of color assertion and mathematical assertion are not given in advance in a rule book. They have to be found in the constraints of ongoing practice, just as the horizon of logic had been found by a careful survey of clear factual assertive usage.

If we cannot comprehend a natural language such as English or German all at once, because of the myriad of uses to which natural languages can be put, we can comprehend special usages and the language that is associated with these usages. In order to understand the sense of a particular use of language (assuming it has a clear sense), we need to note which language game it is associated with on a particular occasion. If it is an assertion, is it empirical or grammatical? What is being talked about? And so on. By locating the appropriate language-game horizon, we can bring any particular bit of language into focus. The variety of language games is enormous, and Wittgenstein cited many that he never investigated in any depth.[30]

When we search for the grammatical horizons of language games, we find two phenomena similar to those that had been noticed for logic in the *Tractatus*. A statement that cannot be located in a language game may be philosophical nonsense, and we also find a form of nonsense when points of pure grammar are located on the horizon of a language game by immanent analysis. Grammatical assertions are necessarily true or false with respect to their associated language games, and their assertion therefore borders on nonsense. Any effort to change these assertions would produce a new language game. For example, we could add the name of a new primary color to those we already have, at least in theory, but this language would be idling philosophical nonsense if we could not find the new color and mix it with others. Wittgenstein's subtlest problem is to link grammar and practice. His survey works at describing current linkage, not at finding possible changes. Ordinary language is in perfect order wherever it is interwoven with successful daily practice, continuing a basic observation of the *Tractatus*.

Language games involve an explicit awareness of the linkage between language and practice. Where practice is sufficiently settled and agreed upon, criteria for the applicability of terms of a language game may be available. Criteria give public means for settling debate on the applicability of terms, and hence they are intimately involved with the grammar of language games. When a criterion exists, deviation from normal usage will appear unintelligible. Symptoms provide, by contrast to criteria, only fallible evidence for the applicability of terms. Philosophical skeptics would hold that only symptoms exist, but this view is an attempt to judge language-game practices by a rigid external epistemological criterion. Of course a language game may have to change in the face of experience, but as it is played, its interweave with life produces practical certainties.

The skeptic fails to note how language is actually used or that we learn the basis for secure statement in many areas when we learn language. We can treat criteria as certain until it is discovered that there are problems. Philosophers want criteria for certainty that could be laid down only by omniscience, and hence their demands are silly, and the satisfaction of those demands is inevitably nonsense.

Wittgenstein notes that criteria for applicability of terms do not usually exist. Where they exist, they are helpful in tracing the lines of grammar, and some criteria are typically available for settling usage somewhere within each language game. When scientists agree that certain tests conclusively establish the existence of certain properties or entities within a scientific language game, they are establishing criteria. A nameplate or manufacturer's number may establish the date when something was manufactured, just as a valid driver's license may be a criterion for whether one may order a drink or cash a check. Problems arise when philosophers attempt to provide criteria to settle all possible epistemological disputes because they cannot live with the legitimate uncertainties of everyday usage. In everyday life, agreement about particular cases is the criterion for whether someone is following a rule. Philosophers produce nonsense if they try to turn this test into a certainty by attempting to make an inner process the real criterion, as no outward, public criteria can be provided for the existence of a conjectured inner process.[31]

We encounter criteria as guides to grammar in our current usage, but usage can diverge from experience. If a critical test for a disease runs into conflict with practice, we may judge that the disease has changed or that the criterion is inadequate and then change our grammar. Criteria are part of the fixed grammatical dimension of many language games, and if they must be adjusted, the relevant game and its grammar also undergo a change. Wittgenstein's perennial problem is that he must discuss adjustments that are forced on us by experience, not in terms of the relationship of language to the world, but in terms of the changing contingent relationship of judgments about criteria to other assertions within a language game.

The fact that language usage with clear sense always takes place within a language game means that there is no clear general language for asserting similarities and differences *between* language games. Just as Wittgenstein had denied that there could be a metalanguage in the *Tractatus*, a higher language within which our language could be modeled, he takes the position in his later work that similarities and differences between language games can be *shown* only by placing language games adjacent to one another. Language games can be related like games themselves. There is no common characteristic of all games, nor are they independent of one another entirely, since we can collect them under the open concept of a game. Games are whatever are sufficiently similar to what we already call games. This similarity cannot be specified in advance, and it cannot be measured. New cases are decided rather uniformly in the absence of an explicit definition.

The best way to express complicated similarities is through the notion of a family resemblance. Family resemblances cannot be logically defined as disjunctions of sets of properties, but we can see resemblances between family members that we cannot spell out, although we can also be fooled.[32] Board games, ball games, games of patience—what do they have in common? Platonism wrongly supposes that there must be an essence of the concept of a game because *game* is applied to so many different things.[33] We can work with open concepts that are gradually filled in with examples, just as well as we can with closed concepts that are completely bound by rules. We simply *do* so in real life. We can play tennis, even though there are no rules about how hard to hit, how high to toss the service, and so forth.[34] The rules of coaches are just rough guides to better performance, leaving a great deal of scope for individual idiosyncrasy. *Mathematics* is an open concept that is filled in with relatively closed language games bearing family resemblances.[35] *Rule, proposition,* and *thinking* are also open concepts to be filled in with relatively closed language games.[36] Wittgenstein's mature structure of language thus contains a tangle of open and closed concepts, the open concepts filled in gradually with articulate and complete language games bearing family resemblances (in terms of the open concept) to one another.

If our actual language is an assemblage of language games, our progress in analysis can be aided by the invention of artificial language games. The *Blue Book* introduces this methodology, suggesting that ideal language games can be used to show (by implicit comparison) that someone has failed to understand the usage of some common word.[37] Ideal language games are the heirs of the sharp logic of the *Tractatus.* A simple ideal language game is a simpler language game than the one we may use, but one that we can imagine as complete. Obviously, we cannot invent concepts more sophisticated than those we already use very easily, so ideal language games will typically seem simpler than those in our actual language. They can be used to show that our language is more complicated than we had realized. A language game must comprise several words or sentences, a fact repeating the logical multiplicity of the assertions in the *Tractatus* and allowing significance to arise out of contrast. The language games we make up are not better or more perfect than those already existing in our language, but they do permit us to make and to notice comparisons. In the philosophical survey of language, we can construct an ideal language game to embody some theory of language perfectly and then see that the theory fails because the language game falls short of the complexity of actual usage.

The builder's language game sketched at the start of the *Investigations* serves such a purpose.[38] Wittgenstein presents a language exhausted by clear factual assertion, at least assuming that the supplies requested are themselves clearly sortable into blocks, pillars, slabs, and beams. We can see that our language is different from this one and different from the account of language in the *Tractatus*, of which this simple language is a caricature. Is it a game? Can it be regarded as the complete linguistic life of some group of people? Whether this language game could be translated into ours in a reasonable way would depend on surrounding ideas of emotional expression, tone of voice, and so forth.[39] We are likely to assume that these people are simple and that they act mechanically.[40] We tend to think of such action as a degenerate or incomplete way of living, probably because we do not normally encounter completely alien societies. Even in anthropology, we tend to think of others as restricted or limited, with respect to ourselves, but we could imagine them as participating in an alternative form of life, provided that we disregard any restrictions on their nonlinguistic behavior and imagine that their linguistic usage is alive in the context of this behavior.[41] As philosophers, however, we are not doing science. We only invent simpler language games as thought experiments designed to show us the nature of our own language games.

Our own language was learned by training in simpler language games. A child could learn a language game like that of the builders. Explanations and sophisticated extensions come later. This observation helps to bring natural and ideal language games together into philosophical therapy. Imagining simpler language games that might have been learned early on, before the full range of current usage, helps us to avoid the haze of general pictures of language. Propositions make sense, as all pictures do, only when they assume a definite place within a language game.[42] The variety of language games and their associated grammars is astonishing. Wittgenstein even describes looking at flowing water as a language game, even though this language game lacks exact description.[43] We do not explain language games as philosophers do—we note their existence. The clear and simple language games that we note are not preparatory studies for a future regularization of language.[44] We normally remain unconscious of the prodigious diversity of language games, even though they occur naturally in our language, because the syntactic clothing of everyday language makes things look too much alike, a temptation exhibited by the *Tractatus* itself. Something new and spontaneous is always a language game, and language itself changes over time by specific alterations and extensions of language games. By thus explicitly noting the possibility of language change, Wittgenstein has provided a framework for discussing language in general, without providing a misleading general philosophical theory of language. It is time to turn to the language games at a more concrete level, beginning with clear factual assertion and the pictures that allow such assertions to have a clear sense.

Five

PICTURING

WITTGENSTEIN never gave an example of anything that he recognized as an elementary proposition because he thought that the elementary propositions of a language would be recognized only after a complicated analysis had been carried out. For his purposes, he was concerned only to show that such analysis was possible, establishing the existence of the relevant horizon. He suggested that the possibility of analysis might be sufficient to locate the precise meaning of a particular proposition and to resolve puzzlement concerning its meaning. He never indicated that a complete analysis of a language such as English could be carried out. Such an analysis would have been inconsistent with his focus on concrete linguistic problems and with the implication of his hermeneutics that no neutral external viewpoint outside language could bé assumed.

Although Wittgenstein did not give examples of elementary propositions, commentators have been fascinated by the question regarding his best guess concerning the nature of elementary propositions. The most unequivocal text from the *Tractatus* states that an elementary proposition would be properly expressed as a concatenation of names.[1] This comment seems clearly to indicate, given the plural term *names,* that an elementary proposition must have an articulate structure involving the concatenation of at least two names.

That two names would be required is suggested by an argument that a single name would be a linguistic segment too impoverished to say anything. We would not know where to look to verify what a single name could be asserting without a considerable auxiliary apparatus of explication. But the elementary proposition can have no background apparatus; we should be able to recognize *exactly* what an elementary proposition is saying, knowing only it and the logical horizon of clear factual assertion. If we grant this basis, matters become complicated in a hurry. Can there be different kinds of names in elementary propositions? On the one hand, the *Tractatus* suggests that all names are somehow grammatically alike, and when Wittgenstein refers to the *Tractatus* in the *Investigations*, he presents a proposition that is a concatenation of names, all of which have a uniform typographical appearance.[2] The names in elementary propositions are said to name objects, suggesting that they have a uniform function, even if only certain names could be admitted to particular configurations.

On the other hand, the use of symbolic logic leads to symbolic expressions such as "aRb" and "Sc" in pursuing the analysis of factual sentences. In these expressions, a, b, and c are taken as names of individuals, but R and S are taken as expressions representing predicates. A predicate is often described as containing "gaps" that need to be filled with a corresponding number of names of individuals (if quantification is not considered) in order to create definite factual assertions. The implied differences in the status of predicates and names of individuals are reflected in the typography of the predicate-logic symbolism. Wittgenstein's assertion that only names would appear in elementary propositions seems to deny the cogency of a metaphysical distinction between the gappiness of predicates and the status of names, implying a criticism of the standard analysis.

Wittgenstein's start on analysis led him immediately to predicate-logic representations of ordinary sentences, but Wittgenstein suggests that these predicate-logic formulations may be misleading, as when he suggests in the *Investigations* that it is pointless for most purposes to "analyze" a broom as consisting of a handle and a brush fitted together in a certain way.[3] Wittgenstein thought that predicate-logic expressions might not appear at all in a full analysis of factual assertions. That the categories *subject* and *predicate* are not essential to language is shown by Wittgenstein's recognition of hieroglyphic language and gesture language. These languages picture, but they do not contain an apparatus of predicate logic that would be exposed in an immanent analysis.

Both the *Notebooks* and the *Tractatus* make it clear that a sentence represented by "aRb" need not be construed as having three names in it.[4] In this discussion, Wittgenstein alludes to the misleading nature of the predicate logic, and the issues are clearly laid out. In a sentence represented by "aRb," the fact that R stands between a and b can be taken as a linguistic representation of the fact that a certain relation holds between a and b in reality. The sign "aRb" can be taken as a concatenation or nexus of just two names, R standing as a piece of linguistic syntax designed to show us which relationship between a and b is being asserted. If R is a spatial relation, a picture of a and b could show the relation R without containing a symbol for it, as a and b could be pictured as standing in the appropriate spatial relationship.[5] In other cases, symbols such as R may code other relationships between a and b. It is clear that instantiated relational predicates of more than two places could be treated similarly. If all elementary propositions turned out to be instantiations of two-place or more than two-place relational predicates, we could imagine all elementary propositions as uniformly a nexus or concatenation of names, provided that they were syntactically displayed in ways that coded the appropriate relationships.

Ordinary sentences that take a simple subject/predicate form in their predicate-logic representation raise additional issues. Consider an expression such as "Tc," which says that the object c has a specific property T, and suppose that such expressions are met at the level of elementary propositions after a complete analysis of factual assertion. Any reading of this expression as a concatenation of two names, one the name of a property and the other the name of an individual, threatens to establish different kinds of names in elementary propositions. Are different kinds of individuals involved in such assertions, and are they the same as those named in everyday discourse? Did Wittgenstein make a slip in the *Tractatus,* asserting indirectly that an elementary proposition could contain only one name, T occurring to the left of c to indicate pictorial form, as in the analysis of relational expressions discussed above, even though this position seems to conflict with the doctrine that an elementary proposition is a concatenation of names? Will "Tc" give way to concatenations of names at the level of elementary propositions, so that the problems with predicate-logic representation are philosophical and can be forgotten when complete analysis is achieved?

Stenius and Bergmann have proposed that different kinds of individuals exist at the ultimate level of analysis.[6] In order to evaluate this claim, an argument called *the simplicity argument* is worth considering. Suppose logical analysis of a language reaches an elementary proposition of the form "Tc," which represents the fact that c is square. This analysis assumes that at least some ordinary predicates will occur in elementary propositions, a supposition that seems compatible with Wittgenstein's claim that we could grasp the sense of elementary propositions when we located them. But an object with a shape typically also has a color, a texture, and so forth. The sorts of objects or individuals that we normally talk about are, in short, not simple at all; they are complex. We do not just name such objects, we can describe them and note their relationships to one another. Retention of ordinary predicates thus seems to force us to suppose that, if the objects whose names are concatenated in elementary propositions are truly simple and can only be named, then they are not like the objects that we are ordinarily familiar with. But Wittgenstein seems never to have entertained the idea that the philosophical analysis of language would result in the discovery of special objects (or special predicates) not known in ordinary life. Furthermore, Wittgenstein never suggests that he entertained the idea that there were different kinds of names in elementary propositions. As the first reading of elementary propositions must assume different kinds of names and special objects that these names stand for, it seems a dead end unless a great deal of confusion is to be attributed to Wittgenstein.

A second reading of "Tc" as the syntax of an elementary proposition suggests that c is the only name in such an expression, T serving merely to say how c is—that is, what kind of a picture of c is being presented. Sellars has suggested that we could imagine a language in which only what were considered names would appear. Such devices as color, typography, and arrangement of these names would then code what was being said and what was being shown.[7] This device means that "aRb" and "Tc" would be printed in this language without the R and the T, respectively, the display or type-face of a, b, and c somehow coding the assertions being put forward. What this language accomplishes is ultimately arbitrary. By printing only the names of individuals, one shows the possibility of a nominalist reading of ordinary predicate logic, but one could also print only the predicate symbols, allowing their colors, typographies, or whatever to code which instantiations of them were being asserted. Such a language would show the possibility of a reading of predicate-logic notation that was not at all nominalistic.

Both of these special languages are functionally interchangeable with predicate-logic notation. The single symbol does not function as the name of a mere simple in either of these languages; it is communicating at least two pieces of information and hence could not be a name in the sense of the *Tractatus*.It may be a sufficient objection to note that these special symbolisms project a philosophical viewpoint about an ontology that serves to correct ordinary understanding. Such strategies want to improve, rather than clarify, the meaning of ordinary language, but in the service of a philosophical program. It hardly seems possible that Wittgenstein was following the dictates of such a philosophical strategy.

Without assuming that Wittgenstein could not have made an error, we can at least try to avoid imposing one on him. Especially since the *Investigations* seems to treat a concatenation of names of the same type as an example of an elementary proposition, we will assume here that Wittgenstein thought that, when he wrote the *Tractatus*, elementary propositions would turn out to be concatenations of names and that predicate-logic representation was but the first step in analysis, and a probably misleading first step. In these terms, R, and especially T, in the examples above, may be taken to stand for particular configurations of names that would stand in their place in fully analyzed elementary propositions. In other words, predicate-logic expressions are only artifacts produced at an early level of analysis.

If elementary propositions are expressed as concatenations of names and if the names all serve the same grammatical role, one may still ask what these names stand for and whether they can stand for something that we are not aware of in ordinary discourse. The verbal answer is that names stand for objects. The sparse textual passages on this point suggest to some that the objects are physical and that the *Tractatus* presents a kind of scientific picture of the universe. They suggest to others that objects are phenomenal and that the *Tractatus* presents a kind of phenomenal picture of the universe based on sense data or similar phenomena presented to our sense apparatus, or to others even that they are universals or properties of some kind. These positions have all been supported in the literature.[8] It is an unimportant argument against properties or universals as objects that they cannot be spatially located themselves, although spatial pictures are used to represent the relationships between objects.[9] But none of these views can be proved decisively wrong, and there remain still other possibilities.

Perhaps Wittgenstein deliberately held open the question of the identity of objects as something that could be discovered only by concrete analysis but could not be determined in advance by the horizon of logic.[10] Furthermore, realism and solipsism are said to be equivalent views in the *Tractatus*, and no strategy for ontological reduction that would privilege one of them is ever discussed by Wittgenstein. He would not have formulated the question of which of the philosophical construals of objects was correct, because the formulation would be philosophical nonsense, and his suspension of belief was therefore not between phenomenalist and physicalist interpretations of the logical machinery of the *Tractatus* but simply a waiting strategy to see how analysis would turn out. Ordinary language speaks of material objects and sense impressions, and Wittgenstein was no doubt waiting to discover what elements of representation would be required at the level of the elementary propositions. Perhaps both kinds of objects would turn up in analysis. The commentaries would force a philosophical interpretation onto a text that is deliberately avoiding one.

Whatever they were, elements of representations would have to be given by common names, that is, names of kinds of things that could occur in various elementary propositions. Names of times, places, colors, and numbers are obviously potential examples. All of them fit into metaphorical spaces within which they single out locations that might be required in a number of different analyses. These items are not properties but locations within an appropriate conceptual space. The analysis of a particular color, for example, could be given as a certain mixture of basic colors, coded by numbers representing the ratio of the basic colors required to produce the specific color. The basic colors would then be represented by names, as the simples of analysis. In Wittgenstein's own sample analysis, given as part of his critique of the *Tractatus* in *Investigations*, 48, the names concatenated to make elementary propositions are common names of colored squares, the same colored square possibly occurring at any point in the visual field when it is regarded as an element of representation.

The elements of representations cannot predicate themselves of themselves, just as the standard meter can be said to be a meter in length only as a kind of joke. We *use* the elements of representation to make assertions; they show what they stand for, and then we can say things on the basis of what is shown. Wittgenstein thought that names would turn up in the immanent analysis of our ordinary languages, but if ordinary language is already in order, names must stand for objects that we can already recognize as immanent in our ordinary conceptual scheme. This position explicitly allows for different kinds of elements of representation to be found in different parts of Wittgenstein's City, a fact that links the analysis of the *Tractatus* with the later discovery of distinct quarters within the City.

Names are concatenated in elementary propositions, but concatenation must be understood as shown. If concatenation itself is articulated by a symbol, it is a vacuous symbol, since the symbolically richer sentences will say no more than they did before. Consequently, the configuration of names in an elementary proposition must show what assertion is being made, without the showing itself being capable of real expression. An ideal notation for elementary propositions would contain configurations of names only, and the meaning of these configurations would rest in a natural understanding of the significance of their structure.

A fully worked-out elementary proposition, naturally understood, has a structure. Suppose that two of the names in the configuration are drawn from different spaces. A permutation of these names may then produce nonsense. The trouble is that, when the significance of the structure of concatenation is recognized in terms of pictorial form, pairs of elementary propositions bear relationships that logic cannot capture, because the structure of elementary propositions contains no logical symbolism. Two elementary propositions differing only in that one name rather than another occurs at a certain point in the concatenation can in some cases not both be true, under the assumption that one of them pictures the world correctly and is therefore true. This inference comes from the picture theory and not from logic, since the logical operators cannot apply directly *inside* the structure of an elementary proposition.[11] When Wittgenstein wrote the *Tractatus,* he seems not to have understood that the analysis of elementary propositions would come out this way. We can rule that elementary propositions remain *logically* independent, by retaining the standard conception of logic, but elementary propositions exclude one another in terms of their internal structure, and analysis needs a way to grasp that fact.

Exclusion between elementary propositions does not itself entail the wreckage of the *Tractatus* program, although that program would have to be supplemented. The problems can produce their own cure. Red is not blue, and four is not two. A study of such structures in color and mathematics produces grammars for the allowable elementary propositions related to such structures, immanent grammars that set different constraints on allowable combinations of elementary propositions. Wittgenstein's City suddenly has diverse quarters, in each of which an important local dialect is spoken, although logic remains everywhere a means of expression. Mathematics, color phenomena, pains, emotions, and so forth begin to assume distinct, indigenous grammatical structures of their own. But two very important aspects of assertion remain intact everywhere. The logical multiplicity of language matches the logical structure of the experienced world, a fact shown in language, and language is still used nearly everywhere to make pictures of the world based on this transcendental isomorphism.

Wittgenstein was not a skeptic. He began with the observation that factual assertion is a clear feature of everyday language. Language would not make clear sense in certain employments unless the world could be experienced in the right multiplicity, and in this sense language and the world mirror one another. If this line of thinking is taken as a Kantian transcendental argument, Wittgenstein is deducing what must be the case if clear factual assertion is to be a possibility, but the tone of Wittgenstein's prose suggests, not a transcendental *argument*, but the claim that a careful *description* of what lies open to view will *show* this mirroring relationship. The *Tractatus* does not describe the world and then language. It describes the world *in* language, and then observes that the structure of description is the same as the structure of language. Language does not copy reality; it reveals a reality that we can notice only insofar as it is touched by language. We cannot sensibly talk, as Kant had attempted to do, about a reality that is inexpressible. Elementary propositions show reality in showing what they say. Interpretation ends in a natural understanding that can grasp this showing without articulating it. Language cannot be used to say everything. The existence of bedrock, of natural understanding, is a permanent feature of Wittgenstein's outlook.

Simplest facts are asserted of reality in language by concatenations of names, and the facts themselves can be considered concatenations of the objects for which the names stand.[12] The links of a chain are not concatenated by something else; they fit together into the chain by themselves, which must be grasped directly. We cannot examine the world to see whether our perception, talk, or thought accurately reflects the world as an independent entity; we just perceive, talk about, or think about the world. The *structure* of our talk is found in the world when we consider it directly in such a way that the truth or falsity of elementary propositions can be settled. (Of course, if the settled propositions have an internal conflict, we must reassess our impressions of where truth lies.) We cannot *say* what the names of elementary propositions stand for. To complete the sentence "*a* designates———" into a clear factual assertion is not possible; for we can know no independent relatum. Philosophy often results from an impulse to say what can only be shown, to attempt to articulate internal connections between language and the world. We learn what names stand for by mastering language in use, not by finding links between it and an external reality. Philosophy, in attempting to fill such blanks, offers a pretentious and misleading restatement of what we must already know.

Before Wittgenstein introduces language as an explicit topic in the *Tractatus*, he speaks of the human ability to picture facts. This activity, like gesturing, need not be overtly linguistic. We can silently draw or sketch pictures, and assertions can be regarded as linguistic pictures.[13] The parts of such a picture may extend to the world to enable us to know whether or not the portrayal in the picture is true of the world. The picture theory is not a theory about how language and the world are related but an account of how we can make pictures, true or false assertions, and how this making is grounded in human gestural understanding.

Every picture must be logical in the sense that it must contain enough elements to stand for objects in reality that it pictures.[14] But a picture may picture by spatial arrangement, by the use of colors, or by other means. This aspect of its picturing is called its *pictorial form*, and the particular way it represents within its pictorial form what it depicts is its *representational form*. When we understand a picture's logic, its pictorial form, and the particular way it represents what it depicts in its representational form, we know what it claims, and we can determine whether it is true or false.[15] The picture cannot *assert* its own logical, pictorial, or representational form; it *shows* them. Explanation of pictures must therefore end in natural understanding.

Suppose I make a black-and-white drawing of my house and garden and use the picture to assert what my property is like. My drawing certain objects in a certain way, in certain sizes and certain relationships, will represent the fact that they exist in certain spatial relationships in reality. The pictorial form may be linear perspective, and the representational form the point from which the perspective is shown. One can discover by looking at my property whether what I am asserting about my house and garden is true. If I want to represent all of the trees in the garden, there must be as many trees sketched as there are trees. If I want to represent the sizes of the trees or their detailed identities and appearances, a more complicated picture will have to be drawn. We can learn to read the relevant facts from such drawings, not because they must be read in one way, but because we do learn to read the relevant facts from such drawings as we learn any language—by studying examples and then applying what we have learned to new cases. The final picture, true or false of reality, may be *logical* (if it has the right number of elements for what I want to depict), *spatial* (if it shows sizes and relationships of objects by using certain conventions of perspective), and *representational* (if there is a viewpoint from which the acknowledged perspectival conventions in use depict things as they are).[16] If we do not grasp what the picture shows, it is for us merely a physical object.

Attaching instructions for interpretation to a picture cannot completely settle the problem of understanding, since the instructions would also need interpretation, and an infinite regress would threaten. When we understand what a picture is saying, we must already have understood what it shows. This understanding can become obscure in linguistic pictures, since the pictorial form of assertions is a logical pictorial form, and the multiplicity of the picture is its logical form. Wittgenstein's use of *logical form* in this connection needs to be noted carefully. Elementary propositions do *not* contain logical structure that could be represented in sentential logic, but they have a logical form in their multiplicity. Wittgenstein was not unaware of the fact that we could grasp the meaning of sentences and pictures that we have never seen before. Our stock of names, by itself, could not explain this ability. But when we recognize the names and the pictorial form of a new sentences or picture, we can grasp what it is saying by means of what is shown, before we know whether it is true. Giving pictorial form to the variable content of names allows us to express and to understand new pictures and new sentences. Later, it is understood that, when we learn language games, we learn what is shown in the language usage that is associated with the games.

The world, as we know it, can be grasped only as an asserted fact, as a giant conjunction of the simplest true propositions reached by analysis. A slight technical problem appears here. If all of the elementary propositions reached in analysis are true, then the world would be represented by the conjunction of all of the true elementary propositions. If some of the elementary propositions happened to be false, the world-fact would be represented by a conjunction some of whose elements would be the negations of the false elementary propositions. Since it cannot be known in advance of analysis whether elementary propositions will be true or false, it is difficult to characterize the conjunction that would represent the world, but we can know in advance that analysis presupposes the existence of such a conjunction. This conjunction could not perhaps be written out, but we can consider the world as having such a logical picture in language. The *Tractatus* begins with this philosophical observation.

When we look at the world or perceive it through another sense modality, we perceive subfacts of the world-fact, and we may perceive incorrectly. I look into the garden and see a yellow flower. If the flower *is* yellow, my description is true of the world. If the flower is *not* yellow, then my description is not true of the world. Nevertheless, my incorrect description at this point need not prejudice my description of other independent subfacts of the world. Their truth or falsity is logically independent of the truth or falsity of the fact that I may have incorrectly described. The color of the next flower is a new fact that is logically independent of the color of the flower that I have just described. Wittgenstein holds the view that we perceive facts, not objects or qualities. Although Wittgenstein's position is clear, Wittgenstein's use of the word *fact* requires special discussion.

Wittgenstein's use of *fact* is based on ordinary usage, but it clashes with the typical use of *fact* by philosophers, which is drawn from another usage. Wittgenstein intends a use akin to the neutral way in which facts are assembled in scientific or legal investigation.[17] Here the originally assembled facts, if they prove internally inconsistent, must be sifted in order to attempt a consistent view of the world. The original facts are simply claims about the world. They are of the kind that can be true or false and are therefore relevant to a coherent description of reality. Wittgenstein opposes the philosophical prejudice that we can infallibly know what is true or false of the world and that the task of epistemology is to find rules and methods for discovering what must be true. While positivists and others held that we are in direct and sometimes infallible nonlinguistic contact with the world and that the problem of epistemology is primarily that of expressing this experiential basis correctly in language, Wittgenstein sides with philosophers such as Kant and Schopenhauer, who thought of perception as generated by categories or theories producing judgmental claims that were then assessed against incoming reality. Wittgenstein gives theory-laden observation a linguistic turn. A fact is what we can know to be true or false, in the sense of ordinary language. It does not have to be true.

Making pictures is within our control. We can recognize pictures and can recognize those pictures that are elementary propositions. In the domain of clear factual assertion given by the *Tractatus* picture theory, a fact is simply what should correspond in reality to a picture. Discrimination between those facts that actually occur in reality and those that do not cannot be certain. An elementary proposition and its negation show two ways the world could be, and experience may determine to our satisfaction which of them is true and which is false. We could say that the elementary proposition or its negation, whichever was in fact true, was a positive fact and that it was a negative fact that the other was not true. In this way, we could draw all of the required distinctions. Contingent complex propositions, when analyzed, would decompose into elementary propositions and their negations in a logical structure in such a way that they would also describe precise ways the world could be, such that a determination of the appropriate positive and negative facts would settle the question of whether the complex proposition was true or false. A particular configuration of such positive and negative facts would stand for a state of affairs, a possible way the world is that is ultimately available to experience and one that makes the complex proposition either true or false. Wittgenstein calls *facts* not the true states of affairs in this sense but the possible states of affairs. His epistemology leaves in our control only that which is in our control—the ability to discern facts in his sense.

A digression on *depicting* and *representing* in the *Tractatus* may be useful.[18] Elements of a picture represent objects, they do not normally depict them. *Depicting* is a rough synonym for *picturing*. Only facts—that is, configurations of objects or names—can picture, and if they picture, they always picture facts. If x depicts y, x and *y* are therefore both facts. Representing is a more general notion. If *x* depicts *y*, then *x* represents *y*, but *x* may represent (or stand for) *y* when *x* is not a fact. We have an illustration in naming, which is a form of representation, but not of depiction. Strictly speaking, statements about representation are nonsensical, since objects do not stand by themselves in Wittgenstein's ontology as things that can be referred to and understood independently of their occurrence in facts. We see the correlation of elements, or names, and objects, but we cannot successfully describe it in language.[19]

The elements of a picture must be the same in number as the objects in the pictured fact. In the pictured fact, the objects are arranged in a definite configuration. In the picture, the elements are also arranged in a definite configuration. For picturing to occur, the configuration of the picture must suitably represent the configuration in the fact. A traditional objection to the picture theory is that it is trivial because any configuration of *n* objects may be taken as a picture of any other configuration of *n* objects. Thus, any portrait of Marilyn Monroe could be taken as a portrait of W. V. O. Quine, under some appropriate correlation between specks in the one and specks in the other. This criticism of the *Tractatus* is valid only if one is considering the philosophically abstract space of all logically possible languages and pictures. Wittgenstein was not. The correlation required to make the portrait of Marilyn Monroe a portrait of W. V. O. Quine is *arbitrary* in the sense that, for each spot and its color, one must specify the color of the correlated spot by inspection and good luck. There is no natural or recursive specification that would allow us to give a reasonably succinct characterization of the method of turning the one portrait into the other.

When Wittgenstein talked about configurations of elements in pictures, he clearly had in mind only natural configurations. Wittgenstein would have considered the correlation just mentioned a pointless philosophical deception, sharing that attitude with the most embittered social critic of the usefulness of analytic philosophy. As applied to language, Wittgenstein would have held that only the normal predicates and relations of natural language could be used for picturing, as well as extensions of these resources whose meaning could be easily grasped on the basis of ordinary-language usage. Wittgenstein did not invent languages that would violate a grounding in what we already understand. As applied to pictures more generally, Wittgenstein would have held that only the normal representational modes exhibited in the paintings and languages of various cultures could picture in his sense. But Wittgenstein is not interested in a general theory of picturing and language as much as he is in a perspicuous presentation of what we already understand. He is interested in removing philosophical perplexities with respect to the linguistic preunderstanding of German-and English-speaking communities.

If one fact is a picture of another, the pictured fact cannot be a picture of its picture as it stands. A picture includes the pictorial form that directs it onto another fact. So even if a picture and what it pictures have the same multiplicity as configurations of objects, picturing is not symmetric. If a pictured fact is in turn used as a picture, as a picture it has a pictorial form that is not a feature of its previous existence as a pictured fact. Unless Wittgenstein's remarks on picturing are constrained by relevant but inexpressible features of natural interpretation, they slide off into paradox.

Nonlinguistic pictures cannot be negated.[20] We can make two pictures of the same house and garden that are not compatible, but one is not the negation of the other without an implied linguistic framework. Pictures of something are never, as we have noted, merely physical objects or merely facts. That the picture is organized or portrayed in some way is a fact, but that it is a picture of reality or the world is not a fact, not something *in* the world. The relationship of a picture to the world is partly mystical or inexpressible.

We cannot describe the "feelers" that show which objects the names in an elementary proposition stand for, and yet they are not private.[21] We can all form and apply pictures, and we recognize in clear cases what is a picture and what it is a picture of. This relation is not typically reversible. Even though a picture and the fact that it pictures share a structure, the picturing relationship is one-way. We could take the fact to be a picture of the picture that pictures it, but now the fact would be functioning as a picture with its own feelers. The direction of picturing is given by a form of life; it itself cannot be stated and discussed in any comprehensive and coherent way.

Suppose we start with an assertion in ordinary language and analyze it into a truth function of elementary propositions. Each elementary proposition, as we have noted, pictures a state of affairs known at this level as an atomic fact, but elementary propositions are not necessarily true. Whether they are true or false cannot be known in advance. An elementary proposition, like a picture, says that the world *is* some way. The sense of the proposition is that it is true or false depending on how the world is. A picture or elementary proposition does not depict its sense; it depicts the world as being some way. The sense, which is shown, enables us to determine whether the elementary proposition is true or false when we know how the world is in the relevant way. For truth functions of elementary propositions, the checking is more complicated. Which elementary propositions we encounter (a given elementary proposition or its negation) may be a matter of how we have analyzed, so the various possibilities that we can reach in analysis may be rather complicated. Much of the complexity of the *Tractatus* when language is explicitly discussed involves these possibilities of logical pictorial form. If all of the elementary propositions we reached were true, then we would have (accidently) encountered the world as we can know it. Reality consists in existing and nonexisting atomic facts. Knowing reality enables us to know which elementary propositions are true and which are false, something that we would also know if we knew which atomic states of affairs existed (for the others would not).

A very slight gap opens here. If we consider an elementary proposition and discover it to be false, perhaps we merely discover that it does not fit reality, so that its negation is true, even though we do not know which atomic fact exists or what elementary proposition might be true in its place. Logical analysis need not come to fit language precisely to the world except in the lucky case where all of the elementary propositions that we find are true. The problems with exclusion between elementary propositions and the emergence of grammar stem from this slight complication, coupled with a shift from analyzing particular complex propositions to raising the more philosophical question concerning which among all the conceivable elementary propositions might be true. But if we know whether each elementary proposition is true or false, we cannot know more. Reality and the world are the same from the standpoint of language; we cannot know the distinction in language. For this reason the *Tractatus* equates reality with the world.[22] Knowing which elementary propositions are true and which are false is equivalent to knowing all that we can know.

In the later philosophy, picturing becomes more complicated. Clear factual assertions are still pictures, but Wittgenstein begins to recognize that we can make pictures of what will happen, as when we say that we expect a friend to come to tea.[23] The expectations are embedded in situations in which the person who comes satisfies the grammar of the expectation when the sentence turns out to be true. Sentences expressing expectations are pictures in advance, and although there are difficulties with saying when these pictures are pictures of what comes to happen, Wittgenstein thinks that the grammatical multiplicity of the expectation can match that of the event that satisfies it.[24] We have to learn to read the multiplicity of a sentential picture from its occasion and use, not from its apparent grammatical multiplicity. In doing so, the picture theory becomes modified in a variety of grammars. Different kinds of pictures are introduced. "That's him" is a picture in which the kind of similarity is quite different from that of the drawing of a house and garden.[25] I can picture bits of an apple but not bits of red, although I can picture red bits.[26] I cannot picture a rod without its having a length.[27] In general, some pictures can be likened to portraits, where historical representation is given in terms of some fixed style, and others to genre pictures, where various wilder and fictional forms of representation are possible.[28]

When we enter a picture with our natural understanding, it does not have different interpretations, if it is a clear picture to begin with. Problems arise for picturing when we philosophize about pictures and attempt to generalize about their relationships to reality.[29] Pictures always contain two objective poles, but they are related to reality in a myriad of ways that escapes an easy philosophical generalization. If a feeling of satisfaction were the arbiter of the pole reaching reality, a command and its opposite or an expectation and its opposite might mean the same thing on a given occasion, if the utterer were to be satisfied with what occurred. Satisfaction or nonsatisfaction of the *grammar* of the picture remains the determiner of the poles and the choice of one of them in experience, but the determination is closely linked to how sentences are used in particular contexts. Psychological states are characterized by pictures over time, not by the idea of a factual mirroring at a single time. Some of the later pictures are films, rather than snapshots. We can picture desire, sensation, and emotion, and we can picture movement over time. We cannot picture the inner feelings that may accompany movement over time, or perhaps it is better to say that inner feelings can be pictured only *by* picturing these movements.[30] Pictures may be complete or incomplete, detailed or general, provided that they are controlled by an appropriate grammar. A picture of something, a calculation or experiment, is just as good as the actual calculation or experiment if we are trying to find grammatical constraints, as opposed to developing empirical content. Pictures have only to be fit into intelligible language games and associated with a clear grammar in order to present reality to us.

Pictures retain their hold on necessity. We do not judge pictures, although we may determine that they are true or false, satisfied or not satisfied, in particular cases.[31] Science and mathematics abound with pictures, just like the pictures of the *Tractatus*, except that, in making pictures of reality to ourselves, we constrain reality more than the *Tractatus* had realized. *Tractatus* pictures allow us to see reality as it is now. Later, pictures are taken more overtly to determine what we can see in advance of confirmation with reality. If we think that the sequence 7777 must occur or not occur in the expansion of π and that no other possibility exists, we are constrained by a picture of the expansion as already existing.[32] The formation of carbon atoms into rings is a picture that allows us to see and discuss organic compounds. The fact that such formation does not merely seem so but is taken as a scientific necessity indicates that it is a picture—part of the grammar of science.[33]

Does the picturing relationship of the *Tractatus* remain part of Wittgenstein's City in the later works? For science and for certain kinds of everyday factual assertion, the picture theory of the *Tractatus* indeed seems to remain entirely in place. The paucity of references to science (as distinct from references to mathematics), as well as the paucity of references to everyday factual assertion other than in newly discovered and developed quarters of the City, would itself suggest that Wittgenstein thought that the *Tractatus* had accomplished this much. Furthermore, his ahistorical and conservative view of science supported this retention of features of the earlier analysis. Wittgenstein does not bend before the new scientific revolutions that would suggest that his view of scientific progress as enlarging the scope of factual discourse belongs to the nineteenth century. He treats Newtonian science, which can be handled appropriately by the *Tractatus* account, as equivalent to science, thus sharing unwittingly with positivism a certain foundational picture of the structure of science.[34]

Darwin's theory is said not to have a special relationship to philosophy, confirming Wittgenstein's general view that there can be no necessity in history. Natural laws cannot be known to be true, and any laws of causality, for example, are just a priori insights that may be useful for generating propositions of a more specific nature. We cannot know what is going to happen. Wittgenstein's probability theory is an a priori measure over truth-functional assertions, assigning them an attribute of logical width that measures their a priori likelihood of being true on certain assumptions. It does not enable us to learn about probable connections in reality. Connections in reality are not affected by the structures of linguistic representation.[35] Therefore no inductive logic can be constructed in terms of Wittgenstein's probability theory. Wittgenstein had a later tendency to split talk of space, time, probability, and other topics into psychological and scientific notions, the former requiring new grammatical exploration, and the latter being placed more closely to the purview of the *Tractatus* conception of science. The scientific notions come from everyday experience, space coming from our possibilities of movement, so scientific concepts get related to everyday activity, as does everything else in Wittgenstein's City. The full force of his later conventionalistic impulses, however, are never directed onto science, which retains a protected location, just as it does in positivism, even if Wittgenstein thinks science to be superficial and trivial with respect to the important issues of life.

In Wittgenstein's later development of the picture theory, he rejects not its basic appropriateness for factual assertions but the notion that there is but one appropriate layer of elementary propositions and one notion of a picture, appropriate for all factual assertion. The remarks on simplicity in the *Investigations* suggest that the significance of the elementary propositions might be relativized to specific analyses for the purpose of eliminating specific confusions of thought. From this point of view, the *Tractatus* account failed because it worked with only a simple view of pictures. Something like the *Tractatus* analysis remains the key to the analysis of factual assertion in the later work, but Wittgenstein introduces new pictures. Different pictures can be compared, and usage, which can always be pictured in a language, can conflict with a specific picture, which allows a variety of kinds of pictures to come into view. The key feature of Wittgenstein's picture theory is not the specific picture theory of factual assertion in the *Tractatus* but the idea that language presents pictures that are or are not consiliant with our experiences of reality or with our ability to perform certain actions.

There are hints of a more sophisticated relationship to science in some of Wittgenstein's later remarks. He later observes that science would not function unless pictures of experiments provided a secure foundation for its investigations.[36] He also notes that Newton's laws might be otherwise than they are.[37] In an explicit mention of relativity theory, he suggests that what he does is like the setting of clocks, only after which certain empirical considerations are meaningful.[38] He explicitly toys with the idea that certain empirical generalities have hardened into pieces of grammar, which then provide the structure for empirical scientific observations. And he notes that our empirical propositions do not form a homogeneous mass, suggesting that many special grammars and language games might exist within the confines of science.[39] These hints could have been developed to present a view of scientific assertions (and even everyday factual assertions) in which many specialized genres of factual pictures could be involved in our use of factual assertive language. Indeed, it is easy to suppose that Wittgenstein would have done so and that Wittgensteinians interested in science should also engage in this activity. The complexity involved in bringing this flexible conception into line with assertive practice does not alter the basic insights of the picture theory of the *Tractatus*. In his own development, Wittgenstein was anxious to press on to the initial exploration of other quarters of the City.

Six

MATHEMATICS

WITTGENSTEIN realized early that mathematics does not have a special subject matter, does not refer to a Platonic realm of eternally unchanging numbers, and does not have pure mathematical propositions that are true or false in virtue of picturing such a realm. These opinions, however, were consistent with the confines of the *Tractatus* account. Mathematics bears an uneasy relationship to logic in Wittgenstein's early view, living piggyback on the existence of logic.[1] Logic cannot be directly applied to ordinary language but is appropriately used to represent its structure. Mathematics can also be directly applied to inference in ordinary language. Like logic, it can take us from sentences that are true or false to other sentences that are true or false.[2] Mathematical statements represent rules of inference or relationships between signs. Mathematics is thus ultimately to be assimilated to logic, not to physics. Physics would suggest mathematics as a kind of superphysics that had been abstracted from all empirical content.[3] Logicism dominates the *Tractatus* account, even if Russell's theory of types and some other aspects of the extant logicist program were rejected as philosophical nonsense. Wittgenstein also rejected the ontological existence of classes. Numbers were taken to be the exponents of operations on signs. Apparently propositions of mathematics are pseudopropositions; mathematical propositions do not express thoughts, they code operations on signs.[4] They can be proved in terms of operations on signs without looking at facts in reality, and they function as ornaments that could be replaced by much more cumbersome logical derivations.[5]

The range of Wittgenstein's mathematics was always rather small. In the *Tractatus*, only the sequence of nonnegative integers is defined, and Wittgenstein seems prepared to countenance no more than this set as a basis for mathematics, plus whatever operations and additional mathematics might prove computationally useful in getting from one statement of simple arithmetic to another. The mathematics permitted on this basis is limited when compared with modern mathematical practice, but Wittgenstein thought that both sufficiency and clarity for scientific and everyday assertions could be provided in this way.

In 1929, Wittgenstein realized that, in order to say that something was twice as red as something else (a simple enough proposition), the number 2—and not merely logical conjunction—needed to appear as an essential constituent of the proposition. The *Investigations* opens with "five red apples," illustrating the diversity of language games, and it is no accident that *five* occurs essentially in this phrase. When the *Tractatus* system broke down, the implied logicism of the *Tractatus* disappeared. The positive integers became an autonomous sequence of signs that we learn by heart, a sequence of signs that has a special use for counting in our language, one that we can learn (typically as children) through training.[6] Mathematical statements are still sharply differentiated from empirical propositions, but because we have been trained to count, we can communicate to one another the quantity of things that we have counted. This ability depends ultimately on certain constancies of experience, but the sequence is no longer taken to be given or defined in logic; it is sui generis now, no matter how useful its applications. The foundations of mathematics in rote learning or training are already a long way from a basis in gesture, although mathematics does belong to the space of communal activity, and it is related to such prelinguistic realizations as that two rabbits make more meals than a single rabbit.

In prelinguistic empirical mathematics, we may treat two piles of coal or potatoes as equal, in spite of the fact that a long process of weighting or counting might establish the fact that they were not, strictly speaking, equal. If mathematics is still protected from its empirical flank as a subject matter with an intrinsic grammar, it is not obtainable by abstraction from empirical assertions. Simple abstraction cannot account for the difference in grammar between empirical mathematics and pure mathematics as it is applied to empirical subject matter. They conflate only in very simple cases. Mathematics is also protected on its logical flank as an autonomous subject matter with different language games and grammars. Pure mathematical statements are not factual assertions, neither are they logical propositions—they do not belong to the language game of assertion at all. When logicism, Platonism, and abstraction from empirical experience are abandoned as analyses of mathematical statements, the status of even the simplest ordinary mathematical propositions needs to be reconsidered.

An immediate problem is encountered on this terrain. Wittgenstein assures us that he wishes to leave ordinary language in place as a medium of expression, looking for a clear view and a precise description of it. The language of mathematics is an extension of ordinary language, but because of the expertise and special training involved, everything that mathematicians say and agree to is likely to appear mystified to philosophers. Philosophers might describe mathematical language but would have no point of view from which they could criticize it. Wittgenstein's project, surprisingly, was to distinguish between legitimate assertion and nonsense *inside* the domain of mathematics, on the basis of his conviction that mathematicians often succumbed to a mystified *philosophical* self-understanding of what they do. On his view, mathematicians frequently produce nonsense by the same techniques that philosophers employ, such as illicit generalization from a few ordinary examples. Wittgenstein's notion of clear description is not passive before scientific or mathematical usage; his description is designed to eliminate nonsense wherever it appears in the guise of philosophical speculation.

We can begin with the simplest kind of example. The statement "2 + 2 = 4" is true in mathematics and is used in practice to derive sums. But if mathematicians then say, " '2 + 2 = 4' is true," they may already be verging on philosophical nonsense. The reason for this judgment is that this mathematical assertion is being quietly assimilated to other clear factual assertions, and this assimilation suggests that the mathematical assertion is true or false depending on a fit with reality. But there are no mathematical facts in this sense, no pictures of numbers to be generated, and this assertion is not true unless the notion of truth involved is understood by some means other than the picture theory developed for factual assertion. Truth in mathematics is quite different. In fact, Wittgenstein's view is that " '2 + 2 = 4' is true" is either nonsense or misleading, and it is plain nonsense if it suggests the assimilation of mathematical assertions to scientific assertions. Logical inference is possible within mathematics, but the grammar of mathematics must rather be understood in its own terms.

Perhaps mathematics was so important to Wittgenstein because it presented the temptation of a spurious clarity, a temptation to which Russell and Frege had succumbed, one that Wittgenstein himself had felt at the time of the *Tractatus*. In one aspect this clarity is genuine. In inventing and developing mathematical calculi, mathematicians do nothing wrong. The problem comes with interpretation. Calculi seem rigorous and pure, and by comparison our ordinary language may seem vague and confused. But to prefer the calculus for its merits is to slide into obscurantism, because the calculus is not a language but just a display of signs that must be interpreted by means of language if it is to have a use. We cannot make a false assertion in mathematical calculations, but only because truth is not at stake in the calculation. A scientific mistake is a different kind of mistake from a mathematical mistake. A mathematical statement in not itself a picture of reality, although we can use it like a picture to guide calculation. In mathematics, we postulate, and a form of truth is a derivative of postulation, whereas in science we construct pictures of reality. Mathematical mistakes may come from not following a rule correctly in a long and tricky calculation, but scientific mistakes can be errors of logical reasoning or mistaken observations. Observational mistakes cannot occur in mathematics as they can in science, since mathematical errors are errors in calculation. At the boundary of logic, the statements of mathematics are not reducible to logic, although we can use logic in mathematical derivations. Logic does not provide the numbers, but we can use logic to manipulate numbers. The application of logic allows mathematical and scientific assertions to share some family resemblances.

Wittgenstein's crucial observation in this area is that mathematical proof, or kinds of mathematical proof, determines whether mathematical assertions can be advanced. The two poles *proven* and *not proven* permit sentential logic a foothold for application. Proofs, of course, do not prove the statements they prove true or false as factual assertions; they are true or false only relative to their assertibility in a specific mathematical language game. The statement proved is not about mathematical objects but concerns a conditional fact. If we accept the premises as assertible in the language game, we must also accept the conclusion proved as belonging to the language game, provided that we accept the proof itself. Because there is no subject matter in reality for mathematics, the proven statements of mathematics can appear in connection with all kinds of

postulated mathematical symbolism. Mathematics is an assemblage
of language games, having no sharp and uniform external boundary,
with potentially confusing and criss-crossing subdisciplines held together by an internal network of analogous proof techniques.

Wittgenstein is not trying to develop a distinct philosophy of
mathematics. He is not rescuing a Kantian view of mathematics,
and he is not supporting intuitionism against Platonism. Wittgenstein is also not a skeptic about mathematics; as we understand
factual assertions in the *Tractatus*, so we understand clear cases of
mathematical usage, and we want to use these cases to find clarity
with respect to more obscure cases. His project is to draw the line
between sense and nonsense in areas of mathematics by employing
relevant notions of proof as an instrument of the survey. This project
is not terribly remote from the *Tractatus* in terms of its guiding
ideas. In the *Tractatus*, one-step hermeneutics yielded the sense of
a clear factual assertion as a display of its truth possibilities in a
structure similar to that given by truth tables. Wittgenstein's later
hermeneutics provides the sense of mathematical propositions by
embedding them in specific proofs. In the most similar case, a fully
analyzed mathematical proposition can be taken to be its own proof,
in that a mathematical analysis does not in such a case involve a
hidden language or a hidden symbolism.[7] When we do not notice
the supporting proof structure, we can become confused regarding
the meaning of a mathematical proposition; and when we suppose
that a proof *must* be available (although we cannot at present produce it or say what it would be like), we are likely to lapse into
mathematical nonsense.

In comparing Wittgenstein's views on mathematics and on science, it is easy to observe that Wittgenstein thought that he had
drawn a line of clarity through science and had explained what clear
factual assertion meant. If he seemed to accept verificationism, it
was because the line drawn by the horizon of truth functions seems

to coincide with verificationist impulses. Scientific theorizing is only conjecture about particular true or false assertions of fact. Although Wittgenstein was clearly not a positivist, his implied analysis of scientific assertion was quite consistent with the positivist philosophical opinions of his day concerning science. Positivists also wanted to eliminate metaphysical extravagance from science, and they also hoped that logic could be used as a tool for this purpose.

In turning to mathematics, philosophers tried either to duplicate the structure of mathematics within logic or to challenge the *entire* structure of mathematics, as in the case of the philosophical intuitionists. Philosophical intuitionism pursued a program of finding a special logic that would express the intuitionist ontology of mathematics. Wittgenstein's criticisms place him closer in spirit to the intuitionists, but he does not work with a systematic ontology of the kind that motivated the intuitionists. He retains his focus on the immanent analysis of particular sentences, looking for the appropriate proof structures that could yield their clear meaning. In drawing a line through mathematics on the basis of what could be proved in terms of local practices, Wittgenstein challenged the philosophical picture of mathematics more profoundly than he had challenged the philosophical picture of science. Science retains a factual basis given by the picture theory, but an analogous basis for mathematics is swept away, and the question of mathematical meaning depends on a local interweave with practice that precludes any grand design.

Wittgenstein is frequently seen as a hopeless tyro in the philosophy of mathematics, perhaps attempting no more than a screening of his ambitions for fame from the burgeoning reputations of Frege, Russell, and Gödel, an ambition that was protected by casting up an aura of constant philosophical puzzlement in the face of accepted mathematical practice.[8] If Wittgenstein drew the line of clear mathematical meaning too narrowly for the taste of most mathematicians and kept it hovering too closely around a coherent relationship to ordinary experience, it is far from clear that such a line cannot be coherently drawn. Russell and Frege, in their own ways, had attempted to curb the paradoxical excesses of Cantorian set theory by means of philosophically controlling axiomatic systems. Wittgenstein can be seen as working even more stringently within the framework of similar ideas. To some extent, Wittgenstein's attitude is quite like that of a mathematician who prefers to work naively with clear intuitive cases, rejecting the formal superstructures of mathematical theorizing as being of dubious clarity.[9]

In Wittgenstein's view, mathematical statements are related ultimately to such everyday activities as counting and measuring. It is possible to develop calculi of signs, but without controlling interpretation, such calculi can be of no philosophical interest. The horizon of a language game of mathematics is determined by the potential and actual use of that language game. If it has a variety of uses, it may be interpreted differently in each use, and the philosopher should consider one interpretation at a time. Wittgenstein's aversion to axiomatic systems, expressed clearly in his treatment of logic in the *Tractatus*, appears here once again. An axiomatic system, besides privileging certain statements arbitrarily as self-evident axioms, attempts to say everything at once that is possible within the horizon. All of its theorems are taken to lie hidden within the axioms and rules, coming clearly into view only when explicit derivations are located. These derivations are *not* the proofs that primarily interest Wittgenstein, and he is not convinced that an axiomatic system immediately establishes a space that we can explore leisurely by finding derivations.

When Wittgenstein had earlier described language as being established immediately, he had not meant that assertions should lie hidden, although puzzlement could require us to trace and recover connections to what is open and obvious. The establishment of a horizon and an associated space was meant to provide the resources for determining the meaning of any clear statement, compatibly with one-step hermeneutics. Applied to mathematical space, the axiomatic method has the wrong kind of structure, because whether or not a sentence can be asserted as a theorem in the space cannot be known until a proof has actually been constructed and until it is known that this proof is consistent with the other possible proofs in the same space. The space is therefore not clear by Wittgenstein's philosophical standards. Possibly hidden problems dominate the thought of axiomatizing mathematicians, especially the problem of contradiction. If a contradiction is hidden in the axiomatic system, such a system is considered ruined in advance, although its ruin cannot be recognized until the contradiction is located. Axiomatic systems raise contradiction to a universal anxiety but provide only delayed and indirect means for relieving the anxiety. Language is not ordinarily used in this way.

Wittgenstein refused to be terrorized by contradiction.[10] Although he did not know of modern proofs for consistency and completeness, he would have found them suspicious, if we may judge from his discussion of Gödel's results. If a mathematical statement has a clear and successful use, we can continue to use it in that way, even if it has a contradiction as a consequence. We ignore the contradiction—we simply do not draw the contradictory consequence in logic nor attempt to apply it. Wittgenstein may have in mind the rather obvious fact that all of our ordinary opinions may be contradictory if all of their consequences are drawn, a philosophical situation that does not paralyze us in everyday life, provided that we know which specific opinion to apply to any particular case. Or taking a case from science, the long dispute between the wave theories and the particle theories of light in physics did not paralyze physical thought; individual physicists were able to apply the different views to specific cases without encountering local contradictions, while the clash itself proved stimulating for the development of physical theory.

The peculiarities of Wittgenstein's views may seem less troubling when they are compared with the way we view games. Chess and mathematics are human creations whose individual configurations do not make factual statements about reality. An illuminating point of analogy is that both are guided by rules, and the rules give their pieces a significance that they do not have themselves. Chess is not about wooden figures, and mathematics is not about signs on paper. An illuminating point of contrast is that there is no winning or losing in mathematics, and arithmetic and geometry have applications to the real world that chess does not normally have.[11] Mathematics can share structure with reality, presenting possibilities in its application that can be realized, but it does not present a hypothetical better world in comparison to which reality is an inferior copy.[12]

Now suppose a game has been successfully played for a long time, and yet, in the playing of a particular game, the rules of the game are discovered to be contradictory. Such a situation occurs, for example, in professional sports, where rules are carefully formulated and studied, but not all eventualities can be foreseen. The discovery of a situation in which the current rules are contradictory does not make all of the games previously played meaningless. Future damage can be blocked from the contradiction by an emendation of the rules that prevents the contradictory position from arising, but the point is that the situation and the emendation may leave all of the previous games intact. One may even decide to resolve the conflict randomly, such as by tossing a coin to choose a single path out of a situation that is recognized as untenable. This normal localizing attitude toward encapsulating contradiction Wittgenstein recognizes as healthy in everyday life but as excluded from axiomatic mathematics by the imposition of overly stringent philosophical criteria.

Let us try to get a crude grasp on Wittgenstein's placement of mathematical statements by considering an arithmetic equation. An equation does not state a fact about reality, and it is not true or false in the manner of factual assertions, although it can be used on specific occasions to create a factual assertion. An equation makes a kind of ersatz statement to the effect that what its sides show is an equivalence.[13] The sense of an equation is thus completely given in its expression, and so an equation alludes directly to the proof of this equivalence. The proof is usually not expressible in logic alone but requires steps that are licensed only by the grammar of a mathematical language game. Whether or not it is true that the sides show an equivalence is relative to an appropriate horizon of proof, given often by a calculus, within which the proof can be rigorously constructed.[14] Relative to the manipulations permitted by this calculus, an equation can be said to be true or false, depending on whether an appropriate proof is constructed. Key terms, such as *truth* and *proof*, are thus clearly established with respect to the kind of horizon associated with one-step hermeneutics. Unlike the single horizon of the *Tractatus*, however, mathematics will have many horizons, each associated with a clear notion of proof techniques. There should not be any unanswerable proper questions in mathematics, since the relevant horizon and the statement in question provide the resources for resolving clear meaning. Nonsense arises when statements are made that have no clear horizon or that are simultaneously resolved against different horizons.

Philosophical nonsense has the same foothold that it had in the *Tractatus* system. "This extension has this number" is philosophical nonsense because an extension and its cardinality have an internal relationship and because the sentence attempts to state what can only be shown. But the autonomy of mathematical language also generates its own problems. If the rules of mathematical syntax generate a seemingly infinite number of possibilities, as when the positive integers are generated by an inductive rule, attempts to talk all at once about all of the numbers so generated are almost certain to depart from clear sense. What such propositions attempt to express is shown in the use of the inductive rule, but an induction cannot properly be given as a statement.[15] An induction cannot lay out all of its cases for our inspection at once. We can inspect only particular instances generated by the induction; we cannot survey all of its consequences. The use of an induction is mystified if it is assimilated to an axiomatic system. An induction is more like a scientific theory, a conjecture about the status of some specific assertions that it can help to generate.

Wittgenstein is quite careful to separate talk of finite numbers from talk of infinity. Finite numbers can, in principle, always be interwoven with practice, by means of counting. Infinite numbers cannot typically be interwoven with practice. "Three things lie in this direction" can be true when interpreted as a factual assertion, and it may be derivably true in the context of a constructive mathematical proof in some particular mathematical language game. "Infinitely many things lie in this direction" has a completely different philosophical grammar, even though the surface assertive grammar may seem similar. Endless time and endless direction exist only as grammatical possibilities or rules for generating specific assertions; they cannot exist in reality.[16] Nonsense arises when this distinction is overlooked. Infinity is related to rules that function as hypotheses did in science, generating more and more specific mathematical assertions. The equation "$m = 2n$" seems to correlate any number with another number twice as large as the first, but it cannot be said to correlate all numbers with all other numbers.[17] *We* have to correlate numbers case by case, using the equation as a guide. Wittgenstein's way with Cantorian paradoxes and with the assertions that give rise to them is to treat them as nonsense whenever they try to assert something about actual infinities. The fact that the symbolism seems to be under syntactic control does not impress Wittgenstein; the symbolism is a mere calculus unless it produces specific mathematical propositions that have clear empirical meanings.

Proofs are proofs of particular propositions, relative to a particular horizon. The propositional sign expressing a proposition may express different propositions in different calculi or in different language games, leading to a complicated variety of cases, each of which, ecproperly understood, can be perfectly clear. A proof must be totally convincing in its context, so that the status of the proved proposition is determined without residue. We cannot say in general how we mean a proof; its acceptance and its import are interwoven with mathematical training when the proof is perspicuous.[18] Its acceptance is a decision based on what it shows; it is not completely a matter of argument. A proof depends on what it shows in its grammar, a fact that carries the distinction between saying and showing over to mathematical propositions. A proof is therefore not an empirical experiment, concerning which reinterpretation always remains a permanent possibility. A proof is like a single thought experiment that is totally convincing and that will be totally convincing to others with similar training.[19] Wittgenstein wants to remove the aura of mystifying power that proofs may seem to have, explicating proofs as a part of our extended natural history that is shaped by a certain kind of training. The philosopher cannot *explain* the coercive power of proofs; the philosophical task is to locate the proofs that are totally convincing and to compare them in detail with proofs that seem confusing or too hastily accepted. The mechanism for generating mathematical nonsense, hasty generalization, is already familiar as the mechanism responsible elsewhere for generating philosophical nonsense from clear factual assertions.

Proofs are autonomous with respect to their horizons; they develop chains of propositions in terms of decisions we seem compelled to make, and yet these choices cannot be checked against reality.[20] It is easy to blur the line between empirical and grammatical considerations if we are not careful. If I measure a table with a yardstick, the logic of the situation is that I could be checking either the length of the table or the length of the yardstick. Accepting the yardstick as fixed—a decision that cannot be proven to be correct—allows determination of the length of the table. If people calculate what they have to pay for things, we can describe their behavior as accepting the calculations as fixed, the calculations determining what is to be paid. We generally pay more for more of what we are paying for, as the amount is determined by weight or volume.[21] But this observation is based on everyday life and its activities. If we paid more because the seller was older or because we were taller than the seller, this behavior would not be less logical or less mathematically correct, although it would seem a strange practice from our normal point of view. Nor could we argue that, because we do it as we do, it is rational, since many of our forms of social interaction are manifestly irrational.[22] Proofs and calculations do not prove anything absolutely; they are accepted or agreed upon as determining certain further actions, based on an interweave with generally accepted social practices. At a given time, the philosopher can only note and develop these points of agreed-upon grammar. Our economic payments flow out of primitive barter where money does not yet change hands.

We do not frequently move suddenly from satisfaction to dissatisfaction with our pictures or our grammars, so their theoretical logical defeasibility should not be a central philosophical concern. When we come to do philosophy, we can begin with fixed points of agreement in grammar and with their associated human practices. These agreements have arisen in history, but we may properly take them as the fixed points that create the current space within which meaningful assertion and interaction take place. Wittgenstein has tried to locate in natural human decisions the force of what had seemed to some earlier philosophers to be a set of synthetic a priori constraints. He could not meaningfully locate that force in a Platonic realm of meanings and their fixed relationships. Mathematicians invent new forms of symbolism and possible description; they do not discover an already existing a priori realm.[23] Mathematics involves logic insofar as its proven propositions can be manipulated within language games by the rules of logic, forming new links between clear and proven mathematical assertions. Wittgenstein is not out to prove that the inventor image is correct and that the discoverer image is wrong. He wishes to attack the inevitability of the discoverer image, an inevitability that cannot stand when mathematical calculi are regarded as the potentially defeasible instruments of human agreement.

With these observations in hand, Wittgenstein is relentlessly careful in accepting standard interpretations of leading results in mathematical logic. As we have seen, mathematical propositions are not factual assertions, but they can be considered true in a derivative sense when they stand at the end of proofs. More specifically, a proposition of Russell's system is true only when it has been proven. Many metamathematical results depend on a more general and Platonic notion of truth. One form of Gödel's results states that there will always be a true but unprovable proposition of elementary number theory with respect to any consistent axiomatization of elementary number theory, showing that all consistent axiomatizations are incomplete. A reference to a potentially infinite series of gradually expanding axiomatic systems should arouse philosophical suspicion. The proof of this result depends on the idea that all of the syntactially well-formed propositions in the syntax of the system must be already true or false, whether they are or are not yet proven in an existing consistent axiomatic system. Wittgenstein objects at this point. Before the proofs are obtained, propositions of this language are not properly regarded as necessarily true or false, because truth values for such propositions exist only when a relevant proof has been constructed within an appropriate language game. The speculation that there is always a true proposition not provable within a given axiomatic system fails to make clear sense, because the notion of truth involved cannot be linked to an existing language-game horizon.[24]

Let us consider another example, that of Cantor's diagonal proof to establish the nonenumerability of the real numbers. The basic strategy of the proof is to imagine an enumerating list of the real numbers between 0 and 1, given as decimal fractions, and then to specify a number not on this list because it differs from the first number in the first place, the second number in the second place, and so on. Wittgenstein argues that no actual real number is generated by this process, since we can have determined only a finite number of its places after any real calculation using this rule, not enough for us to say exactly which real number we are generating. Wittgenstein concedes that the diagonal proof says something about the multiplicity of the concept of a real number but denies that its normal interpretation, which speaks of a relationship of difference in cardinality between two entire infinite sets of numbers, can be clearly carried through. The concept of a real number is only partially determined by the proof. Wittgenstein, in short, is determined to hold statements of metamathematics and set theory to a restricted range of surveyable clarity, arguing that propositions wilder in content must somehow be reducible to this range or must be regarded as nonsense when we attempt to spell out what they say.

This position has seemed to some an expression of sheer ignorance, a failure to grasp the established channels of mathematical practice and the empirical power of its sophisticated results, but the continuing unavailability of consistency and completeness proofs for sophisticated axiomatic systems in these areas is sufficient to indicate that Wittgenstein's criticisms are not completely without point. It must also be remembered that his principal target is not mathematical practice but philosophical interpretations of mathematical practice, including those proposed by mathematicians, that attempt to justify mathematical assertions as necessary truths without relating them to a horizon of clear sense.

Logic itself must be carefully tailored to the details of mathematical language games because apparent truth-functional structure may have to give way to the grammar associated with particular mathematical language games. For example, the law of excluded middle, rejected totally by intuitionists on general philosophical grounds, has some instantiations in the domain of mathematics according to Wittgenstein, but its use requires careful adjustment to local mathematical grammar. Consider again the sequence 7777, one that has not yet been located in the expansion of π. A hasty move is to say that this sequence must occur or must not occur in π and to formulate this assertion as an apparent instance of the law of excluded middle: $P \lor \sim P$. Now if P states that the sequence must occur in the expansion, there are several problems. What is the nature of the necessity? Unless the expansion already exists and we are exploring it (a possibility rejected by Wittgenstein because the expansion is infinite and cannot be completely laid out in advance), there are problems. If P announces the necessity of the sequence's occurring, $\sim P$ must state, not the necessity of the nonoccurrence, but the possibility of the nonoccurrence, since the necessity operator will lie within the scope of the negation as part of P in an instance of excluded middle.[25]

We cannot interpret this sense of possibility, since we cannot be sure that our current rules of expansion give it as a possibility. (Not every sequence need be a possible sequence with respect to the exact rules that we are applying.) If P states merely that the sequence will occur, $P \lor \sim P$ is an instance of excluded middle, but it is then an empirical statement or an empirical projection rather than a purely mathematical proposition. The normative force of the rules laid down in mathematical language games has been lost. We may feel certain that we mean something with respect to an infinite prediction, but feeling certain has been demonstrated repeatedly not to be a sure guide to necessity. In the realm of mathematics, $P \vee \sim P$ cannot have a clear sense if P or $\sim P$ does not have a clear sense, and it may not have a clear sense unless both P and $\sim P$ make clear sense.[26] The law of excluded middle is everywhere applicable in the domain of picturing assertion, as in the *Tractatus*, because such assertions (and their negations) always have a clear sense. It cannot be taken over to mathematics, however, without deciding, case by case, whether the presupposition of clear sense is met both by P and by $\sim P$. Logicism assumes incorrectly that logic may be taken over wholesale into the domain of mathematics, assuming without a discussion that the philosophical grammar of factual assertion and that of mathematical assertion have the same essential structure.

For Wittgenstein, the concept of proof has no general essence and no clear boundary, but particular proofs must meet high standards of perspicuity and surveyability. A convincing proof must be reproducible; it must therefore have a kind of crude but clear structure that is not destroyed by minor deviations and that can be easily remembered. A drawing used to provide a proof in geometry has essential features, but its straight lines need not be straight, nor its circles perfect. Wide latitude in the exact representation will provide the same conviction. A convincing proof must be capable of being grasped all at once, so to speak. Very complicated proofs, whose structure is not surveyable, do not count as genuine proofs. Shortened proofs can help to provide conviction that complicated proofs are correct. A proof pattern that cannot be grasped can be shortened and turned into a proof where there was none before. Wittgenstein's objection to logicism becomes the objection that its supposed proofs fail in not being perspicuous.[27] Russell's proofs do not prove theorems of arithmetic; they prove that arithmetic theorems can be syntactically expressed within Russell's system. The structure of Russell's proofs is often so unperspicuous that survey and checking become an empirical and fallible matter. The real foundation of mathematics is not logic but the fact that different methods of finite counting almost always agree.[28]

A final objection to the Russellian approach is that a reduction to logical notation suggests falsely a uniformity of mathematical practice, just as printed words had suggested a uniformity among factual assertions to the author of the *Tractatus*. Mathematics is not uniformly anything, much less uniformly logic. Mathematics is a motley of techniques of proof, a fact based on its manifold applicability and its importance for a variety of practical aspects. Each proof is unique, showing us something that it alone can demonstrate. When two proofs meet in the same propositional sign, any attempt to say that the two proved propositions are the same must proceed from other connections, not from a mere matching of their syntactic structures. If we can arrive and leave various places in discourse using different proofs interchangeably, equivalence will gradually be established. Proofs help to bring about mutual understanding; experiments presuppose mutual understanding.[29] Of course, mutual understanding may be obtained after experiment, but proofs always establish some item of grammar, while experiments always presuppose some item of grammar.

Calculations can be as perspicuous as proofs, involving no mistakes. The statement "$12 \times 12 = 144$" is a calculation of grammar, indicating a limit point that cannot be in error. The child, learning to calculate, can make mistakes concerning these limit points, but by the same token does not yet calculate. Secure mathematical propositions are so overdetermined by practice and prior decision that they could not be false, and they cannot be falsified by simple observations of fact. We dismiss awkward experiences as not covered by the relevant mathematics, retaining mathematics as the standard of acceptable content.[30]

Wittgenstein's philosophy of mathematics is not designed to provide foundations for mathematics. Foundations already exist in measurement, estimation, training in the number sequence, agreement in counting, and so forth. Parts of the domain of mathematics are sharply marked off from clear factual assertion in Wittgenstein's later work, and the division in discourse is already immanent in the everyday activities that ultimately give rise to the two forms of discourse. There are hybrid assertions, of course, as when we count or measure things in the real world, but the assertions of pure mathematics provide the grammar that makes it possible to articulate hybrid empirical assertions and that enables their refinement.

Wittgenstein's technique is used to probe the limits of clear mathematical assertion from the inside, so to speak, just as the limits of clear factual assertion had been probed from the inside in the *Tractatus*. Wittgenstein finds more philosophical pseudopropositions in mathematics than most philosophers do, but to argue that mathematics is not mystified at all and needs only philosophical foundations is itself to succumb to mystification. Much of mathematics is an exotic extension of ordinary language. Wittgenstein did not intend to revise mathematics but to eliminate from it the rot of philosophical interpretation and speculation, including that produced by mathematicians.

Many of the topics of Wittgenstein's *Remarks on the Foundations of Mathematics* run parallel to topics raised in connection with the philosophy of psychology in the *Investigations*. One of the most important issues is rule following. Wittgenstein's discussion of this

topic has become a much-discussed topic in philosophical commentary on his work.[31] After restricting the *Tractatus* to language
games of factual assertion, Wittgenstein seems for a time to have
taken languages as though they were calculi whose applications were
determined by rules.[32] This device could model the diversity of language games by modeling that diversity of language games by modeling that diversity in terms of different kinds of rules, and many
mathematical language games seem to bear family resemblances to
other kinds of games that are highly constrained by rules. The *Tractatus* could be taken as a special case of such a system. But if Wittgenstein did hold for a time a rigid conception of rules of games as
naturally yielding interpretations and meanings, he quickly recognized a problem with the interpretation of rules. We can and do
follow some rules naturally, showing an understanding of clear rules
by simply acting in accordance with them, a fact that can be noted
but not explained. Such understanding is the clear basis for following
rules in general. We have to interpret rules consciously when they
are new or complicated or even weird. The great failing of philosophers in discussing rules is to hold that we follow rules by interpreting or reading off a private formulation of their meanings in
every case. In saying that the last interpretation of rules is just
following them or acting in accordance with them, Wittgenstein is
attacking philosophical obscurity and preferring the description of
public and coherent agreements that can be noted and discussed as
the foundation of meaning for rule-governed activity.

Wittgenstein typically grounds his discussion of rule following
in clear cases and tries to embarrass what he sees as philosophical nonsense in attempts to *explain* the clearest cases. As human
beings, we can all be trained to follow certain clear cases of rules,
as when we learn how to follow the arrows on a marked hiking
trail. At a level further removed from common activity, Wittgenstein notes as a matter of fact that disputes do not typically break

out among mathematicians regarding whether certain rules are being followed.[33] This observation is taken as clear and basic. Tables, ostensive definitions, and similar instruments can function as rules, if we take them correctly in hand. When we understand a rule, we know how to go on, which means something different with different rules in different circumstances.[34] It is possible that we simply grasp how to go on, that we simply can go on, and that we do not follow a rule by means of an interpretation that tells us how to continue.[35]

In any event, the idea that a complete list of rules can determine an activity or be used to give the meaning of a word is an absurdity. Rules leave some things open, although we can act quite clearly on the basis of rules. It is characteristic of human beings who share a certain form of life that they go on in the same way in the face of certain rules, and the philosopher cannot legitimately do more than describe that fact. We are tempted, when we think philosophically, to talk too much, to try to remove exceptions that we can imagine by refining rules, making them more rigid and precise. If something happens in the brain of the follower of a rule that explains regularity in behavior, that event could be a matter for scientific hypothesis, but it is not a legitimate focus for philosophical conjecture.[36] We can play games without being completely bounded by rules, and the conception of a language game *completely bounded* by rules is a Procrustean philosophical demand.[37]

As Wittgenstein develops his remarks on rules, he notes that their importance in special cases in making behavior more regular can rest only on a natural basis that can only be described. Knowing how to use a rule is like recognizing the color red again. We can do both of these things, and it is pseudoexplanation for philosophy to suggest that this ability is due to an internal representation of the rule or the color, against which each specific application is checked.[38] Another error is to suppose that the individual steps in following a rule are already implicit in the statement of the rule, an error similar to that of supposing that the axioms and rules of an axiomatic system already contain all of its theorems and all of its contradictory consequences, if there are any. We give instruction in a rule by saying "right" or "wrong" to the tyro, stopping when we observe that only right steps are being made. Wittgenstein's point is that performance is critical in the sense that no greater security concerning future agreement than present and past practice is possible. Skepticism is short-circuited by what lies open to view. Even the rule follower's own explanations do not force certainty. The statement that a certain rule is being followed or is being interpreted in some way leaves open the question whether we would agree in every possible case, and the evidence for our agreement reverts back simply to the fact that we agree on the explicit cases that we have jointly considered. A rule is like the mortar between bricks. We do not use another adhesive to join the mortar to the bricks; we simply use the mortar to fit two bricks together. A rule is used to fit two cases together, and it does not typically need an interpretation to join it to the cases.

Quite in the face of textual evidence suggesting that rule following is often clearly given in practice, Wittgenstein is at times interpreted as a skeptic concerning the following of rules.[39] Some have argued that, as he established the idea that internal representation is nonsense, he destroyed the idea that rules could be objectively followed. How can current practice be known to be in conformity with past practice? Even if current practice is uniform, how can it be established that it is correct?[40] Wittgenstein's inability to answer these questions brings a charge based on an assessment against the wrong criteria. Wittgenstein thought that such questions presupposed a philosophically ruinous search for certainty. Of course Wittgenstein knew that accepted practice in the present was not the only criterion of whether a rule is appropriately stated or whether it is being and has been correctly followed. If we agree that we will all write down the same names on individual scraps of paper and look at the scraps after doing so, the scraps may not all have the same names. When a rule is followed, we expect individual behavior to agree, and if the rule is clear, we are astonished by individual variation.

Using a calculus, relating different bits of information consistently to current grammar, explaining what we are doing—all of these activities and more are relevant to the question whether current and expected agreement should be taken for granted.[41] We frequently discuss our agreements and probe the question whether our practice is in conformity with various rules. Legal disputes often raise such discussion to a highly reflective level, where resolution is also expected on the basis of clear past practice in simpler cases. Nothing *makes* an application of a rule correct, certainly not an agreement. Where we cannot be mistaken concerning which rule we are following, we can be convinced that we are not following it correctly when unnoticed aspects of our practice are brought to light. It is absurd to suppose that a good philosophical theory of rule following could make such discussions otiose or even that it could bring about the resolution of such practical problems. The mistake of the philosopher here, as elsewhere, is to want to unmask the future in the present. Sometimes we must be content to wait, just as in everyday life.

If Wittgenstein had been a skeptic about rule following, the simplest mathematical language games as well as the simplest language games in other domains would be infected with the virus of skepticism, since rule following is always interwoven with grammar. Wittgenstein's problems with mathematical statements have nothing to do in general with whether or not we will go on to new mathematical cases in the same way inside a clearly defined language game. Mathematical language games are autonomous from other quarters of the City in that their autonomy and their internal family resemblances depend on the kinds of mathematical proof that are involved in their description. Rule following, clearly involved with the description of mathematical language games, provides an internal grammatical link to the wilder relationships of grammar in other areas of the City.

Seven

SEEING AND COLOR

WE HAVE discussed the extrusion of mathematics from the *Tractatus* system first, for at least one important reason. The mathematical quarter of Wittgenstein's City might have been developed autonomously and somehow added to the *Tractatus* system, forcing only a retraction of the claims to philosophical completeness that describe the success of the *Tractatus* program. When color incompatibilities are recognized, they force deeper changes, for at least two reasons. First, the color attributions of ordinary life remain factual assertions in many cases. Any deep problems with their analysis thus tends to necessitate the division of the apparent domain of the *Tractatus* into autonomous realms, each with its own grammar. This development raises the question whether analysis of still other domains of apparently factual assertions would not be required before an overall crude map of ordinary-language usage would be in sight. The second reason for the depth of the challenge of color is that many color statements turn out to be much more complex than they seem at first. There are the problems that primary colors seem to exclude each other from copresence at a single point and that one surface may seem to be of the same color shade as another, except twice as bright or twice as saturated.

When these two problems are recognized, dozens are knocking at the door. For example: should black and white be regarded as colors in the same sense that red and yellow are? Color seems to be inextricably involved both with certain objective physical structures and also with certain phenomenological structures. We can divide the questions of what color something has and what color it seems to us to have under certain conditions of viewing.[1] Discussions of color draw the self into the world as a contributing factor in the phenomenology of color. Even if the relationships of perceived colors are objective, they are different from many physical relationships of color. Once color statements are to be analyzed in cases that include the phenomenology of color, the self (in some sense) is so firmly part of the world that questions of philosophical psychology are firmly on the agenda of analysis. This factor may be the reason that the analysis of color produced in its wake the entire range of topics of philosophical psychology associated with the later Wittgenstein.

The problems with the original analysis of color can be traced to Wittgenstein's paper of 1929 on logical form, which announces the problems with the completeness of the *Tractatus* system and suggests solutions that Wittgenstein then immediately repudiated.[2] If the *Tractatus* was thought to solve its problems completely, Wittgenstein seemed to realize after he had written this paper to fine-tune the *Tractatus* system that it introduced more problems than it could solve. The *Tractatus,* in the course of illustrating the remark that all necessity was logical, noted that two assertions attributing different colors to precisely the same spot could not be jointly asserted. Some deeper structure of color needed to be found to explain this restriction and to analyze the joint assertion as an explicit contradiction. At this time Wittgenstein took the ordinary color terms to be essential to the analysis of ordinary language, but he recognized that these terms are abstractions, in that there are nonmatching shades of ordinary colors.

Wittgenstein's intuition at the time of the *Tractatus* seems to have been that a term such as *red* would not appear in elementary propositions but would be analyzed as a disjunction of specific shades of red that could be phenomenologically discriminated. Red, attributed to a precise spot, could appear in analysis as a disjunction of attributions of specific shades of red to the spot, and all of the disjunctions would be disjoint from all of the disjunctions involved in the analysis of other primary colors. Just enough sentential structure seems to appear here to suggest that color statements could be further analyzed into color terms that do not lose touch with ordinary experience, as they refer to specific colors that we can match and discriminate. Although this approach might have seemed promising as an anticipated direction of analysis, it is almost embarrassing to note that this analysis cannot be carried through.

Two specific disjuncts referring to specific shades of color, whether both red, for example, or belonging to two different abstract colors, will also exclude one another at the new primitive level. If the incompatibility of two colors such as red and green has been analyzed into more elementary propositions, the problem of grammatical exclusion repeats itself at the new level, which now calls for a further analysis if the *Tractatus* is to be salvaged for color. The relationships *between* the disjuncts comprising colors, relationships of brightness, saturation, and so forth also cannot be given by the supposedly logically disjunctive structure of the colors. Wittgenstein first attempted a revision of the *Tractatus* by modifying logical structure in view of the syntax or grammar of color, but the results were inconclusive and restricted.[3] The crack in the autonomy of logic in the domain of color widens to inspection, finally undoing the validity of the *Tractatus* system for the complete range of color attributions. The case of color forces the emergence of autonomous grammars that completely change the *Tractatus* survey of color.

Wittgenstein next had an idea that achieved a partial solution to the color problem.[4] An element of representation is now taken as analogous to a yardstick rather than as analogous to a name, and the yardstick has a scale that is laid against reality. The picture of a discrete color spectrum of disjunctive colors begins to merge into a continuous spectrum of colors, only one of which touches reality at a point on a given occasion. Reality determines a point on the yardstick, but we are able to see the whole scale of the yardstick and consequently the possible points of the yardstick that reality excludes in selecting a single point of the spectrum.

We know from syntax that reality on a given occasion selects only one point of the yardstick at a point in reality, but the determination of color could otherwise be independent of other determinations at the ultimate level of analysis, say, determinations of time and place. Each could vary, logically independently of the others, in the sense that any place could go with a particular color, and any color with a particular time, and so on, but only one time, one place, and one color would constitute a simplest picture of reality. Again, we could draw no conclusions other than logical necessities about the future. If a place has a fixed color over time, its color could change at any moment. We can now think of the ultimate level of analysis as determining that an elementary proposition is the confrontation of a set of independent yardsticks with reality, each yardstick representing an independent aspect of reality. Reality would then determine a specific point on each of all the yardsticks at each point in logical space. No inferences from yardstick to yardstick would be possible (that is, from the place reality determines on one yardstick to the place it determines on another), and this feature would be the trace of the doctrine of logical independence that was central to the *Tractatus*. We could, however, draw an inference within a yardstick that a determined value excluded other values on the same yardstick, a step that first hints of a grammatical supplement to the *Tractatus* system. In principle, such a solution seems to provide only an addition to the picture of the *Tractatus*, a second dimension of exclusion, so to speak, overcoming Wittgenstein's confusions of 1929 and allowing the *Tractatus* conception to retain a central place.[5]

Trouble unfortunately appears when the phenomenology of color is more deeply probed. Color is not a dimension that can naturally be probed merely by the yardstick metaphor, no matter what the color spectrum might suggest. The color spectrum yields only a determination of hue, and since saturation and intensity must also be represented, a full analysis of even the simplest factual assertions appears in a conceptual space involving a color solid, not merely a yardstick representing the spectrum.

It is sometimes argued that Wittgenstein at first attempted to let factual color phenomena dictate color syntax and that the yardstick metaphor traces the completion of this stage. At one point, he says that the exclusion of one color by another with respect to a spot is not like the exclusion of one man from another with respect to a place on a bench.[6] The former is said to be a grammatical or logical impossibility, the latter a physical impossibility. Such a view can suggest the possibility that there is a sharp break between the two notions of possibility and that Wittgenstein's interests shifted from physical to logical or grammatical possibility, permitting a doctrine of autonomous language games to emerge. Wittgenstein means to retain the distinction between logic (or grammar) and fact, the postulation of the former allowing the latter to be formulated. This position does *not* mean that the rules of grammar, carrying the trace of logical necessity, are nonjustifiable and arbitrary. They are such only because we decide what to make part of grammar, but these decisions are ultimately based on practice. Wittgenstein's point is that the notions *justification* and *arbitrariness* break down in connection with the decision to make an apparent physical impossibility into a grammatical barrier. That two men cannot sit in one spot on a bench becomes grammatically impossible once the men and the spot are coded into elements of representation for certain kinds of factual assertion. We could name types of people with respect to their seating bulk, as well as types of seating places, and thus produce grammatical barriers in a specialized syntax.[7]

When Wittgenstein alludes to other possible grammars, his purpose is to give us a feeling for the shape of our grammar as it is. We do not have a shift from logic to syntax and grammar, as Wittgenstein addresses the color problem, but a gradual recognition that color phenomena involve barriers that are best thought of as grammatical barriers and a recognition that the complexity of these color phenomena seem perfectly wild in comparison with the simple color statements that had exhausted the topic in the *Tractatus*. Philosophical analysis in this area had to involve subtleties of a kind that had completely escaped the Procrustean assertoric measure of the *Tractatus*, and it suggested the open family texture of later analysis of psychological topics.

We will now look at some of the complexities that seep into Wittgenstein's discussions of color, even though Wittgenstein is painfully aware that he barely scratches the surface of the grammar of color. In the later work, analysis is never completed, except for the resolution of some very specific puzzles. In the *Notebooks*, Wittgenstein had already raised some of the crucial problems, but he seems to have repressed them in the writing of the *Tractatus*. He recognizes in the *Notebooks* that a point cannot be red and green at the same time and considered such combination a physical impossibility.[8] This view is taken over into the *Tractatus*, even though the contradiction is analyzed there in terms of relevant elementary propositions of color that refer to specific hues.

Another *Notebooks* problem is that of a colored surface. When we look at a uniformly colored surface, we can see that all of the points of the surface have the same color, even though we do not see each single point of the surface.[9] In this sense, a proposition seems to be able to state something concerning infinitely many points without itself being infinitely complex. Facts about each point do not follow from facts about the surface in truth-functional logic, but they might still be part of a logical analysis. This puzzle may explain why the *Tractatus* is unable to rule out an infinite number of objects and states of affairs.[10] Later, Wittgenstein analyzes an infinite grammatical space of color and a finite space of color perception and associates each of these two spaces with an interwoven grammar. What is infinite belongs to grammar, but grammar will license some of the inferences required for philosophical analysis and therapy. The fact that color belongs to both a physical and a phenomenal space seems inextricably mixed in Wittgenstein's first analyses of color phenomena.

In the *Tractatus*, red belongs to the space of colors that we use to describe things, along with other primary colors.[11] The complexity of colors such as red is then gradually traced out relative to a growing budget of particular language games. In at least one of these games, red remains an element of representation, along with other primary colors. This color system for factual color ascription presents grammatical barriers, but its adoption allows us to make the factual color assertions that we use to describe reality. In this use, color space does not *contain* colors, and it is not *abstracted* from colors. It lays down the grammatical structure within which all color assertion will make sense. Places in this system can be taught ostensively, provided that the existence of this structure and its basic grammar have already been grasped.[12]

According to this system, a reddish-green is not possible because red and green are pure colors at the *end* points of the system, placing a barrier of grammar in the path of joint attribution, although the colors can be mixed to get colors that are not red and green at the same time. We can change this grammar, but we would not know what to do with the new grammar.[13] With the system we have, we can analyze all of the pure hues we encounter as mixtures of the primary colors. Nonprimary colors can be described in terms of the primary colors, but not the primary colors themselves, which can only be exhibited.[14] The grammar of color is not a purely arbitrary convention. Lighter and darker, as well as primary colors, have an anchor in experience that allows the color system to be inclusive of our color experiences and immanent in our ordinary color ascriptions.

Wittgenstein takes the color octahedron to give a bird's-eye view of the factual grammar of pure colors.[15] Pure primary colors stand as end points, and any particular hue that is not primary is assigned a place within the octahedron. This view raises a delicate point about the explicit introduction of grammars in the quarters of Wittgenstein's City. A representation such as the color solid should not be viewed as a philosophical discovery that is used to *explain* the ordinary use of language. If logic is a structure sometimes thought to lie hidden in the ordinary use of language, grammar certainly is not. We already understand the use of primary color terms, as well as many other color terms related to natural objects. It would seem that there might be color gaps in ordinary language because we can experience colors that we do not have names for. But samples of color come into play here as standing for the colors that we may want to discuss, and the samples may be regarded as part of the language of color.[16] I can bring a sample of a wall color to a paint store and then match the color by mixing colors until the match is obtained. Our activities of mixing up colors are sufficient to show that color space can be filled in, even if ordinary language has not provided us with all of the specific names that there might be for colors. None of the colors is therefore missing in ordinary-language usage, but specific names for colors may have to be supplied for particular purposes.

Color space is given in advance, but it is not completely labeled. The horizon is there, and we can understand any particular location within this space. Where names for particular colors are required, as in stamp collecting or interior design, color names can easily be added as names of particular samples. Philosophical grammars do not lie behind ordinary language; they fill in what is immanent in ordinary language, taking careful note of existing grammatical barriers. Science itself grows in this way, many of its specialized language games constituting grammatical extensions of ordinary language that are adapted to local patterns of data.[17] A science may generate an explanatory language to account for features of ordinary language or its extensions, but it is not the job of philosophy to attempt explanations, nor its primary job to analyze extant scientific explanations. Wittgenstein's philosophical grammars lie implicit in ordinary usage and will, when developed, carefully reflect distinctions in this usage that are easily missed in the uniform appearance of language. The color octahedron is part of our language, not an analysis of it.

Wittgenstein spends considerable energy in developing a careful phenomenology of color. We could not understand anyone who said that there were five pure colors. We also cannot say that red is a pure color, since this statement is shown only in our symbolism. We see the pure colors as points that show themselves and that indicate the limits of the grammar. Within the space, we can immediately see and state important relationships of color. We can see that orange is a mixture of red and yellow, for example, and that our finer judgments of fact can build on these crude and inescapable observations.[18] If I have two paint pots—say, of violet and orange—I can shift the color of mixtures toward either end quite smoothly, by altering the mixture, but I cannot produce a pure color by mixing mixtures. The color solid can thus be seen as a convenient and succinct representation of the grammar of color that ultimately matches the multiplicity of our color that ultimately matches the multiplicity of our color experiences, at least where color hues are concerned.

The color octahedron belongs to the physics of color. Matters change drastically when we consider the contextual perception of colors. The grammar of the colored surfaces of bodies is different from the grammar of colored solids, that is, bodies that are colored clear through.[19] Judgments of lightness of color can come from either discourse, and they can be either grammatical or empirical.[20] In the former case, an absolute color can be located in the color solid as a light color, or two locations can be compared, and one found lighter than the other. Such propositions resemble those of the *Tractatus*, because they are true or false in terms of the reality that they stand for. But in a painting or a colored photograph, the sky may be lighter than any other thing, even though it is objectively presented with a fairly dark color. Again, a piece of white paper may be quite dark as its local color is matched to the color solid, although it will still be seen as white, if it is recognized to be white paper. A book with white pages might be darker than a yellow sky, in terms of matching to the color solid, even though the book pages are seen as lighter than the sky.[21]

A psychological component enters inevitably into all judgments of color and lightness in such representations, and it is a component that is of dizzying complexity for philosophical analysis, perhaps capable of analysis only in particular cases in fixed contexts and concerning which particular puzzlements are troubling. Generalization is hard to achieve concerning perceived colors. Red and white can appear to be hot, but brown and gray cannot be hot.[22] A glowing gray does not appear anywhere in either the physics or the psychology of color. A weak white light remains white to perception, especially when it is identifiable as the color of a white object, and it is then never gray.[23] Gold is always a glittering surface color that belongs to the psychology of color because of its glitter. Whether I see a particular spot as white or gray will depend on how I see the illumination and on what I think I am looking at. A gray place can be seen as white in poor light, or gray in good light.

All of these problems are raised by the effect of colors on one another in actual paintings and representations and by the influence of what we know about the appearance of colors in reality. The contextual element is so dramatic that a color can look completely different in a painting and alone on the palette.[24] Someone who picks a spot in a painting and wants to match that color for the walls of a room will find that the meaning of having the same color is here placed under severe pressure. Individual pieces cut from paintings do not at all reveal the colors that we see in the context of the painting. What we think we know about what we think we are looking at introduces a virtually unmanageable component into the phenomenology of color. Having raised these problems, Wittgenstein was never able to solve very many of them at the level of grammar.

Wittgenstein studied the distinction between opaque and transparent colors, one that he traced back to Goethe's theory of colors. Goethe's theory seemed to Wittgenstein a primitive color grammar, rather than a theory of the physics of color.[25] Transparent colors suggest something beyond; they color a more distant field with a color that is being looked through. From this point of view, white is always opaque, a pure transparent white being as inconceivable as transparent milk. The question is why the transparency of other colors will not carry over to white, which indicates that we have run up against a grammatical barrier.[26] Red transparencies cannot be cloudy. We can see a white surface as red through a red glass, or as white, but we cannot see it as black when we look through a black glass.[27] The problem here is that just looking at the color hues in the color solid suggests that colors are alternatives to one another. Looking at hues conceals the real breaks in color grammar that come into view only when we attempt to survey closely what we can intelligently say and lay aside the preconceptions of philosophy.

White occupies a peculiar position in the phenomenology of color, as we have already noted, but white can appear at times on equal footing with other colors, as in flags and patterns. When white is mixed in to weaken colors, the resulting phenomena waver between psychology and grammar.[28] The difficulties are related to the fact that we have several related concepts of the sameness of colors, concepts that require grammatical differentiation and development. Color concepts can be used in statements concerning the abstract hues of the color solid, with the colors of perceived surfaces, with the illumination of surfaces by exterior light, with spots in a visual field, and so forth[29]

Our color concepts do not lie within us because we experience color; they lie in the grammar of the color assertions that we are able to make.[30] I do not say that our world does not have the stable colors that have triggered our basic color grammar of physical description. We know what the basic colors are because we have learned English, German, or some other natural language.[31] Our color grammar exists because we typically can agree in color assertion in certain circumstances, and violent disagreements about such assertions are uncommon.[32] The breaks between color assertions in various contexts are grammatical. When I see in simple circumstances that something is red, I am not hazarding a description of the object or drawing certain conclusions from its appearance. I see that the object is red, and I could not be mistaken.[33] Wittgenstein is not at all concerned with *philosophical* skepticism in sufficiently clear cases. If we say "the color of this object is red" or "the color of this object is brighter than the color of that one," the hypostatization of color here could draw us into philosophical nonsense. We normally say "this is red" or "that's brighter than this."[34] To try to explain color facts in simple cases or to make theoretical assertions about color is to orient ourselves toward inevitable mysticism.

We perhaps cannot resolve the intermingling of psychology and physics into a single grammar of color, not even reach a clear resolution in particular cases. If recognition of the complexity of color phenomena forces a revision of the *Tractatus*, there can be no guarantee afterward that a total grammar of color can ultimately contain the phenomena. And Wittgenstein starts with the most favorable sense modality. There is a physics of color, based on the color solid, to which color reports can be related. A full philosophical grammar must also contain chapters on hearing, smelling, and the other senses, or perhaps, better, chapters on tones, sounds, smells, and the like. In these areas, however, the lack of an analogue of the color solid (although there are some apparently measurable acoustical scales) forebodes continuous difficulty. The grammar in these areas is obscure, and agreement is difficult to obtain.

It is interesting to compare the wealth of Wittgenstein's remarks on color with the relative paucity of his remarks on other sense modalities, whose initial confusions and lack of grammaticality make it difficult for Wittgenstein's method to get a foothold. Wittgenstein notes of smells, for example, that it is difficult to imagine how they could be described. In the *Investigations* he observes that we cannot describe the aroma of coffee and wonders what seems to be lacking in our language.[35] Presumably he had not forgotten the phrase "the aroma of coffee" but realized that there is nothing available for smells comparable to the color solid and its pure color points of reference. Elsewhere, he notes that smells can be pleasant and that what is pleasant about them is not just a matter of sensation.[36] If current knowledge influences what we see, memory also seems capable of influencing the perception of smell, conjuring up pleasant associations that might have been associated with a given smell on a previous occasion, or what we take to have been that smell.[37] In fact we can locate smells only in a kind of flat and disparate space of the smells of certain objects, a space in which grammatical barriers are not easily located. When we encounter a smell, we cannot usually say how it could be produced from other smells by mixing, using the technique that is so adaptable in the case of color. The smell stands there alone, perhaps as the smell of some object, such as turpentine.

Color is an entry point into the inadequacies of the *Tractatus* that forces the psychological to reveal itself, and it is inevitably associated with the more complex question of seeing. In the epistemology of the *Tractatus*, seeing is propositional; we see facts, not complexes. Visual facts not logically contained within a particular seen fact are logically independent of it, quite consistently with the general logical atomism of the *Tractatus*.[38] Later, vision remains propositional, but it assumes psychological dimensions, quite similar in many respects to those that accompany the development of the grammar of color. The intrusion of the psychological is clearly marked in the concept of seeing an aspect, a concept whose grammar fascinated Wittgenstein. If the same object can be seen in two different ways, as having two distinct aspects, this fact is mirrored in a grammar that allows different perspectives to be noted and described. We can train ourselves to switch between such differing aspects, linking vision both to volition and to rule following.[39] As with many topics in the late grammatical investigations, there is an original complexity of observation in the *Notebooks* that emerges again only after the Procrustean aspects of the *Tractatus* have been left behind. The *Notebooks* observe that seeing one spot to the left of another is an objective matter based on an internal relationship, involving forms of space and time, but also that visual space is different in height and breadth, the kind of phenomenological observation that is ruthlessly surpressed in the *Tractatus*.[40]

Relatively clear and isolated problems for perception center in seeing the faces of others. A face need not have a particular expression that I note: I can see directly on many occasions that a face is happy or sad. We can see a face in a context that determines pretty certainly what it shows.[41] A mental interpretation is not required.

I do not consider how I would feel if my face were in that position and infer what the face shows. We can see directly, in many cases, what the eyes are sending out.[42] The eyes speak as they do because of the whole face and the whole situation. If everything but the eyes were to be covered, the eyes alone would be ambiguous in their meaning. Consciousness and its implications can be directly perceived, and yet we do not notice this element in the same way that we do the color of another's eyes.[43] Grief can be directly recognized, for example, in a relevant situation, without an inference from facial features.[44] We can walk up to a person in a certain situation, look at that individual, and know what we should say.[45] Without noticing how a face changes physically, we can keep track of its changing meaning.[46] Pauses to check with evidence from the past or with an inner picture are not involved.

A face upside down (as when we are looking at an inverted photograph) usually cannot be read correctly, even though the picture is completely accurate.[47] On other occasions, we can see a face in a few lines, even in caricature, and we need have no trouble recognizing facial expressions in two-dimensional photographic or film images. The multiplicity and subtlety of our observations is nicely correlated to our expectations, to what we can say. Thinking of a face this way and that is like having a chord modulated into one key or another.[48] We are rarely at a loss for words when we see a face and are aware of the situation in which it is expressing something. If faces had only a small number of expressions, human life would be different, and so would be our language.[49]

These different aspects of seeing faces repeats a pattern of analysis that emerged in the discussion of color. There are a few clear assertions that can be made on certain occasions without fear of error. With these relatively fixed points we meet a modulated set of possibilities that is difficult to survey, although we can often deal with particular instances without confusion. Our language has, however, the multiplicity that seems appropriate for the discriminations that we want and need to make. Whenever this situation exists—and it exists for all phenomena with a psychological component—the grammars of language games will be tangled and complex, and we may be able to analyze only very special puzzlements generated by particular situations. Wittgenstein explicitly describes his investigation as falling short of completeness and notes that its purpose is to yield strategies for finding clarity when encountering specific conceptual difficulties in connection with seeing.[50]

Familiar objects are simply those whose place in linguistic space is obvious when we see them. We do not see familiar things differently; they do not have to have an aura, and we may not even notice that they are familiar.[51] Something is familiar because we immediately recognize the relevant linguistic space in which we can make assertions about it, perhaps because we have encountered it many times before and thoroughly know our way about. Although I can think away the color of something or imagine it with a different color, I cannot intentionally think away familiarity.[52] When I see that a certain handwriting is my handwriting, I cannot will this familiarity to one side.[53] Familiarity is not an external property of an object but a recognition that the relevant descriptions of the object belong to a specific language game and that the relationship could not be changed without changing the object. The fact that familiarity cannot be willed away is a barrier given by grammar.[54]

Visual space differs from physical space, even if there is a partial overlap in simple cases of seeing that are basic for the more complicated grammars of visual and physical space. An infinite number of things can exist in the grammar of physical space, but only a finite number of things can be discriminated in perceived visual space. Polygons of a hundred sides fail to belong to purely phenomenological visual space; they cannot be visually discriminated from polygons with roughly the same number of sides unless sight is aided by counting or perhaps by instrumentation. Perfect circles exist in the grammar of physical space; the circles that we see are usually only more or less circular.[55] Geometrical statements are seemingly made about seeing, such as that a certain form is contained in a certain drawing, but such statements are hybrid assertions whose grammar needs to be treated with great care.[56] Visual space has uncertain contours near its edges, and as the *Notebooks* had observed, the vertical axis of visual space is different from its horizontal axis. Just as a face in a photograph may not be recognized upside down, almost any familiar form may not be recognized, no matter how accurately it is represented, if it is oriented in an odd way.[57] Ordinary print that is printed backward may be virtually impossible to read.

Wittgenstein uses the informal phenomenology of an orientation interwoven with visual space to attack philosophical theories that regard seeing as an interpretation of neutral sense data. Sense data are by definition not oriented; different orientations of the same sense data are equivalent in terms of information, according to sense-data theory. Sense data should not be given a central place in our account of seeing because seeing is not the uniform interpretation of appearance that philosophical epistemology normally makes it out to be.[58] Retinal images do not tell us anything about immediate experience because neither they nor their interpretations have the multiplicity of orientations of our immediate experience. When we see, we may have sense data, but that information is not the whole story. Seeing is a state; it cannot be equivalent to the action (which takes time) of interpreting visual input.[59] Wittgenstein's argument is that we find puzzles about seeing in philosophy because we do not find seeing itself puzzling enough.[60]

Philosophical epistemology smooths over the terrain, creating silly mysteries in its ignoring of the variety of individual cases. Seeing something and seeing a likeness between two things or two facts will also have two different grammars.[61] "I see a patch" and "I see a line" have two different grammars, and the latter may itself have a variety of analyses.[62] *Equality* will mean something different in visual and in physical space; it is transitive in physical space but not in visual space. The latter follows from the fact that we cannot always discriminate lengths, for example, that are slightly different. The multiplicity of seeing statements is like that of expectation, to be discussed below. Visual and physical space are representable in different pictures, and what we mean with our statements is related to those pictures. Disagreement is resolved, where it can be resolved, by public discussion of those pictures.

As in the case of the perception of color, what we see can be involved with what we know. Certain pictures and movements are unambiguous because we know what is going on and because these things are often related to everyday life. We can see galloping horses and recognize pictures of galloping horses, even if we never see a galloping horse frozen in the position that represents a galloping horse in a picture.[63] We can see that a picture is that of a man climbing (and not descending) a mountain because we know that people do not descend mountains by sliding downward in the characteristic posture that we associate with climbing.[64] I may be able to recognize a genuine loving look and to distinguish it from a pretended one but may be incapable of describing the difference.[65] What I already know may fix any of these observations into place without my knowing how it is done.

A major focus of Wittgenstein's later investigations of seeing was directed to the problem of *seeing as*, a problem in which factual assertion and understanding are completely interwoven. Suppose some apparatus is described as though it were part of an experiment. Then I am told that the experiment is part of a scene in a play. Everything seems different, and yet the apparatus and its physical arrangement are exactly the same.[66] If seeing something *as* something is explained as a private psychic perspective, a familiar form of philosophical nonsense threatens.

In a complicated linkage to his other attempts to rule out private mental entities, Wittgenstein is concerned to present seeing in a manner that can be presented and discussed in the public domain. Rather than construing *seeing as* to be a relationship between me and what I see, *seeing as* is taken to be a relationship between what is seen and a certain public visual reference space, and if something can be said to be seen in two different ways, it is because there are two public visual reference spaces in which the object in question can be placed. Wittgenstein consistently struggles to avoid the claim that there is a single object that is *interpreted* differently in the two spaces. The object in one space is different from the object in the other space, and we should stop with that basic observation. The language of *seeing as* bears some relationships to situations in which an object is seen from two different points in space, so that the very same object has a different appearance from each of these two points; the grammar of *seeing as* is somewhat different. The common object drops out. When we see something *as* something, a space metaphor is involved, but a linguistic space is at issue, rather than a physical or a visual space. I can say that I see a figure in a certain way and communicate what I mean by pointing or by sketching my impression of what I see. This action is sufficient to place my impression into a relevant linguistic space.

One does not always see things *as* something; in fact this experience usually occurs only after analysis or after having learned something.[67] Seeing an aspect shows us a certain possibility. There are a number of drawings—the duck-rabbit, the Necker Cube, a square whose corners are connected by two pairs of lines—that can be seen in at least two ways. The first can be seen as a duck or as a rabbit, the second as oriented up or oriented down, and the third as a flat design or as the top view of a pyramid. If one sees just the rabbit, for example, one is not seeing it *as* something; only someone aware of both possibilities might describe it in this way.[68] There is an asymmetry here linking this observation to the grammar of other psychological concepts; a first-person report and a third-person report can differ, in that the third-person one recognizing both possibilities can report that someone sees something *as* something, when the first-person assertion would be wrong, if the perceiver does not see the two possibilities. How can we defeat the temptation to say that, when I see something as something, it is a private experience? If we surround any of these objects with other objects related to only one of the possibilities, providing a context that warps perception in one of the possible directions, we can express aspect clearly in the public realm. The duck-rabbit surrounded by pictures of ducks only or by pictures of rabbits only looks different, and in fact it is different, as these contexts place it into two different linguistic spaces in which aspect is clarified.[69] I see the figure as the limit, now of one series, now as the limit of another, or I can see the figure as embedded in two different series.[70]

We cannot ask that a circle be seen as a rectangle; there is no aspect in which that possibility emerges, no context in which it can be brought out, because grammar rules out the possibility in every context. We can ask that a circle be seen as an ellipse, however, because an object may in fact be seen as a circle or as an ellipse. We cannot say of the duck-rabbit that we see it as a rabbit and in some other way that we do not yet recognize and then, after learning about ducks, assert that we had a duck in mind.[71] A schematic cube can be seen as a box but not as a tin box, except under special circumstances.[72] If there are causes for these phenomena, they are of interest solely for scientists, until scientific discovery changes ordinary language. The philosopher can properly deal with only their current conceptual location. *Seeing as* is not part of pure perception. It is like seeing, but again it is different, because of the aspects of knowledge and volition that may accompany it. The criterion of the meaning of all visual experiences—experiences of seeing or seeing as—is an appropriate public presentation of what is seen.[73]

When we see something first this way and then that way, as this or as that, the differentiation of meaning can be shown in the consequences of the different possible uses of the object represented.[74] It could hardly be clearer, when context is considered, that meaning is not in the object or in our minds but in the location of the object within a language-game horizon. When an object has two possible locations within two different horizons, a location need not force itself on us, such as the location of a simple attribution of color to an object. The location becomes a matter of conscious choice and is subject to will. With practice, for example, we can get the ambiguous drawings referred to above to assume either aspect, by a conscious shift of gaze or focus. We see the object conformably with a successful *act* of interpretation, and so aspect is related to knowledge and thought and shows the same grammatical barriers.[75]

Moving from the relatively settled language games of color attribution to the confusing and jagged domains of perception, one encounters rough terrain quite different from the clean outlines of mathematical language games and their associated concepts of surveyable proofs. Color language games, leading into general problems of perception, connect the stark logic of the *Tractatus* to the explosive complexity of the language games of philosophical psychology. If mathematics could be adjoined to the *Tractatus* system, color and perception language force a major reassessment of its limited domain of applicability. Wittgenstein moved quickly over this terrain, noticing differences but achieving a crude survey of only a few language games. Unfortunately, he was robbed of the time he needed to find solutions for the problems he had uncovered, but the path of progress for Wittgensteinians could hardly be more clearly indicated.

Wittgenstein's discussion of seeing thus places clearly on the agenda a set of problems that are pervasive in Wittgenstein's attacks on philosophical nonsense in psychology. We have seen how the supposedly private aspects of seeing have been systematically moved into the public realm by Wittgenstein. The connection between these topics and those to come in philosophical psychology is explicitly noted by Wittgenstein.[76] When grammar becomes the object of attention, only the public realm need be consulted. The philosophical temptation to postulate psychic acts as the containers of meaning or interpretation for the grammar is broken by Wittgenstein in favor of comparisons and contexts and behavior that can be publicly exhibited and discussed. In this way, in spite of changes in detail, the *Tractatus* drive for public clarity remains undiminished in intensity in the philosophical psychology.

Eight

FEELING

IN THIS chapter we will consider feelings as consisting of sensations, emotions, and pain, with pain being an important bridging concept between sensations and emotions. Although these topics do not exhaust Wittgenstein's philosophical psychology, Wittgenstein saw the grammars of the feelings as rather clearly organized and closely related and as presenting a major set of problems for philosophical psychology. In seeing, for example, we met a motley of specialized grammars crisscrossing major internal divisions, such as that between physical space and visual space. In moving to the grammar of feelings, we encounter a fairly detailed map of this quarter of the City.[1] This large-scale map is introduced as a plan for the treatment of psychological concepts. The major features of this plan are given as features of grammar, and there is even a link to the topic of seeing, in that seeing is, on some occasions, a sensation.

Psychological concepts are expressed by psychological verbs that display the differentiating grammatical peculiarity that the first-person singular and third-person singular of the present tense of such verbs have different grammars. In perhaps the most famous instance discussed by Wittgenstein, "I am in pain" and "he is in pain" require completely different grammatical placement within the horizon of psychological assertions, even where the same person seems to be referred to in the two assertions. Wittgenstein notes as a crude characterization of the difference that the third-person case often approximates a factual assertion, that is, presents a claim that others can verify by observation or infer from evidence. The first-person case is akin to an *expression* of the speaker's pain, the entire sentence standing for a natural expression of pain. Such a claim does not present a possibly incorrect inference on the part of the speaker, an inference from private feelings to the existence of pain somewhere in his body, but it often directly expresses an appropriate situation. The differing meanings of first- and third-person statements and their relationships are a constant thread running through the discussion of psychological topics, and we have already noted its appearance in connection with seeing an aspect. This difference is a major element in the family resemblance among psychological assertions, as mathematical proof had been for mathematical assertions.

Both sensations and emotions have duration (that is, they exist over time), but sensations are typically impressed upon us, while we express our emotions. They may well occur together, characteristic sensations accompanying certain emotions. Sensations have degrees, varying from scarcely perceptible to unendurable, and they tend to be localized. Emotions run a course, and although they are not localized, they are not diffuse, either. One reason for the relative complexity of the grammar of emotions is that there are directed and undirected emotions. Fear is a directed emotion, usually directed at an identifiable object, while anxiety is an undirected emotion and may have no discernible object. The typical localization of feeling in the body when sensations occur is related to the normal sense modalities, although there are some residual puzzles concerning the feelings that inform us (sometimes without our noticing) of the position of our bodies and of their contact with other objects. A kinesthetic sense has been postulated to account for this capacity by students of Wittgenstein, but the parallels to sensations of seeing and hearing are obscure, starting with the unknown location of the supposed kinesthetic receptors. At the same time, the phenomenology of sensation cannot be limited to the sensations attached to normal sense modalities. Sensations shade off into images, pictures that are subject to the will. Emotions, by contrast, give little or no information about the external world, and their course, in many cases, moves more slowly and deliberately, allowing time for them to develop a deeper expression.[2]

Pain is seen by Wittgenstein as the important connecting link between sensations and emotions.[3] Pain resembles a sensation in that it can be localized, has a duration, and has an intensity and quality quite like that of other sensations. At the same time, we express pain as we express emotions, through a characteristic course of bodily behavior (facial expressions, gestures, noises) or through specific kinds of assertions that express pain. No doubt Wittgenstein felt that success in the philosophical analysis of the grammar of pain would derive valuable benefits for the more amorphous domains of the sensations and the emotions. Wittgenstein's early concern with solipsism and the question of whether the solipsist could express unsharable feelings leads later to the grammar of pain taking on a pivotal significance.

Each of us can distinguish the intensity and location of felt pain. We can know how others feel, but we cannot have *their* feelings, except in the grammatical sense that we can both have pains, for example, a toothache. I cannot differentiate my pain from that of others; all the pain that I feel is my pain. If I could distinguish the owner of a pain from among its possible owners, then a mistake in the attribution of pain would be possible. But all *felt* pain is my pain, which I cannot clearly and coherently say, since it is a grammatical assertion. In the grammatical sense, we can recognize that others are feeling pain and even that they are feeling similar pains, but the grammar needs careful analysis.

Philosophical nonsense starts when I suppose that, when I attribute pain to others, I am asserting that they are *feeling* exactly what

I feel when I experience pain. I can attribute the same *pain* to them grammatically, since I can report my pain and also attribute the same grammatical pain to others. But if I assume that my statement means that they have the feeling that I do, a foothold for skepticism has been given, since I do not have access to the inner feelings of others, and I have no way to find out that my feelings and theirs are identical. No possible criterion for the correct grammatical attribution of shared pain can appear in terms of this point of view. Wittgenstein is out to undercut this model. The meaning of our talk about pain must be different from what this model suggests. The meaning of our own pain talk cannot be clarified if we hold that such talk reports our feelings of pain. Reports of pain are expressions of pain, not reports of feelings. If the model based on feelings is adopted, the language of pain becomes incomprehensible.

We can begin by noting that pain behavior is often appropriately attached to particular occasions. When we suddenly hurt ourselves, it can be natural to cry or to scream and to touch the affected parts of the body. This natural expression is particularly noticeable in children. Adults may learn to stifle or to conceal overt behavior, pain behavior in particular. A *person* feels and expresses pain, and nothing less. There are no detached pains or pains ascribed to inanimate objects, except in special fictional settings. The inanimate parts of the human body (the hair, for example) cannot be said to feel pain. People can hurt themselves, but chairs cannot.[4] There is some uncertainty about whether animals can feel pain. This uncertainty lessens when animals can be seen as resembling humans.[5] Fictional animals—teddy bears or the like—can feel pain, provided that they are presented as humanlike in stories.

The point of these first remarks is to localize pain in certain situations where humans are hurting or injured and to connect these situations with natural behavior, natural gestures such as crying, that no language need accompany. Wittgenstein's crudest analysis of pain language is that it can simply replace natural pain behavior on many occasions. Instead of crying, rubbing a hurting spot, or striking out at the cause, one can express pain by saying that one is in pain. The language game of pain is an extension of pain behavior, and its horizon must be traced back to that behavior.[6] Pain behavior is like the reaction to other sensations; it is like blinking in bright light or withdrawing one's hands from a hot object.[7] It gets replaced by linguistic expression, but linguistic expression can also accompany natural expression. "I have a toothache" can take the place of a moan, perhaps to explain why I am acting as I am, but it does not *mean* "I'm moaning" (which could be false), "I would be moaning if I weren't civilized and sensitive to your feelings," or anything of the kind.[8] The whole sentence, as a block of language, replaces the behavior. When I say that I am in pain, I do not *name* a person to whom I attribute pain, just as I do not name anyone when I groan. I can draw attention to myself by moaning.[9] I do not draw attention to the person moaning to identify that person as the one who is moaning. I do not stand in an external relation to my behavior. My behavior necessarily expresses *me*.

When sentences replace behavior, they have the multiplicity of the replaced behavior, not the multiplicity given by their apparent grammatical features, which can be quite different. "I have a pain in my foot" and "I have a thorn in my foot" have completely different philosophical grammars. The thorn might or might not be there. I might have to look to see if it is there, just as a doctor might have to. But "I have a pain in my foot" is not something I verify by looking to see whether there is a pain in my foot. If a rock has just fallen on my foot and demonstrably bruised it, neither you nor I may be in doubt that I am in pain. I feel it, and you recognize it directly in the circumstances.

Ordinary language is quite troublesome here, especially for philosophical analyses. If I say that I feel my pain, such a statement is nonsense if it is taken to have a grammar something like "I feel my slippers under the couch." The latter is an empirical statement that can well be false. "I feel a pain in my toe" could be false, if sincerely uttered, only under odd circumstances, such as when the relevant leg has been amputated. Wittgenstein is well aware that there are many puzzles about pain, and he is concerned to eliminate the most misleading philosophical puzzles and to work at weirder puzzlements on a case-by-case basis. "I feel my pain" is a strange assertion, probably nonsense.[10] It is on the border of what we can say of pain. Crude behaviorism tries to support the idea that such sentences are nonsense, but at the price of denying the obvious existence of feelings. Wittgenstein is not concerned to eliminate normal reports of feeling pain. The point is that there is a grammatical barrier, and the philosopher should consider genuinely normal assertion, not artificial situations. Perhaps I could feel pain in your tooth if we were wired together in a strange experiment, but it seems a matter of empirical fact that I do not; in any case I could not feel *your* toothache.

If we are asked by our doctor or dentist whether something he or she is doing is hurting us, we may not be able to say whether it hurts or not, although it may be clearly unpleasant. Similarly, we may not be able to identify our precise feelings in many real-life situations. For Wittgenstein, the important issue is not these borderline cases, which may have no clear general analysis, but the fact that there are clear cases where I am in pain and cases where I can see that others are in pain. These clear cases are paradigmatic of the meaning of pain assertion. The fact that we feel pain but also express it gives it a complex grammatical place between sensation and emotion. The behavior or expression of pain is not entirely voluntary; it is embedded in certain external circumstances.[11] The picture of behavior does not give us the concept of pain; rather, the picture of pain does, that is, the idea of pain behavior in the right circumstances.[12]

We learn the concept *pain* when we learn language—specifically, when we learn the occasions for the appropriate use of this piece of language. We do not learn to use *pain* by guessing which of our inner feelings are appropriately labeled as pain. By an extension of language that is similar to the development of linguistic sophistication elsewhere, we may learn to express pain linguistically, even when no sharp feeling of physical injury occurs, as when we comment that the political maneuverings of our colleagues are causing us great pain. In any event, grammar rules out statements such as "I appear to be in frightful pain" in serious circumstances, even if there are occasions on which it may be problematic whether we truly are in pain. Anesthesia can also cast up a budget of problems about when it is properly said that someone is feeling pain. The difficulty of locating pain on certain occasions may tempt us into making a feeling of pain the criterion for the existence of pain, or at least attempting to do so, so that the question of pain would always seem to have a uniform theoretical basis.[13] Philosophy tries this strategy for reducing anxiety before the multiplicity of cases. Perhaps neurophysiology could settle the question definitely by finding a physiological correlate of pain feelings, but such an approach abandons philosophical grammar for a pointless philosophical anticipation of the scientific future. A philosophical conjecture here is pointless because it cannot point to the details of the next development along this path.

If I see someone writhing in pain with evident cause, I do not think of that person's feelings as hidden from me.[14] Such an experience is the clearest case of seeing the pain that others feel. It is a primitive reaction to help others who are in such situations.[15] This helping need not involve language, but where language exists, it can be used to articulate perceptions of the situation and desires to help. Nothing changes whether or not I suppose that an injured person has feelings exactly like those that I would have (or have had). If I know what it means to say that it is five o'clock here, that does not mean that I know what it means to say it is five o'clock everywhere else.[16] Identity cannot be carried across all situations. It depends on a complex web of background invariance. The words *above* and *below* may similarly have clear local significance but not a global significance. We want to say "pain is pain," no matter who has it, but although firmly enunciated, this sentence can still be nonsense. If I know what pain is here and now in my human community and what to do about it, that knowledge is quite sufficient until I encounter genuinely novel events, such as the appearance of beings from outer space. If these beings say that they are in horrible pain but show no corresponding circumstances of its cause or behavioral symptoms, they must be very clever at concealing their feelings, or perhaps they speak a different language, in which *pain* has a different meaning.[17] Wittgenstein's attitude here is like his stance toward contradiction in formal systems. Until we encounter problems, there is nothing wrong with the language game we are playing, and after we encounter problems, we can still play the language game we are familiar with if we can extend our game in an appropriate manner.

There are, of course, pain episodes that occur in slow wasting diseases, and these long-term repeating episodes are difficult for behaviorism to describe. Wittgenstein discusses such cases infrequently, but they cause no problem for his theory, especially as they function in medical detection, and he is not committed to denying the occurrence of feelings of pain. If pain talk replaces the natural expression of pain, this fact alone precludes a philosophical analysis of pain assertions as always referring to inner feelings, and yet not all pain language could replace the natural expression of pain. By refinement and extension, the language of pain becomes autonomous, and we learn extensions of pain language that help us to express how we feel in new contexts. The possibilities of the grammar of pain now determine the limits of what we can say. We can now turn to emotions and sensations.

Emotions are grouped together as feelings having natural expressions that can be replaced with linguistic expressions, connecting to one aspect of the analysis of pain.[18] Although emotions overlap with sensations in the case of pain, other emotional expressions are typically unlike sensations in that they give us no information about the external world, as pain often does. Emotions can influence or color thought. Thoughts are not toothachy, but they can be painful (in an extended sense), angry, loving, fearful, and so forth.[19] The expression of emotions can issue in complicated thoughts and actions, even artistic production, whereas pain issues primarily in action designed to bring about its termination.[20] Emotions are thus chiefly differentiated from sensations in that they are expressed analogously to the way in which pain is expressed, and they are chiefly differentiated from the bridging concept of pain in that they are involved with thought. Like pain, many emotions are also attributable to animals and to fictional characters of various kinds in situations bearing sufficient resemblances to human circumstances. For example, animals seem to us to be fearful in many situations.

"I hate him" can replace behavior rooted in hate, just as "I'm angry" or "I'm angry with him" can stand in the place of angry behavior.[21] Language games of emotion can be taken to replace attack or avoidance behavior of varying intensity and complication. The grammar of emotional reports therefore shares with pain the notion that language can replace the natural expression of emotion. As a result, the language of emotion is not always a description of the inner emotional life. Indeed, the inner life is often inarticulate before we attempt to express it in language.[22] Inner emotional life becomes differentiated and articulate only in language, but always in the context of specific situations whose articulation contributes to meaning.

When we are afraid or angry, various cases can be spelled out, modulated by special expressions and tones of voice. I can speak of kinds of anger, and I can speak of angry voices that may or may not be associated with real anger.[23] Pointing to different parts of the body (the head, the heart) helps to differentiate emotion, but it does not mean that the emotion is located there. All such observations have their place in the language games of emotion. Emotions, like pain, are frequently tied closely to specific states of affairs in real life. We typically do not feel emotions in our bodies, although feelings may accompany anger, fear, or sorrow. Emotions are related to situations in which they are appropriate, and they are subtly gradated with respect to the range of those situations.[24] Sometimes, of course, our emotions are inappropriate, because they arise in the wrong circumstances. If emotions regularly alternated or if we had only a few emotions with fixed intensities, our emotional life would be completely different from what it is.[25]

What differentiates the course of the expression of emotions from the expression of pain is the typically longer, modulated, complicated, and at times prescribed course of emotional expression. I cannot feel deep grief in the same space of time that I feel momentary pain. Short-term deep grief would have to be rare, perhaps an onslaught that is terminated by a sudden realization that the situation thought to cause it had been mistaken or misunderstood. We do not observe our grief, sorrow, joy, love, or fear in the same way that others do, nor do we feel it with a special sense. We can, surprisingly, observe empirically that its course has modulated over time. For example, we can observe that our grief must be less than it was a year ago because we are now able to do things that we could not do a year ago, making an inference about emotional intensity over time within a language game of empirical assertion.[26] Except for the complications brought on by the typically complex course of emotional expression, the philosophical patterns of nonsense with respect to psychological assertion—for example, the postulation of inner emotional states as criteria of identity for the emotions—must be fought with the same weapons in the case of emotions as they were fought in the case of pain.

On the other side of pain from emotions, so to speak, are sensations and sense impressions. Sensations are often immediately given and concrete, episodes that are produced by recognizable physical stimuli.[27] Fear or anger can have a specific object and stimulus, but the temporal spread of emotions is typically longer than the duration of sensations. There can be natural reactions to sensations, such as expressing attraction to, or avoidance of, the stimulus. We shudder on occasion in response to a sudden chilly sensation. The words "I'm shuddering" or "it's making me shudder" are linguistic expressions of the shudder. Because it seems involuntary on most occasions, we report shuddering, rather than replacing shuddering with a linguistic equivalent. Here linguistic expression is closely tied to natural expression, reporting it when it seems useful, rather than replacing it entirely. These observations are sufficient to establish the fact that pain does not neatly divide the sensations and the emotions; it clearly participates in paradigm features of both.

Most characteristically, sensations or sense impressions are closely related to the language games surrounding the objects that give rise to them.[28] In describing objects, we can simply describe our sensations, at least on many occasions. These reports can be nearly independent of other features of the situation in which they are made. The relationships between physical object language games and sensation or sense impression language games are multifarious and complicated, and they cannot be reduced to a simple formula. In the case of directed emotions, we tend to react to a mediated aspect of the stimulus object—its beauty, ugliness, horror, or whatever. In the case of sensations, we tend to react to more immediate physical properties, creating the permanent temptation to report our expressions of sensations as though they were clear factual assertions. Following this temptation produces error, because testing, confirmation, and doubt apply to the language game of assertion, while the language game of sensation almost always bears some characteristic marks of the grammar of the psychological.[29]

The asymmetry between first- and third-person reports in the case of sensation is that I may simply report seeing something, while I see *that* others see.[30] How do we know what we are seeing and what others are seeing? I do not *know* what I am seeing except in special cases, in which my seeing is the result of an expertise that I have acquired and others may have to learn. In simple cases, I see directly. Now if, when I see something red and so does someone else, we reach agreement that we are seeing exactly the same color by pointing to the same color chip as a referent, our reports are closely assimilated to factual assertions. An expression of a sensation or feeling commits us to having a sensation or feeling, but not to there being a sensation or feeling that we possess and surely not to the existence of a sensation or feeling that gives the meaning of our expression. Intonation and gestures give the grammatical meaning without the need for such hypostatizations.[31]

If private sense data are introduced to preserve the asymmetry of certainty in my case and uncertainty about others, the whole philosophical nonsense of skepticism threatens. We could not know the relationship of someone else's sense datum to a color chip, other than what is said about that relationship. The notion of possibly different sense data in different people originates because there are circumstances when we seem to see different things when we are apparently looking at the same thing. There must be a contrast between such cases and a basis in clear cases where the problem does not arise. Supposing that we could always be in doubt about others but could never be in doubt about our own perceptions is to propose what could never be verified. Sense data are private, which is the major rule of their apparent grammar. For the same reason they are also a useless philosophical fiction.[32] We cannot know even the relationship of our own sense data to a color chip. Pointing to the chip, however, asserts my claim and places it where others can check their own impressions. We have a complicated terrain of psychological and physical languages of sensations whose grammars are sometimes coincident and sometimes divergent. Such complicated relationships need to be explored in all sensory modalities in order to begin to map out the grammar of sensation.

At this point, we have found a location in the City that we have met before. Visual sensations identifiable as triggered by the external world belong to the grammar of seeing. The grammar of physically seen color, closely related to factual assertion, was linked by language games to seeing as and to seeing the point of things, thus moving the concept of seeing ultimately into the complex language games of philosophical psychology. Somewhere along the way, sensations of color, also fairly close to factual assertive statements in grammatical structure, belong to this familial sequence of language games. Sensations are also involved in the other sense modalities, and they produce various paths toward inner experiences that are not so clearly interwoven with cognitive structures.

There are many sensations not localized or attributable to specific physical stimuli but that are experienced too passively to be considered emotions. Pleasure seems to be passively experienced as a sensation, at least on many occasions, although the patterns of pleasure are complicated.[33] Pleasure in music can have a natural expression in bodily movements, but the course of these movements is related to the hearing of the music, so that pleasure does not have the same temporal extension that is associated with other emotional expression. Pleasure in other fine arts can be accompanied by a total lack of any sensations of pleasure taken to be caused by specific physical features of, say, the work of art. But pleasure can always be terminated abruptly by a new sensation or by the onset of a conflicting emotion. Pleasure is passive and of limited duration, suggesting that it is a kind of sensation. We speak of pleasurable sensations, but the physical cause is typically remote or mediated when compared with that of other sensations. Enjoyment seems to overlap what is pleasurable but also to suggest a course of expression more like that of an emotion. All of these remarks about pleasure can apply only to various passive pleasures and would require further augmentation to allow for pleasure in the participation of sports and other less intellectual forms of enjoyment.

A difficult case is presented by our ability to feel the position of our bodies. We can feel our movements, but this awareness is not comparable to a sensation of taste or temperature in its concreteness. The postulation of a kinesthetic sense is a purely verbal move, provided it is not a scientific postulation of a distinct sensory apparatus, since I can move my fingers, describing their movements exactly, even though I cannot describe the sensations that reveal this movement.[34] Philosophical psychology here runs against its limits. What we can be conscious of, and what we can describe in our language, is probably only a small portion of all of the neural processing that results in our judgments and assertions. Some of this processing seems to erupt into consciousness without revealing its origins, no matter how conservative one's opinion with respect to the existence of unconscious processing.[35] The importance of processing not accessible to consciousness seems unavoidable, which means that philosophical psychology can pose questions that it cannot answer with its own resources, its resources being sufficient only to block overt philosophical nonsense. But where it must refrain from asking questions or providing explanations, there may well be a place for scientific enlargement of our current linguistic resources.

The clarity of our linguistic resources is severely strained by a cluster of problems surrounding images, imaging, and imagining. When we think these pictures, we can have a sort of internal picture or image, even if it is not clearly presented to consciousness. Internal imagery may accompany thought or feeling, which Wittgenstein never denies. He attacks the view that internal imagery must constitute the meaning of thought or of feeling. Where thought is clear, the internal image can be given as a definite, describable picture. Its content can be given in a straightforward assertion subject to public recognition and discussion. Where sensation is clear, the internal image can be given as a reference to a public item (a sample, for example). In both cases the public item, the sentence or sample, settles the questions of reference insofar as they can be settled, and the question of how these items could match private episodes of meaning or feeling drops out as a piece of philosophy, an appeal to what is at best redundant for analysis. But this account is sufficient to show that coherent images can be linked both to pictures and to sensations. Wittgenstein will attempt to show that insofar as images or imaginings can make sense and insofar as they can be talked about, they must be taken as related either to pictures or to sensations. He wishes to empty the concept of images or imaginings except for this possibility of control.

Wittgenstein cannot simply ignore or deny the existence of images and imaginings. The language games that Wittgenstein uses in the *Investigations* only imagine the linguistic usage of other human beings. These language games are not put forward in a manner that would allow us to look for them in reality. Images create possibilities that may or may not exist in reality, and Wittgenstein needs these possibilities for his critique of philosophy. An image does not instruct us about the real world in the sense that it makes an assertion about reality.[36] What is imagined can be talked about, but it may not be thought through to complete clarity. An image does not have to be true or false. When we think through an image, it could turn out to be nonsense, or it could turn out to be empirically unrealizable. An image functions like a surrogate reality that is subject to the constraints of our language because it can be talked about and possibly made more precise through description and discussion. In such a conjectural language game, we get an image of the life and the language involved, and we can describe and discuss this language game up to the limits of its language. The relationship of such a hypothetical language game to our language and the relative rigidity or simplicity of the language game may show itself only partially, but we can articulate the structures that contrast with one another. Images are ultimately constrained by the limits of our language. As hypothetical facts, their clarity has to be captured in our language. Some images can be described or discussed or drawn or painted just as well as imagined. These images are not ultimately private; like sensations, these images can be transferred descriptively into the public realm, subject to the constraints of our language.

We cannot imagine what color-blind people see because we cannot paint what they see.[37] We can understand that such individuals cannot make our discriminations, but their feelings or images involve a gap that we cannot imagine. On the other hand, an Escher drawing may present an image that cannot be thought through globally in a consistent manner.[38] We can discuss it, but the discussion always finds a gap between the drawing and reality. The possibility of an image of an infinite row of marbles or trees presents a similar interesting problem. How could such an infinity be drawn or painted, and how could it be used?[39] These problem images are the exact analogue of the problems with infinity that are encountered in mathematical propositions. When we articulate the image, it points to a language game that cannot refer to reality; these images therefore threaten to slip out of grammatical control.

To see what is common to the language game of imaging, we can think of people who imagine by drawing on paper. When we ask what they mean by their image, their answer would be to point to a use of the drawing; the meaning does not lie in the drawing, and it is not in an experience that one has while looking at the drawing.

The meaning is not the image, but a use to which an image is put.[40] At the same time, an intended usage cannot, by itself, make an image into an image of anybody or anything. The fact that it is drawn as it is, by comparison with other drawings, is relevant but not decisive for legitimate intended reference.[41] An image thus functions like a verbal description, and it is not any more mysterious than a verbal description when it is properly understood, but its understanding depends on a clear use.[42] Images can come and go, like the doodlings or scribblings we may do in a pad while we speak or listen.[43] What we imagine is typically related to what we are doing or saying or thinking or experiencing. Imagination is not free; it is constrained by the situation and the limits of our language. Clear and coherent images cannot go beyond what we are able to describe, and their clarity is ultimately determined by the limits of what can be said about them.

If images are not free, they are nonetheless voluntary, as is our speech. We can think about and conjure up images, but they do not typically color thought itself in the way that emotions do. Images can have intensity and duration, like sensations, but they are not sensations.[44] Afterimages are the closest to sensations in some respects. They simply appear, but we do not mistake these images for sensations.[45] We can imagine a shining gold ball but cannot *imagine* that it is hollow. In thought or in a dream, we could *think* of it as hollow. Imagining is thus close to picturing, even if a hollow ball can be pictured in a special representation. We can imagine wishing as a picture of a man leaning with gestures of longing toward a picture of that for which he wishes. Imaging is making a picture, and the picture can be described, even if it has only a marginal use. We do not come across images as we do reality; we generate images, using our will. Imaging is something that we *do*.[46] That imagination is subject to the will is a grammatical observation, not an empirical discovery.[47] Images can beset us, but the will can then struggle against them. The same description can represent both what I see and what I imagine, as can a painted picture. The difference is that I can imagine things differently from the way in which I see them, and I can do so deliberately.[48] Seeing and imagining are different language games, but they hang together. Images are not pictures. The object imagined is not picked out by the resemblance between it and the object (which may indeed not exist). But the provision of a picture can answer the question of what one is imagining.[49]

Seeing an aspect and imaging are also closely linked, even though an aspect is not a mental image.[50] If we cannot imagine just the surface of an object, we lack a typical human ability. We need imagination to see a man in a boulder, or a horse in a cloud, but not to see a true-to-life picture of a dog as a dog.[51] The power of imagination can substitute for an available picture or a missing demonstration. We can imagine something changed, without actually changing it, thus bringing a picture of something else into view. An aspect may be more stable, as though an image came into contact with an impression and remained in contact with it for awhile.[52] We can talk about the aspects of things that we notice. Imaging and imagining may be claimed without any sense that a mental image is actually formed, whereas aspects are more clearly in the public domain. What is imagined can be described but not necessarily recognized by others. We can stop imagining something. Aspects are more robust. Once noticed, they remain open to inspection. Nonetheless, the boundary between imagination and seeing aspects is very jagged, and it needs to be traced in detail within specific language games where both may be involved.

Imaging shades into the question of dream and memory images, topics that Wittgenstein investigates in a very disjointed manner. In both areas, Wittgenstein continues his strategy of studying images in grammatically controllable language, while recognizing that auras surrounding dreams and memory prevent this strategy from achieving more than partial success. Some people seem to remember by seeing or hearing something internally and then by reading it off or looking at it or listening to it.[53] People also have behavioral memories (often inarticulate) of how to do something.[54] These two situations alone present a temptation to generalize nonsensically. A memory of how to do something suggests that memory is a physical trace, but except in metaphor, we do not say that machines with traces remember what they can repeat. Remembering is psychological, having a first- and third-person asymmetry. I do not justify my memory to myself, nor typically construct it from hints and traces; I often just remember. Is memory the memory of an experience? It seems propositional; I do not remember my exact behavior or my exact feelings—I remember my pain.[55]

Memory is not usually like looking up pictures, although we sometimes do see pictures, and the propositional content involves a picture. It is easier to remember and to reproduce pure red, green, and so on than a particular shade of reddish brown, a fact possibly connected to the simplicity of linguistic recall in such cases.[56] We may think that we have a color image in memory, but to get at a color, we really need to know how to reproduce it—how to generate it from primary colors, white, and black by a process of mixing that we can describe and control. I can verify my good memory to others and to myself by checking my memory of specific facts against charts, tables, maps, or whatever, all of which suggests that much of memory is essentially verbal or propositional.[57] Once something is remembered, the memory does not linger and does not have a duration and an intensity, in the manner of an emotion or a sensation.[58]

It ought not to strike us as so matter-of-course that memory reveals both inner and outer episodes from the past. Only linguistic phenomena can appear in both places, and the words with which I express my memory are essentially my memory reaction.[59] This sense of memory, one closely tied to knowledge, is relevant to philosophical claims that memory reproduces the past. Memory of this kind is given in assertion. When someone says that they remember something, one should not ask *what* they remember, for that question steers thought away from the assertion toward another kind of picture.[60] One should ask rather *why* the memory is being reported. Memory does not show us the past, anymore than our senses show us the present. Nor does memory furnish us with a past and hence a source of time recognition, although its pronouncements can be interpreted as a picture of the past.[61]

Clearly Wittgenstein is here brushing up against the limits of his method. The relevant ordinary use of language is infused with the philosophically suspect notion that we can directly remember the past. This idea may be related to the extensive written and photographical apparatus that supports and corrects our assertions of memory. Wittgenstein says that we can externalize our memories in reporting them, but he does little with the fact that our memories are already externalized in objects and images surrounding us. The notion of common behavior and common language providing a public space for discussion cannot ground meaning in abstraction from the particular methods we use to keep a record of the past. If Wittgenstein's methods can avoid silly forms of skepticism and if they can avoid philosophical nonsense about memory images or physical memory traces, they are not historically concrete enough to explain why ordinary usage should seem inevitably tainted with philosophical proclivities. Memory will have a mysterious aura when attention is focused on memory reports and the circumstances in which they are produced, while ignoring the cultural apparatus against which many claims about the past can be decisively verified.

Dream images also enter with an aura of mystery. Wittgenstein attempts to suggest that quite ordinary things can have a mysterious air and that the phenomenon of dreaming can be discussed as impassionately as the appearance of an old and familiar table, which may also carry an aura.[62] Dreaming is a special language game. If a dream is not just a dream narrative, dreams are communicated solely through narrative reports to which the normal accounts of assertoric truth and falsity cannot apply.[63] There seems to be no typical present tense of the verb *to dream*, although people might, of course, say "I'm dreaming" in their sleep while they were dreaming. Dreams are reported in the past tense, and Wittgenstein wants merely to describe the use of dream language. We cannot point directly to the content of an occurring dream. What one says becomes the only source of description of dreams, and it is typically accepted, since no independent check is available.[64] The language game is this: when people waken, they report experiences that they have dreamed. People can be asked whether they have dreamed, and they will respond affirmatively or negatively to such requests. In this manner dreaming appears in language in our form of life. Although Wittgenstein allows that it could make sense to ask whether dreams actually take place during sleep, the language game of reporting and discussing dreams takes this turn. The language game places us outside of dreams, presenting dreams as narratives that require interpretation. The dream can become embedded in a developed account, but this account cannot be compared to scientific assertion, since the dream data base remains conjectural.

As he did with memory, Wittgenstein is again running against the limits of what he can say. Some philosophers have suggested that Wittgenstein's assertions are rendered dubious or can even be falsified by scientific research. Recent research has indicated that memory is more variable than older philosophical accounts recognized and that it involves a physiological process that can be interrupted or distorted in various ways. Other research has indicated that dreaming episodes, associated with rapid eye movement in sleep, occur during specific physiological cycles while one is sleeping, although whether they are or can be reported on waking depends on such factors as when, in the dream cycle, the dreamer is awakened.[65] This sort of information is not an embarrassment to Wittgenstein, who is attempting to describe current usage, not attempting to guess at empirical facts about memory and dreaming or to produce scientific hypotheses to account for those facts. Current usage cannot be wrong, even if it turns out to be incompatible with scientific research. Should it become generally recognized that we all typically dream several times a night, we may stop asking whether someone has dreamed and simply ask whether they can recall what they dreamed. The language game would then be somewhat different. Wittgenstein's observations need fear neither scientific research nor change in usage, although Wittgensteinian analysis would have to be altered in details on these topics after a change in ordinary usage. The crucial question, as before, is whether Wittgenstein can succeed in marking the borders of philosophical nonsense surrounding clear usage in everyday life.

With dreaming, the problem is not so much the seeming oddity that Wittgenstein concentrates on the peculiar and unusual nature of the content of dream reports but that the peculiar and unusual *nature* of dream reports escapes Wittgenstein's concentration on their epistemological status.[66] To note that our dreams are seldom realized makes it sound as if dream material is ordinary narrative and overlooks the weird material in dreams that must be laid to one side as nonsense or taken up for interpretation with special techniques. What dreams reveal seems to demand of dreams, even in ordinary usage, the special kind of interpretation that is extended into psychoanalytic readings. This temptation to analyze cannot be checked by observing that Freudian interpretations in many cases contain within them aspects that look like the philosophical nonsense that Wittgenstein took it as his first priority to combat. We already recognize that many of our dreams are nonsensical. The *apparent* nonsense of dream content forces upon us some extraordinary account of dreams as natural phenomena, provided only that we take seriously what dream reports seem to say.

The problems with dreams are the vestibule to the problems with complex human mental functions that are inevitably associated with discussions of psychology and philosophy. Before turning to these topics, we can perhaps usefully summarize the search for the horizons located in the languages of clear factual assertion, mathematics, color, and feeling. Wittgenstein recognized a basis in animal behavior for the crudest discriminations to be found in each of these areas, although a basis in diverse discriminations. Distinctly human behavior is associated with autonomous grammars and with the linguistic horizons of meaning to be associated with these grammars. We do not need grammar to note that the sun is shining, that one pile of rocks is larger than another, that one color is brighter than another, or that a heavy stone has fallen on us. Animals show by their behavior that they also recognize these situations.

Grammar enters when we articulate these recognitions in communicable language as part of the recognition. When language extends the natural basis, domains of truth-functional assertion and mathematical proof become associated with the clear linguistic horizons of specific language games. The horizons that come with the language of color and the language of feeling are not as precise. At times, as when we are comparing two hues, the grammatical device of the color solid controls the limits of assertion. Similarly, in the case of directed anger, a description of the object of anger can differentiate both the nature of the anger and its intensity. In this case, the general grammatical criterion of psychological domains, first- and third-person asymmetry, is under relatively clear control. For feelings in general, however, we may have to grope to express ourselves within the scope of clear and relevant usage associated with a language game.

Wittgenstein's naturalism is concerned to trace how language brings order into our interactions with the world by tracing the limits of clear language usage and by examining the interweave of usage with ordinary life. The *Tractatus* was tainted with a transcendental viewpoint that could not ultimately be defended. The later philosophy quite consciously attempts to circumvent that transcendental viewpoint with an immanent pluralism of language games. But the claim that clear meaning will always be enclosed in the horizon of a language game is not innocent. Feelings, memories, and dreams place great pressure on this assumption and raise the possibility that, if Wittgenstein had had more time, language-game hermeneutics would have brought him once more to a basic reconsideration of his analytical strategy.

Nine

PSYCHOLOGY

IF IMAGING is voluntary and yet if images can be described and talked about, a philosopher must also be interested in thoughts and in the process called *thinking*. Thoughts prove to be as complicated in their overview as images. If images can be related to sense impressions, thoughts can be related to propositions. When they are expressed in language, they can be discussed and evaluated in the public domain. This fact provides a robust check on their significance, a check of the sort that Wittgenstein's search for clarity demands.

Thought is ordinary. We frequently say that we are thinking or are having thoughts. At the same time, thinking is ascribed only to humans (or to some of them) and to animate objects sharing characteristics with humans in fictional contexts.[1] A table cannot grow or think. A teddy bear can do both. Thoughts are closely linked to the other features of our lives, especially to speaking and writing, and to their production. Thinking occurs in certain specific kinds of situations—situations causing puzzlement, for example—which seem to call thinking forth as a harsh blow may call forth pain. Wittgenstein asks, with an eye on other psychological phenomena, what the behavior appropriate to thought is, as well as what occasions are linked to this behavior. Clutching the head, making a movement not to be disturbed, and a characteristic hesitation or shaking of the head are important kinds of natural behavior associated with thinking. It is crucial to understanding thought to recognize that we can think out loud. We can also think to ourselves and then reveal what we are thinking about when we are asked. Thinking out loud is itself a form of speech characterized by a certain pace and hesitation, especially in circumstances that call forth puzzlement. The pace and timing of thinking out loud can be compared with that of recitation, for example. People with mental problems often speak more mechanically than do typical adults.[2]

Thinking to oneself can partly be considered an interior monologue or dialogue. A person with an obvious problem, say, someone searching through a pile of flagstones for one to fit into a certain place, may be said to be thinking, but even these public nonlinguistic episodes seem bound to language. We can imagine the seeker describing the place to be filled by describing it to themselves and using that description to guide choice. Animals can solve problems, but we are more hesitant to ascribe thought than pain to them, which is probably related to the firmer linkage of thought and language. In the case of thought, we cannot exploit the replacement of clear prelinguistic natural behavior with the linguistic expression of thinking. Thinking, in all areas, seems to begin with language.

The possibility of interior thought suggests that thought can be completely concealed, raising obvious problems for philosophical analysis. Privacy of thought is connected to the observation that we cannot always guess what others are thinking. We can sometimes convince others that we know what they are thinking, but the privacy of thoughts and feelings seems to mean that successful pretense, total concealment of thought, is a possibility. Unless a public anchor for thought can be found, mental imagery seems ready to make a comeback in the analysis of thought. We are tempted to think that experience, feelings, and even images can exist before language and that language simply enables us to communicate these inner episodes.[3] Since this idea could hardly be disproved, and surely could not be disproved in philosophy, Wittgenstein attempts to disarm this temptation. The idea that these episodes can occur first or that thought can be complete before its linguistic expression is suggested by the fact that we can come back to say what we were going to say, after an interruption.[4] But our ability to pick up where we left off does not seem wired to thought in that we can come back to complete a physical activity after interruption. A more difficult problem with the view to be disarmed is that thinking is so variegated a concept that no synoptic view really seems possible—unless interior mental episodes can provide such a view. But synoptic strength is coupled with analytical weakness in specific cases.

Wittgenstein's views on thinking shifted more than is the case with some of his views in other areas. Within the *Tractatus* language game of clear factual assertion, thoughts play a uniform role; they are propositions, or pictures of states of affairs. All psychological phenomena, including believing, thinking, and saying, are analyzed there as correlations between propositions uttered by the language speaker and internally related facts in reality.[5] The *Tractatus* account is difficult to match to ordinary usage concerning *knowledge* and *belief*. Because language reaches right to the world, we can know that clear factual assertions are true or false. At the same time, we only *believe* hypotheses, and we can also believe or conjecture that clear factual assertions are true or false before we check them out. Knowledge and belief are discriminated in this context by what they are directed toward, not as differing attitudes toward the same sentences or propositions. Wittgenstein later brings knowledge and belief closer together, arguing that knowledge cannot apply except where belief can apply as well.

Wittgenstein was fascinated early on by the problem of how we can think what is not the case.[6] The answer in the *Tractatus* language game of assertion is that we can make a picture that is not the picture of an existing state of affairs. This solution becomes generalized when mathematics, color phenomena, intentionality, and so forth are found in language games that picture in another way. Thought and what is said become decoupled. We can speak about one thing while thinking about something else, although speech may not be thoughtful under these circumstances.[7] And we can certainly speak, even reflexively, without thinking at all.[8] There are differences between talking without thinking and talking thoughtfully, but the differences themselves are not explained by thinking—they embody thinking. Thinking is not an inner mental state nor its expression. It has a sui generis outline quite different from that of having or expressing pain, feeling and expressing emotion, and so on.[9] As we can think by speaking to ourselves, thinking has no essential connection with overt behavior, and it is hard to find circumstances that must call forth thought as injury in certain circumstances must call forth pain.

Wittgenstein gradually abandons the *Notebooks* idea that thinking must be a kind of speaking. It is not completely wrong to call speaking the instrument of thinking, at least on those occasions in which our thought is revealed in our speech.[10] The problem is precisely that thought need not terminate in speaking, and there is no basis other than postulation for supposing that thought *must be* inner speech or structurally equivalent to it. Where linguistic expression replaces behavior, inner states need not be postulated to explain linguistic meaning. Where the connection between linguistic expression and behavior is broken, we need to see again that there is no need to postulate inner states to explain meaning. It is sufficient that we can state and defend our thoughts; it is not necessary in general to suppose that thought had already existed in a complete, inner, preformed fashion that was then translated into speech or writing.

Thinking occurs in many ways. There can be lightning-quick thoughts that are clothed in words later. The major contrast for thought is that of thoughtful activity contrasted with mechanical action or action in a stupor.[11] Dogs cannot talk, nor presumably think.[12] Dolls and spirits can talk and think because they are sufficiently like human beings. These points represent grammatical barriers, even if the recent development of computers is putting pressure on the barriers previously associated with machines. It is possible that the greater contemporary pressure on the grammatical barrier for machines is due partly to the fact that computers have been presented as humanlike robots in many modern movies and stories about space and that we can now interact with computers. Thinking is not always complete or successful. A boiler, made to carefully thought-out engineering standards, can still explode. If I have thought, I could be wrong in my thinking, but I should be able to say what I have thought. Thinking sometimes pays, and we may think toward a goal, but we do not always think for utilitarian purposes.[13]

Understanding is knowing how to move about in a language game. "I understand" is an utterance advancing the claim that one has the ability to go on and that one can move appropriately.[14] Understanding may or may not be accompanied by thinking. Mental calculation proves itself in public understanding. What we think we have thought through correctly can be discovered in exposition to be wrong, as every teacher knows. We are not so much interested in the process of thinking as we are in what is thought.[15] I can choose a language and think in it, but I do not really seem to think apart from a language. Trying to think in a foreign language demonstrably slows one down, a gentle suggestion that thought occurs in some linguistic space before or during its embodiment in language.[16] Would it be imaginable for someone to learn to do sums in the head only, without *ever* doing written or oral sums in public, subject to correction? It does not seem likely.[17] We learn to think correctly by early training in thought in the public arena. Thought leads us inevitably into the question of whether one can understand and know, that is, the question of whether expressed thoughts are defensible. Philosophical activity should occur at this point, and we should be prepared to discover that understanding and knowing will be as variegated as the grammars of the language games in which the material that is said to be understood or known is expressed.[18]

Wittgenstein also denies that knowing can be explained as an appropriate inner state, perhaps a feeling of certainty. The picture of a mental process is a picture produced by our desire to distinguish humans from animals.[19] Mental process is invoked to explain the picture, without which its supposition would have no foundation. Knowing is frequently enough a state of a person, sometimes an ability, and knowing has a grammar that is closely linked to understanding. As a state, knowing something is rather like having a piece of paper on which what is known is written.[20] A claim to know can be challenged, and the appropriate response is to articulate and expand the knowledge that one claims to have.

The distinction between inner and outer is itself a picture, and a common one. Knowledge cannot be based on the inner; reference to hidden physiological signs would make its existence perpetually dubious and would introduce a generalized philosophical skepticism.[21] The logic of knowing is not that of inner states; it is the logic of bodies of discourse, relative to which particular assertions can be justified.[22] We do not translate preexistent knowledge into words, even if we express our knowledge *in* words. I can say how high something is (if I know), but not necessarily how a clarinet sounds, even if I know the sound of a clarinet and cannot be mistaken that I am listening to one.[23] In the language game of the *Tractatus*, this possibility of difference did not exist. At the start of the *Investigations*, the speakers of the language game may be said to know that certain things are building blocks, even if they lack the linguistic resources to say that they know it. The *Tractatus* doctrines are considerably relaxed in the process, and knowing is not restricted to true factual assertion.

Ordinary grammar makes various kinds of knowing seem too alike. Various statements of knowledge belong in fact to different language games. The difference between "I know what 97×78 is" and "I know that $97 \times 78 = 7,566$" is already striking. In the former case, we are dealing not with a statement of mathematics but with the claim to possess the ability to do a certain piece of mathematics, or perhaps with a claim that the mathematics has been done, and the speaker is asserting an accurate memory of the result. On another occasion, Wittgenstein compares the following four knowledge claims as assertions belonging to four different language games:

> I know that he arrived yesterday,
> I know that $2 \times 2 = 4$,
> I know that he had pain, *and*
> I know that there is a table standing there.[24]

The first statement is a claim about memory, the second about mathematics, the third about pain, and the fourth about a visual experience. We have already noted differences between these language games, as well as the criteria for necessity in connection with each of them.[25] Wittgenstein's critique of philosophical epistemology is precisely that it allows the obvious syntatic grammatical similarities of English or German sentences to override the complexity and differentiations of philosophical grammar.

In a clear factual assertion, the claim to know is simply firm assertion, and the explicit reference to knowledge could be dropped. For example, it makes little difference in certain contexts whether I say "I know this path leads over there," or simply "this path leads over there." Of course, the negations of the two are different, since the negation of a knowledge claim is an expression of dubiety and the negation of a simple fact is another factual assertion. This difference need not come into play on a specific occasion.[26] But if I say, "I know where this path leads to," I might be able to add, "but I'm not telling," because I want to keep a secret or I want to tease or I want you to make it attractive for me to tell you.[27] This possibility would hardly apply to the earlier assertion that the path leads to a definite place. The jagged nature of the grammar of knowledge claims is shown by the fact that sometimes knowledge asserts personal authority and demands trust, sometimes it offers simply a feeling of personal surety, and sometimes it offers a report about the way in which something was learned.[28] As in the case of thought, pretense is possible, but it is difficult to know something and yet consistently act as though one did not. Knowledge claims in a language game of factual assertion do not express natural behavior, and so a pretense not to know may be successful on a single occasion, but larger, subtler links between knowledge and behavior over time are inescapable.

Knowledge and belief are obviously closely related. In many cases, whether I can be said to know or only to believe something is a matter of evidence and situation. Sometimes, as with expressions of pain or emotion, neither belief nor knowledge seems to be in question, because the notion of evidence has no real purchase on the situation. These remarks are sufficient to indicate that, while both knowledge and belief have the grammatical variations of the other psychological verbs, their detailed philosophical grammar involves close attention to the context of usage.

Some similarities of grammar between knowing and believing are straightforward. If "I know that p" means roughly "p" on many occasions, so does "I believe that p" The picture of p can seem involved in both cases.[29] "I believe" does not make a statement about a brain state or a state of mind. It communicates something about reality or reveals an attitude of the person speaking. Both knowledge and belief are more permanent than any accompanying mental state that could be adduced to explain them.[30] We can be said to know or to believe things that we are not thinking about, even when we are asleep or unconscious. Dispositional theories trade on this fact, although dispositional theories run into difficulties with their contention that we are permanently disposed to reveal what we know or believe on appropriate occasions.

In response to a question regarding whether "*p*," I might say either "I know that *p*" or "I believe that *p*" in order to indicate the nature of my conviction. In these circumstances, knowing and believing exclude one another. If I am certain that it is going to rain, I express that certainty not by saying that I *believe* it is going to rain but by saying, more appropriately in most cases, that I *know* it is going to rain. Both "I know that *p* and yet I don't know that *p*" and "I believe that *p* and yet I don't believe that *p*" escape outright contradiction in special circumstances.[31] The second assertion can mean that *p*'s coming true is just so wonderful that I cannot really believe it will happen, and the former may suggest that appropriate standards for knowing in some language game have been met, and yet I do not feel completely certain or comfortable about my discovery or calculation. At the same time, "*p*, but I don't know that *p*," seems harder to tie to an appropriate occasion than "*p*, but I don't believe that *p*," the latter once again expressing excitement that *p* seems to be coming true.[32]

This last observation directs us toward the differences between knowing and believing. A challenge to a knowledge claim must be capable of being answered, and yet we may believe something without convincing evidence or much of anything in the way of supporting grounds for belief. Believing is not thinking, nor need it involve thought. The concepts of believing, expecting, and hoping cluster together, as do the concepts of knowing, thinking, and understanding.[33] Knowing seems typically to involve a history of training or learning that brings one into a position to know. Belief, on the other hand, seems related to doubting. Animals look closely at something until they are sure of what it is, and we can resolve doubt into belief in the same way.[34] Believing that someone is in pain and doubting that someone is in pain are natural and related kinds of behavior towards others.

Believing and doubting can be traced to a basis in natural behavior in other areas of human life. When I say in certain circumstances that I know something to be so, only through a special kind of blindness can I be wrong.[35] When I believe something to be so, I can simply be wrong, unless the situation is structured by special epistemological constraints and expectations, as in scientific investigation. Knowing typically implies not doubting, but it does not imply that doubt would be inappropriate. Doubt may have been triggered by some circumstances unforseen in training. Knowing and believing tend to be linked possibilities, the one excluding the other in particular circumstances. Wittgenstein seems to allow exceptions to this rule only in the case of mathematics. I can see that mathematical propositions are true when a surveyable proof has been located. I do not believe mathematical propositions (as opposed to hypotheses) once a surveyable proof is present. I may, on the other hand, believe that I can prove a propsition and then set out to do so. Perhaps I have discovered that my previous proofs have been wrong. Then I could believe that I have made a mistake in a new surveyable proof, even though I cannot find it; this situation, however, would be rather unusual.

Believing and knowing show the distinctive first- and-third person asymmetries of the psychological verbs. I do not turn to myself and observe myself to know whether I believe something.[36] We cannot usually say "I believe that I believe," although we can say "I believe that he believes" or "I believe that I believed."[37] The language game of reporting knowledge can be given a turn in which the report is taken to be about the person making it.[38] We can then say "I know that I know" in order to suggest complete confidence that I could meet any objection to my knowledge claim. Attributions of knowledge and belief to others can rest on evidence but not on self-attributions; we *express* our knowledge and our beliefs.

We can clearly know or believe something only against the background horizon of a grammar that establishes what it means. A belief is formed when its grounds come up to the standards (which may be probabilistic) of some language game. The standards will be given by the grammar involved in that game and cannot be legitimated by yet further grounds. Justification by experience comes to an end, otherwise it would not be justification. Doubting also has an end; when the end is reached, reasonable doubt is laid aside. The end of grounds is action, not an epistemic state, and we are satisfied when we can act with a clear mind. The reasonable person simply does not have certain general doubts. One cannot doubt at will.[39] General philosophical doubt is pathological. Philosophical doubt is an affectation that expresses a pathological disconnection from action. Similarly, a refusal to express greater conviction than belief everywhere is strange. To say that we *believe* that our name is such-and-such or that we *believe* that we can recognize a close friend is weird.

Knowledge and belief are appropriately in play with respect to systems of propositions and their immanent horizons. Knowledge and belief deal with an ability to get around in such systems, not merely with an ability to grasp the meaning of isolated propositions. Our convictions are collected into language games into which weird convictions (such as having taken a ride on a spaceship with alien creatures) do not fit.[40] A system has certain fixed points and grammatical barriers, and what we can know or believe is warped into conformity with the pictures that provide these barriers. A mistake is a wrong move within a system. A sufficiently weird assertion is a sign of mental disturbance, and it is different from a mere mistake within a system.[41] The normal truth of my statements in playing a language game expresses my understanding of the language game. Certain false statements would suggest failure to understand the system.

Propositions of grammar are completely exempt from doubt within relevant language games and lie apart from the path of normal inquiry.[42] Knowledge and belief are not apposite for such propositions; we come to recognize them and to see that they must be so in the course of developing the philosophical grammar of a language game. This fact permits Wittgenstein to recognize that the bounds of language games can be burst and hence that there can arise occasions on which new language games need to be organized. Wittgenstein notes, at the time of his writing, that claiming to have been on the moon would be classed with the weird assertions, even if it was logically possible to reach the moon.[43] The actual attainment of moon landings has changed the status of this observation, turning an implausible fiction into reality. Philosophical grammar is concerned to mark out the practical horizons within which we actually move, not the space of logical possibility. When these horizons change—and they will change unexpectedly and inexplicably for grammar—a new survey is needed. When I sit down on a certain chair, no thought that it could collapse occurs to me.[44] When I say that I *believe* that someone is not an automaton, this utterance can be only a joke, because having souls is attributed to humans as a fixed point of our grammar.[45] Either or both of these grammatical observations could shift in the future. It is not, however, the concern of philosophy to predict the course of such shifts.

Philosophical grammar traces the fault lines observed by the mature and knowledgeable speaker of a language, but we are not born capable of self-conscious epistemological assertion, and it is not used by humans until a great deal of language is already in place. A child does not believe that milk exists, nor does it know that milk exists, anymore than a cat knows that a mouse exists. The child and the cat are somehow sure of certain things, on the basis of which they act.[46] Children's actions and reactions are followed later by an acquired awareness of names and sentences, then by gradually coming to know certain things consciously, and finally by the sophisticated assertion of belief.[47] Variations and certain kinds of dubiety come with an increasing mastery of language. The core to this development is the notion of training.

As children or as language learners, we are trained to form letters, to make certain sounds, and to produce simple sentences. By training, we learn certain stabilities and barriers and differences as norms, and alterations and extensions are hazarded later on this secure basis.[48] It would be a misunderstanding to suppose that training causes the person trained to choose among meanings that are already present.[49] Training produces correct behavior. Children first learning their native language are trained in it; it cannot be explained to them until after they acquire a certain facility with the language they are learning. Training creates the mechanisms of stable structure, in terms of which meaning comes into view.[50]

Wittgenstein's objection early in the *Investigations* to the Augustinian account of language that he cites at the start of the *Investigations* is precisely that Augustine supposes the child is already sophisticated enough to form correct images of the objects named by the child's elders in the child's presence.[51] This level of awareness could be only retrospective, after the nonlinguistic episodes of training have set certain language regularities into place. All rule following is based ultimately on the fact that training into regular behavior is a natural feature of human life. We learn to act as though we were acting in accordance with consciously formulated rules long before we can articulate the rules that provide a description of our behavior. Children can be taught by example to follow a rule, without ever explicitly mentioning a rule.[52] A child could not be so clever as to learn certainties if it were already able to doubt everything. The child learns by believing, by trusting adults. Doubt comes afterward. General certainty can be turned into doubt, but doubt can be turned into certainty only against the background of assumed certainties. All of these remarks are equally legitimate for adults learning new language games.

Philosophers have generated their usual nonsense by ignoring the variegated usages of "I know" and "I believe." Saying that I know something, even if I am certain of it, is often silly or misleading. But the philosophical thesis that we may not know anything cannot be seriously maintained. We want to say "rubbish!" to someone objecting to propositions beyond doubt, such as to someone who says that a common game has never been played right.[53] I normally do not find out what I am thinking, how many hands I have, what I want, whether I am in pain, whether I am grabbing at a towel, or whether I am sitting in a chair. If one of *these* things became confused—for example, whether I had two hands—then I would not be able to trust my senses either.[54] Sometimes we know by introspection what we are thinking or what we believe, but the occasions are rare. To say that we know what we want signals determination to obtain it, not a discovery about our goals.[55] Similarly, stating that we know we are sitting in a chair is likely to be an expression of annoyance, not a considered announcement of epistemological certainty.[56] Philosophers must avoid a lazy epistemology that assumes that "I know" and "I believe" are always in order and that the truth values of assertions of belief and knowledge are just a matter of the security of the evidence known to support what one claims to believe.

In the *Tractatus* language game of factual assertion, the future is contingent. We have to wait to find out what will happen. With the emergence of philosophical psychology, we still cannot know what the future will bring, but there are noncontingent lines of connection between the present and the future. If we expect something or if we intend to do something, we divide the future into events that will satisfy our expectations or intentions and those that will not. This division takes place in grammar, the sentence of expectation or of intention providing the separation into what accords with it and what does not. Although the expectation and the fact satisfying it seem to fit together somehow, this fit is not always given in advance, as when we make a physical container for some particular object.[57] Someone with an expectation or intention does not have to have a precise picture of what will satisfy the current expression of intention or expectation.[58] The chain of events may terminate with a *decision* that expectation has been satisfied by the course of events.[59] Just as we do not have all of the instances of meanings or all of the applications of rules given in advance, an expectation or intention channels attention but leaves some room open concerning what will satisfy the expectation or intention. At the same time, it provides a basis for determining whether satisfaction can be said to have taken place. The grammatical expectation is the basis of differentiation, but not a prevision, of what happens. Intention and expectation exist in a situation. I can intend to play a game of chess or expect to win from a certain position because the game already exists, just as I can intend to say something because the language in which I am expressing my intention already exists. Intention and expectation are states not of the soul or of the mind but of the entire person in a certain kind of situation.[60]

The natural expression of an intention or expectation is given by the behavior of a cat stalking a bird or a beast trying to escape from a trap.[61] Like other examples of natural expression extended into language, this behavior can be replaced, extended, and refined by linguistic usage. Language has the right multiplicity for connecting sophisticated expectations and fulfillments. By nature and by training, we are disposed to give spontaneous expression of wishes in certain circumstances, although these wishes may, especially at first, be vague and difficult to articulate. How we learn to express expectation and intention is a very subtle matter. In the variety of humankind, however, we do not meet people lacking a conception of what they are going to do.[62] The simplest language game at the start of the *Investigations* already contains an implicit reference to the future.[63] Intention and expectation are not emotions, moods, sensations, images, or states of consciousness. When they are expressed in language, they have a nearly unique status.[64] No constant thoughts of satisfaction need occur between the announcement of an expectation and its fulfillment. I watch a slow fuse burning as it approaches an explosive. I expect the explosion, but I can think of anything during this period, returning my attention to the fuse from time to time.[65] We can say "I'm expecting him" both when we are eagerly awaiting him and when we are not. We perhaps would be surprised if he did not come or perhaps we really intensely want him to come. In both cases, but particularly the former, my thoughts can wander before his anticipated arrival.

The assertion of intention can be separated from the intention of a particular and identified person. We can say "this appliance is intended to be a brake" as a description of manifest function, without wondering whose intention it might first have been to create the braking mechanism, a concept that does not come into play here.[66] Obviously, such assertions depend on a background of grammatical possibility. Not everything is done intentionally, but the expected norms of human behavior allow a large role for intention. When we intend or expect something, we are *in* the pictures that our language provides. We interpret these pictures in a natural manner whose horizon precludes certain doubts.[67] If we step outside the picture, we can produce philosophical nonsense about the connection between intention and fulfillment or expectation and fulfillment.

In the *Notebooks*, the course of the world is said to be independent of our wills. An act of will is not capable of description, so that the *Notebooks* present willing as an ineffable act. Still, the *Notebooks* contain the seeds of later doctrines. The will must have a foothold in the world: we cannot will something that we are unaware of, nor can we carry out an act of will without knowing that we have done so.[68] A wish need not terminate in action, by contrast, partly because it may not be subject to clear articulation. An act of will does not precede an action, so that it could occur without the action following; it is part of the action.[69] In the *Tractatus,* the contingency of the world is stressed with respect to our will, and although the exercise of the will is said to alter the limits of the world, the result of the coherent exercise of the will cannot be stated within the language game of assertion. Its inclusion would require describing a link between the act and the act of will, but the latter does not exist in the world that can be described in our language. At this time, Wittgenstein had not conceived the language games of intending and expecting that could provide an internal link between these activities and their satisfaction. Wittgenstein's increasing subtlety concerning the use of language allows the early intuitions of the *Notebooks* regarding the will to develop into a more sophisticated and articulate focus.

If I raise my arm, then my arm goes up. I do not try to raise it and then see it rise, and I do not use an instrument to cause it to rise because I want it raised.[70] Voluntary movement is marked, typically, by the absence of surprise, but it points us toward nonsense to ask why surprise is absent. If I say, for example, that I am raising my arm (perhaps you cannot see me), I do not describe my action—I express it, as I could by making sounds of exertion if lifting it were difficult. When people are philosophically skeptical about foreknowledge, they have forgotten such simple cases of voluntary action.[71] The training for physical prediction is quite different from that of learning to control our actions. In the former case, we wait to see what has happened. In the latter case, we learn to do what we want to do. I may just do something, but others must draw inferences or react naturally to evidential signs of what is coming. We shut our eyes in the face of doubt with respect to our simple voluntary actions, so that the language games of knowing and believing do not even come into play.[72] If we say "I believe I can bend this bar," then bending the bar is not voluntary; trying to bend it can be voluntary. Philosophy, in seeking a perfectly general account of willing, produces skepticism by losing touch with the immanent features of simple voluntary action.

Wittgenstein found typical philosophical attitudes toward free will to be the product of ignoring the particular circumstances in which willing occurs. The distinction between voluntary and involuntary action is based on the particular surroundings of action and on their weave with the rest of human life, not on a difference in inner states. No act of volition separates voluntary from involuntary acts. Voluntary action depends on certain movements made with their normal surroundings of intention, learning, trying, and so forth.[73] We can change our minds, and we can make unforced decisions. If we play the piano from a score, the score does not cause our manner of playing. We can learn to play the same score better.[74] In this way we use expressions of freedom concerning our actions. We can say only what lies within the scope of language; but within the scope of language we can say many things. Whatever causal processes are involved is a matter for science to investigate, not for philosophy to guess at. The asymmetries of the language of willing are typically ignored in philosophical doctrine. Both determinism and forms of free will, as philosophical doctrines, are the result of lazy generalization from a few cases within only the variegated language of intention. For Wittgenstein, this criticism is sufficient.

The fact that we cannot achieve an external view of ourselves is tied to Wittgenstein's repeated assertions that indexicals are not names, in particular that "I" is not typically the *name* of the person who utters it. In both the *Notebooks* and the *Tractatus*, Wittgenstein points out that, when he uses "I," it is not a reference to Ludwig Wittgenstein. The subject of avowals and assertions about self is not a simple, so "I" cannot be a name in the sense of the *Tractatus*, and

yet it is not a complex or a fact, because its organization and activities do not show the contingency of those facts that exist in the
world. The metaphysical self is not in the world; it cannot be described along with the rest of what is found to be in the world.[75]
Wittgenstein thought at that time that the self could be entirely
excluded from the language game of factual assertion. Instead of
saying "I think," one could just as easily say "it thinks" or "there
is thinking," thus avoiding a misleading use of "I." I can note my
body in the world, but I cannot note myself.

The same doctrine, although considerably refined, is retained in
the later philosophy. When "I have a toothache" replaces the natural
expression of pain, it does not describe an external relationship between a person and a toothache, and "I" still does not function as
a name. But philosophical grammar has given the complete expression of toothache a place in a language game. The difference between
myself and others is now shown by means of the grammar of relevant
utterances, and the relevant statements can be understood only in
terms of the interweave of this grammar with behavior. The content
of my consciousness is revealed by my behavior and by my language.
It must lie open to view if we know how to look.

One of Wittgenstein's strongest expressions of this point of view
is his observation that a private language, whose meanings could
not be communicated to others, must lie outside what we can coherently consider language. This observation has generated an enormous literature on the so-called Private-Language Argument, but it
seems unlikely that Wittgenstein thought that there was a basis for
proving the impossibility of a private language. Rather, Wittgenstein
seems to have proceeded by suggesting that any attempt to state
exactly what such a private language would be like would show us
that we would not recognize it as belonging to the assemblage of
language games that we use to coordinate our lives.[76] A private
language would establish all meanings as correlations between pub-

lic words and private feelings or images. As we have seen, Wittgenstein develops in detail language games that suggest that there are no private languages of pain, intending, color, mathematics, assertion, and so forth, and we have seen his particular suggestions that we can imagine our normal language use in these areas quite consistently without postulating inner mental episodes.

In suggesting in the *Investigations* that no part of our language could be private, Wittgenstein himself brushes against the limits of language in a manner that threatens unintelligibility. His purpose is not to prove the correctness of his views but to use the possibility of his views to undercut the philosophical account of language that sees meanings necessarily to be private mental episodes. We could never move from private images to public meanings, and Wittgenstein uses the fact that we can successfully communicate in the public realm to rebut the skepticism that the philosophical picture must yield. He is not forging an alternative philosophical position; he is arguing that what we need to know about meaning is already available to us.

A public event—my doing or saying something—is subject to an appropriate public standard, and it can be checked for consistency with past practice against records, recordings, or whatever, in the usual way of checking the correctness of memory. Consider a successful dowser who claims to predict the depth of water from a feeling. It is fine if a physiological correlate can be found, but there is no necessity for thinking that there must be such a correlate.[77] The dowser could be reacting to situational cues that neither the dowser nor onlookers consciously recognize, and perhaps the dowser is just lucky. If people seem to describe things uniformly over time, it explains nothing merely to suppose that they do so because they can refer to an internal standard that justifies their usage. The philosophy of language has a tendency to consider only the speaker, the assertion, and what seems referred to by the assertion. A vast web of usage and activity is thereby typically ignored. Pragmatics, when considered, begins to provide an awareness of the crucial dimension of context and normal practice.

A private language cannot be established on Wittgenstein's view of language learning. On Wittgenstein's conception, repetitive training is followed by linguistic elaboration and flexibility. Names are mastered as standing for external objects, objects in the public realm. Words for feelings occur in complete sentences that replace and elaborate public behavior. A private-language picture would require that all terms function as names, including those that are alleged to name inner feelings. But an inward glance at feelings cannot establish correlations, and such correlations could never be taught or established by training.[78] Being the same and seeming to be the same cannot be distinguished with respect to inner sensations that are at best a private "mirror" of public language.[79] Inner feelings cannot be brought into the public realm for appraisal and discussion. They are thus decoupled from any functional role in language. We normally can discuss our feelings in public without an air of mystery or incomprehension. Truly inner feelings are related only to a private-language conception that philosophers require to support other forms of nonsense.

These points need to be related to Wittgenstein's insistence that the human soul appears in the human body, at least sufficiently to remove the mystery from the notion of a completely private language.[80] In certain circumstances, fury is as clear in another's face as it is in one's own breast. It is confusing to suppose that we observe other humans as we observe substances in science, making hypothetical inferences to their hidden structures. The relevance of the private object to meaning and to language can be eliminated by supposing that it constantly alters, even in our own case, and that memory is unreliable.[81] This elimination of the private object can be consistently imagined, and yet our language usage would be perfectly intelligible in terms of its public anchors.

Conjecturing states in others is a temptation already present in everyday language when we are not sure whether someone else is trying to deceive us, but it becomes organized madness in philosophy. In everyday life we recognize the fact that some people are transparent to us and that others are opaque, but if I think that I cannot know what is going on inside anyone else, a philosophical generalization has captured my imagination.[82] The subtleties of transparency have been covered over by a uniform philosophical doctrine. An inner process stands in need of an outward criterion, in that, if we are to note its existence, it must be apparent at least sometimes in human behavior and in the situations that provoke behavior.[83] If I explain in full detail how my friend behaved and the situation that provoked the behavior, there may be no doubt concerning the nature of the related feelings. This certainty carries over to fictional settings. We have no trouble reading the feelings of King Lear, even though they are produced in a fictional setting.[84]

Wittgenstein is not a behaviorist. He does not deny that we have feelings, and he insists that we can communicate our feelings. His denial is that feelings are private, that they cannot be shown or communicated at all. Behaviorism would also regiment ordinary language in a way that Wittgenstein never contemplates, producing a deliriously negative philosophical psychology. Behaviorism misses the social dimension of Wittgenstein's views completely. If we cannot find a criterion for the existence of feelings in others because pretense is always possible, this observation fails to show that feelings are private. We do see, them in public, and what we see is not always merely evidence for something that is inescapably hidden. Behaviorism overreacts to the problem of the missing general criterion for the existence of feelings. Behaviorism describes the brushstrokes, but not what we see in the painting.[85] What may seem behavioristic in Wittgenstein's descriptions and his discussion of criteria is his insistence on the public dimension, but Wittgenstein describes behavior *in a context*. There could be a language with a word standing for pain behavior only and not pain, but it is not our language.[86] We *participate* in human life; we do not view it as we view a film, from the outside.[87] Our participation in life allows us to understand a film and also to understand language, allowing us to choose public-language games and their immanent horizons in order to close the Wittgensteinian hermeneutical circle of clear meaning.

Ten

PHILOSOPHY

THE BASIC thrust of Wittgenstein's view of philosophy as a descriptive critique of language remains in place as his survey reveals more and more of the City. Wittgenstein's philosophers function as a sanitation corps within the City. They speak the local language while they sweep up and dispose of the trash, leaving the City clean and orderly. Philosophy is not the teaching of a set of philosophical doctrines but the *activity* of putting the City in order. At one point, Wittgenstein compares philosophy to arranging the books of a library, in which putting a few books on the same topic together is a modest sign of progress.[1] In the same way, when order is established in any part of the City, the condition of the whole City is improved.

A philosophical description of our language and its production, beyond a few casual observations, is difficult to formulate. Thought is not mysterious while we are thinking, but it becomes mysterious if we are thinking about thought. Our language is primarily adapted for us to use in ordinary settings. In philosophy, when we talk about talk, we lose control of our language in generalizing about what we can say. The context that gives language stability disappears, we become giddy, and we are tempted to react by inventing new and ultimately nonsensical forms of discourse to paper over uncertainty. Philosophers make this error when they investigate language, using artificial calculi and making the calculi into the measure of the language. Wittgenstein's problem is to separate nonsensical philosophical generalization from the legitimate generalization that may go on in ordinary life or in science. Here at least the vocabulary remains under the surveyable control of observation, if it is done right. Normally we know our way around in our language, but when we try to do philosophy, we lose our bearings.

Wittgenstein wanted relentlessly to fix signposts turning us back from the thicket of philosophical jargon toward solid ground, back toward our coherent ordinary usage (including scientific usage). The meaning of a specific word, at least in a context, can often be given by context and example until a particular use is understood. The philosopher may ask what the meaning of a word is, in general, but this question has no legitimate answer. Even to suppose that such questions can be answered, the philosopher must assimilate disparate, fascinating phenomena into a single, misleading pattern.[2] The ways in which words are used are remarkably different across languages, even *within* such a simplified language game as that suggested at the start of the *Investigations.*

When Wittgenstein attempts to deal with questions of meaning, he stops short of full generality. For a large class of cases—but not all, he notes—the meaning of a word is given by its use in a language, and this restricted formula refers not to syntactic patterns but to the interweave of life and language, the situation in which the use of a word is appropriate.[3] Description renounces theoretical abstraction. Wittgenstein wants to keep the differences, the jagged edges, and accept what is obviously fragmentary, contextual, and incomplete. The problem in philosophy is to stop at the right point and to recognize that a description, a reminder, is the appropriate solution to a conceptual knot. Unlike the ordinary use of language, which is always connected to the past and to expectations of the future and is interwoven with life, good philosophy issues in "terminal" remarks that disperse an existing fog; we do not go on to *say* more about philosophical remarks after they accomplish this kind of clarification. Philosophers who ignore this warning are the victims of grammatical jokes.[4] "Where does the candle flame go when it's blown out?"[5] This sort of perplexity initiates typical philosophical mystification. A child may be mystified by this question, as may a philosopher who hypostatizes an unseen candle flame somewhere. That this observation has relevance can be seen from the many philosophers who have postulated other worlds and stuffed them with mysterious entities in order to solve the grammatical perplexities triggered by our all too human language.

For Wittgenstein, good philosophy is clarification and insight—something that allows a grammatical knot to be untied and set to one side. It does not create new doctrines that we need to remember and apply. We cannot *do* anything with philosophy except relieve the puzzlement caused by overhasty grammatical generalization. Good philosophy is therapeutic. Its techniques can be applied to specific problems of language in order to relieve them, and its reminders of what we already know can restore balance where there is conceptual excess. If someone has been overly impressed by the supposed huge size of the earth, this excess can be attacked by means of the following thought experiment. Imagine a rope stretched tightly around the circumference of the earth. Thirty-six inches is now added to the length of this rope, and it is held equally far from the earth's surface throughout its length. How far will it then be from the surface? The perhaps surprising answer is that it will be nearly six inches from the earth's surface![6] This exercise puts the size of the earth back into perspective, on the basis of information that is already available to us. It produces a jarring shift in opinion, wonder at the earth's immensity has been corrected by an observation that brings the earth back to its true size, so to speak. Wittgenstein's therapy amounts to a deflation of the pretensions of philosophy by confronting them with facts already within our grasp that introduce a correcting perspective.

Wittgenstein's early intellectual milieu was Vienna at the turn of the century. For various reasons, the enormous intellectual ferment in Vienna at that time was partly fueled by a feeling that language was exhausted, or useless. There are two general reactions possible in this situation. One is to look for a new start with a new language, assuming that the old language is played out and that all of its variations are exhausted. There is a sense in which Freud and Schoenberg, both Viennese contemporaries of Wittgenstein, chose this route, finding new phenomena and also associated languages with which to express and study such phenomena. The other route is to see the exhaustion of language as due to an overlay of useless ornamentation that has gradually come to conceal its essentially sound basic structures. This way is Wittgenstein's. Ornamentation is to be removed and taken to the junkyard, revealing the true and beautiful basic structure. His drive for simplicity and clarity expressed itself in his life, in his architecture, and in his philosophy.[7] Wittgenstein is a sort of archaeologist, stripping away the verbal ornaments of philosophy until layers of language are exposed whose connection with life gives them a solid meaning grounded in common human behavior.

Science belongs to Wittgenstein's City, certainly the science that underlies successful engineering and technology, given the practical interweave of these activities with human necessities such as housing and transportation. Wittgenstein's opinion of the more exotic branches of scientific theorizing is not known. For the most part, he shows no awareness of such branches of science as relativity theory or quantum theory, and his remarks on Freud are somewhat unclear in their intent. It is probably symptomatic, however, that Wittgenstein did not consider Freud to be making a bold new scientific breakthrough. A total reliance on science, however, is the foundation of an empty and confused culture. At one point, Wittgenstein compares the belief that science will necessarily improve human life with the earlier belief that kings could command rain, in a remark of unusually bitter, explicit pessimism.[8] Science and mathematics had to be subjected to the same salvage operation that affected the City elsewhere. Whereas the positivists accepted facts from science and mathematics and attempted to fit these facts into a consistent logical structure, Wittgenstein's notion of grammar was a filter on facts, permitting only some of them to withstand clarification of their relationship to the common understanding of human beings.

We are perhaps now situated to resolve a supposed tension that has often been thought to vitiate Wittgenstein's undertaking. Pure description should leave everything as it is, and yet Wittgenstein's conception of doing philosophy pronounces judgment on some of the things that we ordinarily say, consigning them to the category of nonsense. We are to withdraw sentences that are not sufficiently clear because they are counterfeit. Reformism and conservatism meet in the realization that description will leave everything in place that is substantial and will eliminate only the fog and the ghosts that are created by philosophical tendencies. A sentence is not an acoustic sequence. Every sentence that actually says something stays; every apparent sentence goes. Wittgenstein is not a relativist. He does not build the City, nor does he find a hitherto unknown City by a voyage of discovery. As with programs to rationalize the architecture of existing cities in real life, meaningful buildings are to remain and insubstantial constructions are to be carried away. Wittgenstein *reveals* the City in which we already live, by paying close attention to its substantial outline. Reformism and conservatism collapse into one, as they often do in real life. The good philosopher does not have special tools, special insights, or special knowledge. The good philosopher applies, incorruptibly and consistently, the standards of clear sense that are accessible to all of us.

Philosophical commentary is at times incomprehensible on Wittgenstein on philosophy. Kenny, for example, quotes Wittgenstein to the effect that the philosopher is not a citizen of any human community and also quotes him as saying that people must do philosphy *individually*, deciding for themselves how to deal with their own pressing conceptual puzzlements.[9] This clash of opinions seems to muddle Wittgenstein's position, and the former opinion must give way. We are all tempted, at times, into bad philosophy, and we need to overcome our own temptations. The philosopher, however, lives *in* the human community, inside the City. Accurate citation reveals that Wittgenstein held that the philosopher is not a citizen of any particular community of ideas, that is, is not the apologist for any particular interests or ideologies.[10] The philosopher is free to root out nonsense anywhere. The bad philosopher may play the role of cheerleader for science and in his or her adulation may not have a basis for turning a critical eye on scientific assertion.

A somewhat subtler problem concerns the relationship of philosophers to ordinary citizens. Kenny, again, takes the "plain man" to be vulnerable to the persuasions of bad philosophers and scientists and suggests a sort of priestly role for philosophers, who can assist plain people in resistance and repentance in the face of such temptations.[11] This role seems a reverse valuation of any line of discrimination that might be drawn by Wittgenstein. Kenny's plain man is Wittgenstein's candidate for the least likely to be duped by bad philosophy. The philosopher is typically the victim of bad philosophy, taking it more seriously than it deserves. In fact, however, there is no discrimination. Every human being can be tempted into philosophy, at least at times. Language itself conceals differences in a uniform appearance and abstracts away from the rough edges of experience in order to facilitate easy communication. Our memory, affected by linguistic coding, simplifies, abstracts, and distorts what may once have been experienced. And like the temptation for any theme, no matter how grim, to be exploited in musical or floral themes, language itself offers ornament as a flourish to celebrate apparent progress. The philosopher is not an expert who can cure others by prescribing philosophical medicine. Individuals must solve their own problems. But the philosopher, in solving personal puzzlements, can show others with similar puzzlements how to deal with their own problems. The philosopher does not assess the problems and provide the solutions for others and does not function as an analyst. The philosopher teaches by example and by finding useful techniques.

If people solve their own problems, no relativism is intended. We all speak the same language, and we all inhabit the same City. When people are confused, they may be in the same spot of the City where others have been confused. Private languages have been ruled out, and unknown languages are to be interpreted in terms of the common behavior of humankind.[12] Wittgenstein believes we are all engaged in restoring and maintaining the same City, and the existence of the City ultimately is the arbiter of disputes over the meaning of language. What seem to be theses in philosophy are properly matters of considered universal agreement.[13] They cannot properly be stated as knowledge claims, because they show what we all presuppose in the correct use of our language.

But does not Wittgenstein finally fall back into doing bad philosophy himself, despite his announced intentions? Must he not do so because he criticizes other philosophers and does not permanently retreat into the silence suggested at the end of the *Tractatus*? Does not the later survey of the City itself generalize about the usage of language? Wittgenstein does generalize. At the level of specific language games, generalizations can be offered that do not carry over to language in general, because they cannot automatically carry over to other language games. At the level of specific language games, the control over generalization is provided by the specific interweave of that game with specific practices in real life. This practice is not yet the level of bad philosophy, because we speak and use language games in everyday life. Hypothetical language games, described and imagined within our language, can be produced to show the rigidities of philosophical doctrine. This activity comes closer to playing at the game of philosophy, but it is a way of reminding ourselves of the complexities of our language usage.

Could philosophy itself be a language game? Bad philosophy typically wishes to say something about all of language, and this desire had been the rot of the *Tractatus*. We cannot generalize about all of language, because the array of language games contains a diversity that defeats substantive generalization. Philosophy can best survey language games in an effort to straighten out their connections to life, hoping that a survey of the appropriate language game will resolve any particular linguistic perplexity. The chapter headings of a book in linguistic philosophy would cite areas of the City, the chapters describing their language games.[14] There would simply be no final, summarizing chapter. A good book on philosophy would have the structure of a dictionary, not that of a logical system.

The quarters of Wittgenstein's City represent tormenting puzzles for him. Initial efforts to understand mathematics, color, feelings, emotions, and so forth, especially when clear factual assertion is taken as the paradigm of controlled linguistic usage, cause our heads to spin because of the complexity of the phenomena. In none of these cases did Wittgenstein feel that he had provided more than investigatory tools, and his generalizations have the force of assembling a range of examples to defeat philosophical doctrine, without settling all issues in the range of simple language games. Wittgenstein does not play in a single language game, or he would ultimately be ensnared in bad philosophical generalization. When Wittgenstein talks about colors and their mixtures, for example, the language is tied to actual experience with pigments and colored light, and it is the language of ordinary assertion that Wittgenstein uses to discuss ordinary assertion about color. Wittgenstein's assertions can be put to the test of everyday experience and common understanding.

To illustrate how a Procrustean philosophical hermeneutics constantly works at making Wittgenstein a bad philosopher, one can take almost any word used by Wittgenstein that has been subjected to commentary—for example, *criterion*—and study the expository readings. If it is asked, "What does Wittgenstein mean by the word *criterion*?" serious confusion already exists, for there should be no presumption that Wittgenstein has a fixed meaning for such terms and no presumption that he has a special philosophical meaning that only sustained analysis can reveal. A criterion is normally a test, standard, or rule of some kind that settles whether something is present or whether a word can properly be applied. The concept *criterion* is part of everyday language. Criteria will vary across practices, where they exist, sometimes being hardened into sure tests and sometimes functioning merely as the best standard available, the standard on which we make a decision. In medicine, for example, a serological test may be the criterion for the presence of an antigen and hence for treatment, even if the test is known or suspected to be less than perfect. A criterion resolves ordinary doubt into action, when doubt is present.

The variability of the notion of a criterion is recognized by Wittgenstein, and he uses the word with its standard range of meanings. Wittgenstein recognizes that criteria may or may not exist in particular language games, and he recognizes that the surety and nature of criteria are highly context dependent. If one searches for Wittgenstein's meaning, looking to define *criterion* precisely in all of the locations in which it appears in his texts, Wittgenstein will seem obscure or wavering.[15] He is not making ordinary language more precise. He is using ordinary language to reveal the complexities of real-language use against the superficiality and trickery of philosophical doctrine. If he were using a reformed natural language to discuss language games, he would fall straightaway into a crippling inconsistency.

Philosophers are tempted to read philosophy into Wittgenstein's texts by looking for special meanings, in spite of the clear signposts pointing back to everyday usage and the humble linguistic style of the texts themselves. Wittgenstein's use of the easily grasped expression *language game* in the *Investigations* is not defined, although it may signal his one special expression, an expression designed to code the highest level of philosophical generality about language.[16] Language games are immanent in the language use of human beings or can be easily imagined where they are invented. Wittgenstein uses this expression to catch the attention of philosophers, indicating to them the highest level of generality that is compatible with an immanent analysis of real usage.

Except for their philosophical errors, there is a sense in which we seem to learn little of the inhabitants of the City. Their language games are talked about, as are the practices with which these games are interwoven. But ethics, aesthetics, and religion are like philosophy in that they are not mentioned as language games. Wittgenstein held that ethics, aesthetics, and religion could not be represented in the propositions of language games because there was a failure of appropriate multiplicity in their propositions. Ethics is private and does not treat of the world, as was already noted in the *Notebooks*. Propositions of ethics are impossible because absolute values are not in the world. Ethical values cannot lie in consequences but exist only in the spirit with which actions are carried out.[17]

Wittgenstein's biography is a sufficient illustration of his unity of theory and practice. Several times he left comfortable and even privileged circumstances to do volunteer work and to teach in elementary schools. One simply saw that these things needed to be done; any attempt to provide rational grounds for doing them was an expression of confusion and weakness of will. Nor was Wittgenstein embarrassed by the existence and use of the word *good* in ordinary language. This sense of *good*, as he observed, meant that something came up to a certain predetermined standard and was hence relative to that standard.[18] Such instrumental uses of *good* could appear in language games because they are independent of ethics and aesthetics, areas that are concerned with absolute values, which are inexpressible. Humans are united in wanting to behave better, but the philosopher has no guidelines for this task, and neither does science.[19] To wonder and to improve, we need to escape the domains of science and philosophy. Ethics is not a matter of agreement or disagreement between people. There is no mechanism for expressing or settling ethical and aesthetic disputes, and the inexpressibility of absolute values also means that ethics and aesthetics cannot be sharply separated.[20]

The importance of religion is also hidden in Wittgenstein's work for those who do not understand that relative silence can be a clue to importance. A look at the tortured Foreword to the *Philosophical Remarks* is sufficient to establish the importance but inexpressibility of religion.[21] The consciousness of sin and the taint of vanity are to be felt as deviations of the will but cannot be expressed as doctrine or proposition. Religion provides imperatives for action, but it cannot provide a rational discursive justification for these imperatives without becoming superficial and repellent.[22] We do not discourse with God, but we can hear him if he speaks to us.[23] A theology that attempts to express this discourse in fixed phrases clarifies nothing and violates grammatical restrictions. If God's talking to just one of us were expressible, it would be in a private language, which is not possible. Consistency here demands inexpressibility. Doctrine is useless; religion demands that a wretched life be changed.[24] Wittgenstein's remarks on religion are restricted to Christian conceptual resources. Wittgenstein was interested in religion only insofar as it showed itself in improvement of conduct and in good works.[25] Philosophy and its accepted branches of ethics and aesthetics, along with religion, are sufficient to establish that Wittgenstein is not a language-game relativist.

Poets and the insane are excluded from the City. Wittgenstein's varied list of language games also shows that the variety has constraints imposed by the demand for clarity. Wittgenstein's *On Certainty* provides a context within which the discourse of the mad can apparently be assessed. G. H. von Wright has analyzed the insights of this book from the standpoint of a philosopher and has suggested that knowledge can occur only in the context of pre-knowledge, a set of common assumptions within which human judgment occurs.[26] Wright takes these assumptions to be expressible as propositions and to form a system. They are derived as necessary conditions of what is judged to be true or false by a process of philosophical analysis. The trouble with this procedure is that it loses touch with the immanent nature of Wittgenstein's analysis; the propositions derived as belonging to preknowledge can be stated, discussed, and questioned. Wittgenstein seems to claim not simply that we do not question assertions on the grammatical horizon of a language game but that we cannot question them without changing the game. It would be mad to try to question seriously the deepest roots of our knowledge, those that are interwoven with our practices. Wittgenstein's point here is a clear continuation of the notion that some things can be only shown and not said. Whatever preknowledge would be, it is interwoven with life at a prepropositional level, at the level of movement and gesture.

A central example is that of knowing one's own name, of knowing who one is.[27] One cannot be in error, but one is also not infallible. The poignancy, rather than the contradiction in this remark, is illustrated in madness. The normal conflation of self-appraisal and public appraisal of one's identity is presupposed in everything one says, and Wittgenstein's City, by his own admission, would break down without it. It might also be noted that this observation avoids the trap of philosophical generality in that, speaking normally as father, professor, soccer coach, and so forth, my identity can appropriately shift with the relevant language games, while my name remains acoustically the same. What I can appropriately say in these various roles varies in a manner that maintains the conflation of private and public appraisals of identity. By identifying with our names, we become part of the human world. Wittgenstein's appraisal of this practice as a condition of residency is a sign of conventionality in that it completely overlooks the difficulties, if not the impossibility of success, that is associated with taking a name in the modern literature of psychoanalytic theory.[28]

A bland philosophical assertion would be that Wittgenstein holds that the use of language by a speaker or writer always presupposes the self-awareness of one's name (one's self-identity) that is expected on the part of the speaker or writer. But this comment does not address the "depth" of this presupposition, compared, say, with the presupposition that one knows roughly where one is and is certain about it. One can be mistaken about where one is without dropping out of human society. If we are mistaken about who we are, in certain ways, we are no longer in the human community. A critical, but penetrating, remark might be that Wittgenstein here comes upon an extremely important insight that he does not have the resources to develop.

In a similar way, original poets working with new usages of language are excluded from the City. Original poets do not use the language as it is already spoken; they produce new sounds that may or may not become part of the imagery of the language. One-step hermeneutics is dumbfounded. Serious attempts to take Wittgenstein over into literary theory and criticism have encountered the problem that his analysis of language applies only to literal expression and its surroundings.[29] The problem is that, although Wittgenstein recognizes that language changes and that language games can come and go, he does not seem to feel that language games can actually conflict, *forcing* changes in language.[30] His conception of language change is a flexible catalog of language games, one that varies with changing human practices. Language games can drop out and others can be added.

Wittgenstein's methods are designed to survey existent language games at a point in time, and he does not see it as the task of philosophers to explain change. Missing is any notion of the dynamics forcing language change, including internal friction and simply playing with language. The family-resemblance metaphor suggests that language games are simply there and that their differences can be explored without triggering a revisionary impulse beyond that suggested by the task of clarification. Although Wittgenstein uses metaphors, he never analyzes the way in which they and other tropes at the disposal of the serious thinker force semantic changes in language. Without generalizing too much, a specific description of the mechanism of change in particular cases, especially mechanisms that merge and divide language games, could well add to our understanding of language. In spite of the variety of language games, once the excitement of eliminating bad philosophy has diminished, Wittgenstein's City threatens to be a pretty dull place in which to live.

One question often pressed onto Wittgenstein is not easily avoided. Why do certain empirical relationships harden into grammar, while others remain uncertain and contingent? Wittgenstein undoubtedly supposed that this sort of historical question could best be attacked by scientific methods. Without assuming that there are historical laws that determine such matters, however, a *description* of the changing relationships of human practice and language games over time might well prove revealing in this regard, and Wittgenstein's tools allow for this kind of description. Wittgenstein's self-imposed limits cannot deal with the real history of these situations, nor with differences or conflicts between language games.

Wittgenstein's City is static. The comparative age of some language games or their relative distance from behavioral roots may be noticed, but Wittgenstein does not talk historically, except to note changes in philosophical views, especially his own. No shift in ordinary usage as a language game, relative to a practice, is ever observed. Language games that are alternatives to those that currently exist are described in our language, even if they suggest alternative language games and alternative practices. Thought is not creative; when used clearly, it organizes what we already know and can experience. The potential resources of our language are sufficient to reach understanding with other human beings, even if at first they are difficult for us to comprehend.

Wittgenstein cites the common behavior of humankind as the system of reference by means of which we interpret an unknown language, by which he clearly means *any* unknown language. Wittgenstein refers constantly to actual language, our language, and so on, as if there were only one. No remarks suggest that there are different cities, between which some relationship must be found. Wittgenstein speaks of humanity as though it were the same in all human beings. These points are present in the first aphorism of *Culture and Value*.[31] One takes Chinese to be inarticulate gurgling unless one understands Chinese, and then one recognizes language— not *another* language, but *language*. Furthermore, we often cannot at first understand the humanity in another, although, by implication, if we come to understand them, we will. Does Wittgenstein lapse here into ignoring differences and doing bad philosophy? Not if he is right that there is only *one* language, consisting of an assemblage of language games at any point in time, and not if there is only one common human behavior.

Wittgenstein is often cited as referring to *forms of life,* as though other human beings could participate in other, different forms of life.[32] This comment is followed in the *Investigations* by a remark that humans generally agree in their judgments of color, a denial of color relativity.[33] Clearly, there are nonhuman forms of life. A lion, if it could talk, could not be understood, and the subjunctive mood of this observation indicates that lion language, unlike Chinese, could not be learned by humans.[34] Earlier, in connection with the builder's language at the start of the *Investigations*, Wittgenstein says that to imagine a language is to imagine a form of life.[35] This statement seems to mean that a clearly imagined language (or language game) is conceived of as interwoven with the practices of life.[36] We imagine not only how people talk but how they live and how their lives are connected with their language. The crucial question is whether an imagined language game is a form of life or only an imagined form of life, one that provides the only means within our language for an examination of our form of life by showing a contrast. That the latter interpretation is more likely correct is shown in another place, where the form of life is identified with language, already conceived of as a single system interwoven with the common behavior of human beings.[37]

The one remaining explicit citation from the *Investigations* may at first sight seem at odds with this reading.[38] Wittgenstein says that only those who have mastered the use of a language can hope, which seems to suggest that there are various languages, or at least various language games. But the next sentence refers to "this complicated form of life," clearly in context the human form of life that includes human language. The occurrences of the expression *form of life* are not that numerous, and they are compatible with there being but one form of human life, even if imagined forms of life within the capabilities of human language are essential to the only philosophical understanding of ourselves that is possible. The position that there is but one City will survive a close scrutiny of the relevant texts.

Wittgenstein cannot distinguish emerging science from nonsense or from original poetry, because his concept of history is that of a reshuffling of language games, with individual games occasionally introduced or eliminated from the deck. His foundational view of science cannot describe adequately what happens in the originating periods of a scientific development such as relativity theory, quantum theory, or plasma physics, in which the experimental practice and the novel data seem hopelessly baffling. His remarks on science grow from a typical philosophical privileging of the physical sciences and from a late nineteenth-century conception of their clarity and growth. There are no explicit remarks on economics or sociology, for example, and psychology is treated as in a state of conceptual confusion that philosophy might help to put right.[39] Change in science is conceptualized on the basis of mathematical change, in which new language games can be postulated out of whole cloth by new definitions, or on the model of more and more complete description within a language such as that of Newtonian physics. The impact of new instruments and the onslaught of incomprehensible data play no role in mathematical development.[40]

When Wittgenstein turns to psychology, he views it in the mode of physics and mathematics. It is not more closely related to philosophy because it deals with the self; the self that it can observe is *in* the world, and psychology is just another experimental science.[41] Psychological phenomena may at least in some cases not have physiological correlates, but this limitation does not prevent experimentation at the physiological level.[42] Philosophical psychology, the study of the grammar of our assertions about emotions, feelings, sensations, and so forth, can be carried out using philosophical methods, introducing the conceptual clarity required to interpret experiments, which are otherwise of uncertain significance.

It may not be possible to understand precisely how Wittgenstein thought experiment and conceptual clarification, the latter undertaken with philosophical methods, would always mesh, unless he assumed a view of psychology as a static discipline, one that would enlarge its accepted propositions only on a firm conceptual foundation, as in the case of mathematics and physics. The nature of appropriate experimentation is at stake here, a much more obscure subject than the nature of appropriately surveyable mathematical proof.[43] Wittgenstein does not discuss very much what might be regarded as comprehensive psychological theorizing. Although Wittgenstein finds Freud interesting—but also shallow and as not having extended the borders of science—Wittgenstein's resources permit no explanation of the *persistence* of philosophical delusions. Delusions are, perhaps, a secular sin, but Wittgenstein failed to observe how doggedly bad philosophers hang on to their delusions. If Wittgenstein diagnoses the nature of philosophical disease, he cannot explain its grip. Freud at least shows us the darker corners of the human mind that are unavailable to Wittgenstein's optimistic therapeutics.

By comparison with many other philosophers, Wittgenstein's account of human knowledge has an irredeemably social aspect. The refusal of the possibility of private languages, as well as the interweave of language with human social life, means that Wittgenstein does not present the problems of philosophy as though an individual had to create science, mathematics, and all other forms of knowledge from private moments of epistemological certainty. Some philosophers have been provoked by Wittgenstein's social basis, linking Wittgenstein to Marx or to defensible foundations for the social sciences, but such extensions need to be constructed on a quite slender basis. The social comes rather shyly and politely into view in Wittgenstein, as in the later Husserl. Language demands social life if its objectivity is to be grounded in common practice rather than in a referential semantics that makes no reference to group practices. The social life that we find in Wittgenstein, however, has no divisions, no conflict, and no incommensurable discourses. Wittgenstein's City lacks any political or social structure. It is populated by *human beings* who speak *language,* and here at last we find a bit of bad philosophy, a vestige of bloodless and hasty generalization completely removed from the harsh particularity of human social existence. Wittgenstein has no resources for investigating ideology in language, the *deliberate* concealment for purposes of domination of real features of the world. Ideology is shown when language games clash, but the social divisions involved are never mentioned as a feature of the City.

Wittgenstein talks about giving orders and commands, *and obeying them,* but there is not a word about the legitimacy of orders or commands. The language games of giving orders and obeying them do not contain the possibility of dispute.[44] The City has no political structure, and Wittgenstein has no genuine social and political philosophy. There is no city hall, police force, jail, criminality, or political discourse. The language of the citizens is interwoven with their practices, but their practices are as consistent and cooperative as their language. What if the builder says "slab" and his assistant refuses to budge without a pay raise? In the builder's language, only orders are given. The assistant does not speak; he just brings the right item. In the more articulate City, it is not clear why wills cannot clash or why demands will not conflict.

Surely Wittgenstein did not think that there was a science of such matters, and his individualistic ethics of absolute values provides no forms for the resolution of such conflict, even if one party can be seen not to be recognizing absolute values. Any attempt to bring Wittgenstein to bear on social and political issues will require that one attempt to do what Wittgenstein did not do, to discuss whether the discourses involved in social and political theory can be illuminated by his methods. Attempts to do so have largely analyzed the discourses of social and political theorists that turn on philosophical unclarity and have concluded that sensitive conceptual readings of various positions will reveal grains of truth in all of them and perhaps the fact that debates frequently turn on unnoticed subtleties of language.[45] This "conclusion" is merely tap dancing. By itself it does not resolve any dispute. The same might be said of clashes between ethical philosophies, and we know what Wittgenstein held there. All of the rationalizations of philosophy in the realm of absolute ethical imperatives are repellent verbiage. One suspects that Wittgenstein would have held the same opinion of social and political philosophies. The question that must be put is the status of substantive nonphilosophical clashes of demands, especially in the light of scarcity. Social and political philosophy have shown that these questions have no purely scientific answer. Perhaps Wittgenstein thought that we should simply act, as we should in the domain of ethics, on our insights, but he never says how. In this area, in which he could not speak, he did keep silence.

If there are scientists in Wittgenstein's City, there should also be substantive arguments between them. The scientists of the City must be hammering out new languages to adapt to new data at the edges of their disciplines, and this process is not a matter of simple clarification.[46] Wittgenstein comes close to suggesting that there is a Platonic realm of mutually consistent language games from among which humans have chosen a subset at any given time. Mathematical history, which allows older language games to be retained by the insulation of definitions that restrict them to narrower domains, gives only a partial picture of change, a picture that emphasizes the preservation of consistency with the past. Twentieth-century science has shown that this picture will not work for scientific progress, where language games clash and demand deep refashioning. Ultimately, Wittgenstein accepts more of the Augustinian picture of language than he seems to realize. His children do come to speak the language that was the language of their elders, even if Augustine's picture of the language and of its learning is in some respects challenged. The rapid rate of scientific change requires at the least a more detailed description of how language is forced to accommodate the new data that breaks the old vessels. Unless one is a rigid determinist—and Wittgenstein was not—this issue cannot be escaped by consigning the problem of change to the domain of science.

Wittgenstein's scope of attack—a single sentence, a few sentences, a language game with its horizon, or at most an assemblage of mutually consistent language games, even given that they are interwoven with a consistent common behavior—is so restricted that it precludes the discovery of any significant seams in the web of language. He was pessimistic about science, about modern culture, about philosophy, and, at times, about his own abilities. He consistently wanted to stop short of philosophical theorizing. But he does assume that the grammar of color, mathematics, emotion, and other areas can be sorted out clearly. Perhaps the legacy of Wittgenstein has run thin, perhaps it has turned into the hermeneutical problems of his texts or has flowered in movements inspired by his insights but grafted into the service of alien goals, because the resolution of genuine conflict in our language and in our lives was not allowed a substantial place in the direction of his thought. We may need to learn more about ourselves and our societies by means of historical studies that recognize such conflicts before we can grasp some of the subtler features of our language games. Such studies will recognize differences in the grammar of terms as standing for other differences, so that our philosophical ontology becomes more complex and troublesome than simply that of human beings speaking language.

If Wittgenstein has no social and political philosophy, if Wittgenstein has no account of the dynamics of language change in science and elsewhere, and if Wittgenstein rests too easily with an account of human nature exhausted by the conscious, literal assertions of language games and their immanent grammars, he is still a great philosopher, and a greater philosopher than many who have dealt with all of these topics. He succeeded in doing what he set out to do, carrying out his task with an unparalleled intensity and self-consistent rigor, and his task was important. He drew the boundary around literal language and exposed the poverty of the bad philosophy that engages in ideological apologetics for the ornamentations of this language. His greatness lies in providing the resources for identifying a widespread kind of philosophical nonsense. No matter that he could not bring the nonsense to a stop. Because of his efforts, we can recognize it, and we can refuse it. We are free to turn to other things and to leave the dominant style of philosophy behind. At least one philosopher is grateful to him for having shown the way out of a living death.

NOTES

Chapter 1: Panorama

1 The British patent application, number 27.087, dated 22 November 1910, shows the construction. Wittgenstein's propeller system was meant to be of use for any aerial machine, not necessarily just airplanes. Gaseous fuel was to be admitted into the arms of the engine (arms shaped as propeller blades) and the gas drawn to the ends of the arms by the centrifugal force of rotation, where it would be ignited and then exhausted through jets at the ends of the arms. The jet effect was designed to boost the rotation velocity. Whether such a device was ever built and run satisfactorily seems not to be known. The device is misdescribed in many biographical sketches.

2 Wittgenstein's work on his sister's house is the subject of a documentary showing plans and photographs for the house in Leitner, *The Architecture of Ludwig Wittgenstein*. A comprehensive study of Wittgenstein's life, with many photographs, is to be found in Nedo and Ranchetti, *Ludwig Wittgenstein*. The details of Wittgenstein's life are interesting, especially the anecdotes regarding his eccentricities. There are also such matters as allusions to his possible homosexuality, but even to begin on these issues would threaten the proportions of the survey of the City to be undertaken.

3 Wittgenstein's own apparent preference for the *Investigations* is usually accepted, certainly by adherents of the ordinary-language movements that flourished on reworking material from the *Investigations*. Russell, Bergmann, Rosenberg, and Sellars are among the distinguished philosophers who see a decline in philosophical achievement in the later publication.

4 Because Wittgenstein prepared the *Tractatus* for publication and had almost completed the *Investigations* for publication before he died and since he apparently did not regard the intervening work as suitable for publication, there are immediate biographical grounds for considering that only these two works demand close interpretation. My first claim is that these two works are not as dissimilar as they seem if one considers the intervening work. Review of this work is thus essential to

understanding the proper relationship of the *Tractatus* to the *Investigations*. I also claim that Wittgenstein was rushing through a large-scale survey of the quarters of the City and that, as he found the keys to various quarters, he regarded the detailed survey of less interest than fresh exploration. I argue this point explicitly for mathematics and color in the text below. A survey of general books on Wittgenstein will reveal that many deal with only the *Tractatus* or the *Investigations*, thus basically accepting the legitimacy of the twin-tower skyline. Kenny's *Wittgenstein* is an important exception to this tendency, but Kenny still concentrates on the change in doctrines from the *Tractatus* to the *Investigations* and says little about color and mathematics.

5   *Investigations*, 18.

6   This publication, *Wörterbuch für Volksschulen*, is sometimes misrepresented as a dictionary, probably because of its title. It is, technically, the second book (after the *Tractatus*) that Wittgenstein published in his lifetime. A little more than three thousand common words are entered in correct spelling, with the intention of improving the writing of his students. It is interesting here that Wittgenstein does not accept common but incorrect spelling of words but wishes to convey correct spelling to each individual student. The meaning and use of these common words is assumed to be known.

7   See Wittgenstein, "Some Remarks on Logical Form." This paper, which was not actually read to the Aristotelian Society, is crucial for grasping the disintegration of the certainties of the *Tractatus*.

8   See the Bibliography for all titles attributed to Wittgenstein in the text.

9   The *Blue Book* and the *Brown Book* were dictated (in English) in 1933–35 to students at Cambridge. They represent Wittgenstein's turn to the subject matter that sustained his interest until his death.

10   *Blue Book*, pp. 46–47.

11   Additional material by Wittgenstein remains to be published, but the difficulty of consulting these fragments has made it seem necessary to introduce references to the quarters of Wittgenstein's City from the published sources, which are now sufficient for large-scale survey work.

12   I allude here to the so-called hermeneutical circle, which claims that the meaning of a sentence (or any part of a text) must be determined ultimately by considering it in a larger context that reduces obscurity and ambiguity in the part, while the part contributes to the meaning of the larger context. At least from his reading and citation of Heidegger, we know that Wittgenstein must have been aware of this central topic in hermeneutical theory.

13   Failure to note the horizon would produce a reading of Wittgenstein in which he objects to the factlike nature of sentences on the grounds that isolated sentences say only one thing from our point of view, thus assuming without question that there could be only one relevant horizon. For an example of this error in a very sophisticated philosopher, see Dummett, "Frege and Wittgenstein," p. 37.

14   The special connotations of the terms *rule, criterion, picture,* etc. that have been developed in the secondary literature could not have been intended by Wittgenstein, who found ordinary terms serviceable. Exhaustively surveying this literature in detail against Wittgenstein's texts would completely miss Wittgenstein's attitudes, an error I wish to avoid in what follows.

15   *Culture and Value,* p. 66. See the remarks about raisins near the bottom of the page, where Wittgenstein explicitly compares his remarks with the aphorisms of Karl Kraus. One suggestion of this passage is that neither the aphorisms nor the remarks constitute a cake, that is, a philosophy.

Chapter 2: Thickets

1   See *Tractatus,* 5.5563, for a clear assertion that everyday language is in perfect working order and that exposing the logical structure of its clear assertions is a concrete problem. This latter comment means presumably that the sentence is not replaced by its analysis but forces its precise analysis in the philosophical effort to resolve particular puzzlement. All efforts to state ethical demands are an error, according to the *Tractatus,* yet the importance of ethical demands were shown in Wittgenstein's life. Wittgenstein's exasperation with the triviality of philosophical talk is part of the legend. On at least one occasion, he whistled to a group of assembled philosophers instead of delivering a paper, expressing this exasperation and perhaps commenting on what passed for thought, in his mind, on most such occasions.

2   It is necessary only to recall some of the simplest terminology involved, such as *illocutionary act* or *conversational implicature,* or the fact that speech-act theorists work on something that they call *speech-act theory.* Without making any comparative evaluations, I note how clearly this orientation diverges from Wittgenstein's project. The technical terms of speech-act theory are initially baffling and need explication. Wittgenstein, to put it simply, avoids the trappings of such theorizing.

3   Winch, Pitkin, and Phillips have relativized assertions in anthropology, political discourse, and religious discourse, respectively, according to such a device. The Azande cannot be understood or criticized from a scientific perspective, Socrates cannot be understood or criticized from the perspective of Thrasymachus, and the

believer cannot be understood or criticized from the perspective of the atheist. (See Winch, "Understanding a Primitive Society"; Pitkin, *Wittgenstein and Justice*; and Phillips, *The Concept of Prayer*.) That Wittgenstein was no automatic relativist can be seen in his trenchant attacks on various forms of philosophical discourse.

4   See *Investigations*, 206. A strange language is to be understood against the backdrop of the common behavior of humankind. There is no presumption that people who converse with one another are making sense. Philosophers should always be kept in mind. For a discussion of the expression *common behavior*, see Haller, "Die gemeinsame menschliche Handlungsweise."

5   Drury, *The Danger of Words*, p. ix.

6   *Zettel*, 40.

7   Whether or not the picture theory is retained, Wittgenstein no longer accepted the picture theory of the *Tractatus* in its full generality as an account of the meaning of all sentences. But the later pictures also have poles; mathematical sentences do or do not have surveyable proofs, and expectations are or are not fulfilled. The picture theory seems to be retained in the sense that the multiplicity of language continues to fit reality. For discussion, see Hacker, "Laying the Ghost of the *Tractatus*" and "Rise and Fall of Picture Theory"; Kenny, "The Ghost of the *Tractatus*"; and Stenius, "Picture Theory and Wittgenstein's Later Attitude."

8   *Grammar*, 85. See also the slightly wilder retention of the idea in paragraph 132.

9   Looking at the existing literature from the point of view of minimizing the break in Wittgenstein's development, I note that Kenny's *Wittgenstein* is particularly relevant, as well as various essays by Cavell, especially "Availability of Wittgenstein's Later Philosophy." Both the *Tractatus* and the *Investigations* claim that there are no philosophical doctrines or theories. Clear, meaningful assertion always lies outside philosophy. Wittgenstein does not refute the *Tractatus* (except in terms of its specious philosophical generality)—he later offers a more subtle and detailed picture of language. In both works, knowledge is not extended: assertions of knowledge are analyzed and described in the context of their use. Both books depend heavily on the idea that *showing* is naturally understood and that explanations come to an end finally in the bedrock of natural understanding. Where the unities have been noted, they have always been qualified. For example, Winch considers the idea that the *Tractatus* describes but one quarter of Wittgenstein's City, that of factual propositions, but rejects it on the grounds that the *Investigations* protests the idea that factual assertion can have a single analysis ("The Unity of Wittgenstein's Philosophy," p. 17). Winch wants to stress the complete diversity of language games so as

to defeat any philosophical generalizations. He seems to miss the point that the later horizons of languages games can contain analyses similar to the *Tractatus* analysis of factual assertion into truth functions of more elementary propositions. These later language games are associated with different kinds of elementary propositions. The *Investigations* does reject the claim that a single concrete analysis of all factual assertion is available. Wittgenstein, unlike Winch, is not afraid of all generalization, and he claims that language-game horizons can bear relationships of intersection and enclosure, generalizations analogous to scientific generalizations in their concreteness. Particular cases can be studied in the details of usage. Winch rejects his own suggestion in terms of a prejudice for a particular view of the *Investigations* that tempts him into an unsubtle analysis of the repudiation of the *Tractatus*.

10   *Investigations*, 422–27.

11   Ibid., p. x.

12   Ibid., 11–14, argues the vacuity of the *Tractatus* analysis, not its outright falsity. Taking words to be uniform in use, one must invent strange philosophical notions of reference. The better way is to notice directly the variety of words and to relate this variety to diverse usage on various occasions, dispensing with the idling technicalities of philosophical explanation.

Chapter 3: Language

1   *King/Lee Lectures*, p. 9.

2   *Tractatus*, 2.1514–2.1515. Only a mind can recognize these feelers, but the objectivity of the feelers is meant to preclude psychologism.

3   The language-game horizon allows us to gain a sufficient anticipatory grasp of what lies within it for practical purposes. But not everything can be foreseen. In mathematical language games, as noted in the text below, Wittgenstein held that contradiction by itself did not destroy their significance.

4   Wittgenstein's repudiation of type theories was based on his opinion that we cannot get outside language by means of semantic ascent.

5   *Tractatus*, 4.0312, states that the fundamental idea of the *Tractatus* is that logical signs are not names, although they function to determine the truth conditions for sentences in which they appear. The fact that ordinary-language propositions do not consist of just names and logical signs is related to the necessity of expressing pictorial form in language. *Tractatus*, 3.1432, seems to say that, in the ordinary-language expression formally represented as "*aRb*," *a* and *b* can function as names, while *R*, placed between them, expresses the fact that they stand in a certain rela-

tionship. We can perhaps state this fact only by saying "*aRb*" in our language. It is assumed here that "*aRb*" expresses a simple relationship such as "Boston is north of New York City."

6 *Grammar*, 104.

7 *Psychology* 1:372 (vol. 1, paragraph 372).

8 A burgeoning literature compares Wittgenstein with Kant, but Wittgenstein seems to be a Kantian only in limited respects. The argument to the existence of objects in the *Tractatus* may seem a transcendental argument, but the question here is whether these objects would be unknowable apart from this argument. See the text below for the considerations that suggest that Wittgenstein's objects were meant to be objects that we are already aware of. Wittgenstein produces no morality comparable to Kant's, and the whole effort at assimilation reduces the force of Wittgenstein's critique of philosophy (no matter that Kant's philosophy was also critical of philosophical practice before him). Wittgenstein is not attempting a synthesis of past traditions. Wittgenstein's unique feature is his refusal to coin special vocabulary to communicate philosophical insights. This point of difference seems more significant than occasional parallels or anything that Wittgenstein says about Kant. (See *Culture and Value*, p. 10, for an enigmatic example.) On Wittgenstein and transcendental argument, see Leinfellner et al., *Language, Logic, and Philosophy*, Sec. 4, pp. 259–74. Wittgenstein's possible Kantian background and his connections to phenomenology are studied in Gier, *Wittgenstein and Phenomenology*. On phenomenology, see also Spiegelberg, "The Puzzle of Wittgenstein's Phänomenologie." For an interesting set of related perspectives on Kant and Wittgenstein, see Bachmaier, *Wittgenstein und Kant*; Fromm, *Wittgensteins Erkenntnisspiele contra Kants Erkenntnislehre*; and Thiele, *Die Verwicklungen im Denken Wittgensteins*, especially pp. 18–19. Thiele notes that Fromm's Kant is Wittgenstein, and Bachmaier's Wittgenstein is Kant. As Wittgenstein hardly refers to Kant and does not mention Kant at all in the *Investigations*, Thiele is concerned to develop a possible Wittgenstein critique of Kant, which seems a plausible undertaking.

9 *Psychology* 2:312–17.

10 *Certainty*, 475.

11 *Culture and Value*, p. 15.

12 *Investigations*, 491. One must assume that the cryptic last remark here is also to be *denied*, like the remark opening the paragraph. Wittgenstein believed that animals, without speaking and writing, are perfectly capable of communicating.

13 *Zettel*, 223.

14 *Blue Book*, p. 1.

15 *Psychology* 1:664.

16 See Marshack, "Paleolithic Symbolic Evidence," which notes that early artifacts are often not the crude beginnings postulated by armchair philosophical anthropology. A subtle logical space may have antedated systems of speaking and writing. Wittgenstein's point is not hopelessly at odds with scientific opinion in this area.

17 *Zettel*, 524, and *Psychology* 1:229–30. In these examples, psychological verbs could be applied to animals, but without using the crucial human distinction between first person and third person.

18 This important point is discussed in a variety of papers. See especially Malcolm, "Wittgenstein"; Rhees, "Wittgenstein on Language and Ritual"; and Winch, "Im Anfang war die Tat."

19 *Brown Book*, p. 178. What is shown in music is mentioned at *Notebooks*, p. 41, entry of 11.4.15.

20 *Color*, p. 46, 213. (References to *Color* include both page number and paragraph number.)

21 *Psychology* 1:22, 517, 995.

22 Ibid. 2:696.

23 Ibid. 1:332, 683; 2:259.

24 "Some Remarks on Logical Form," p. 32.

25 *Zettel*, 379.

26 *Investigations*, 2, presents a primitive language game far removed from the language games we normally participate in. As it is a language consisting only of names, it serves to show the inadequacy of theories of language (both the *Tractatus* theory and other philosophical accounts) that would analyze language into logic and concatenations of names. Despite its simplicity, the language game of *Investigations*, 1, is sufficient to show that words can have remarkably different uses.

Chapter 4: Logic and Grammar

1 The observation is frequently made that Wittgenstein managed to say a great deal about showing, as though he had violated his own observation, but Wittgenstein formally avoids this trap by insisting that his sentences in the *Tractatus* lie on the horizon of assertion, showing logical structure. We cannot speak unless we command a language; our original language learning, however, involves coming to understand what language shows without explicit instruction, which we can do because we are

human. Our language learning cannot take place solely through instruction, without a diachronic paradox. We cannot speak before we learn to speak. Wittgenstein thus objects to the Augustinian account of language learning at the start of the *Investigations* because it presupposes that the learner already knows a language in learning a first language. Just how explicitly Wittgenstein had understood this issue at the time of the *Tractatus* is problematic.

2   See *Tractatus*, 4.3, passim. Wittgenstein's logic is not axiomatized and consists rather of analyses of individual assertive sentences to see whether they are tautologies, contradictions, or contingencies. Somewhat more technically, Wittgenstein presents a form of functional logic whose properties are not always completely grasped in the commentaries, but exchanging this logic for the standard truth-functional logics in analyzing particular sentences would create no problems. See Koenne, "Rekursive Techniken und der Tractat," for a sophisticated discussion.

3   To explain these logical points would require detailed treatment, but the basic idea here is as follows. The axiom of infinity attempted to express the idea that there were an infinite number of things (or numbers). Wittgenstein felt that an existential assertion of this kind was a factual assertion that could not be expressed in purely logical notation. The theory of types attempted to say things about languages that were properly shown only in the symbolism of a language, such as that various signs designated certain kinds of objects. These problems arise when logic attempts to mirror mathematics, rather than being restricted to providing the horizon for the structure of clear factual assertion.

4   In finite domains of the sort that concerned Wittgenstein, universal quantification is always equivalent to some finite conjunction of elementary propositions, and existential quantification to some finite disjunction. Wittgenstein's remarks on quantifiers, however, will not pass muster by modern standards. See Hintikka, "Wittgensteinian Investigations," pp. 95–99. There are also problems with other aspects of Wittgenstein's logical notation. See Daniels and Davidson, "Ontology and Method in Wittgenstein's *Tractatus*"; Fogelin, *Wittgenstein*, pp. 34–77; and Ishiguro, "Wittgenstein and the Theory of Types." Wittgenstein's treatment of quantifiers, defensible in his time, would now require an extensive formal elaboration.

5   *Tractatus*, 4.123, 6.3751.

6   "Some Remarks on Logical Form," especially p. 33.

7   Ibid. and *Remarks*, 78.

8   See *Notebooks*, pp. 2–3, entries of 3.9.14 and 4.9.14, pp. 98–99, for the first point; and pp. 62–63, entry of 17.6.15, and p. 67, entry of 20.6.15, for the second point.

9 Wittgenstein's move from logic to grammar is traced in the *Grammar* and in the *Remarks*. For this observation, see *Grammar*, pp. 205–6.

10 *Grammar*, pp. 210–11. This passage shows an explicit recognition that color propositions will not accept the same analysis as other assertions and cannot be analyzed by the scheme of the *Tractatus*. Other horizons will be developed below.

11 *Grammar* p. 244.

12 Ibid., pp. 247–48.

13 Ibid., pp. 251–52.

14 Ibid., pp. 259–60.

15 *Remarks*, 82.

16 Ibid., 92–93, 116–40.

17 Ibid., 143–44.

18 *Psychology* 1:274.

19 Ibid., 37, 40, 269.

20 Ibid., 38.

21 *Investigations*, 81, 89, 100–106.

22 *Mathematics*, pp. 35–36, 118. (References to *Mathematics* and *Mathematics* [rev.] include page number followed by paragraph number.)

23 *Investigations*, 81, 108–9.

24 Ibid., 551.

25 Ibid., 558.

26 *Mathematics*, p. 37, 122.

27 Ibid., p. 121, 29.

28 *Mathematics* (rev.), p. 397, 30.

29 See the discussion titled "Language Games" in Baker and Hacker, *Wittgenstein*, pp. 89–98.

30 See *Investigations*, 23, for Wittgenstein's description of the multiplicity of language games. Not all of these language games are explicitly discussed by Wittgenstein.

31 Ibid., 580.

32 *Psychology* 2:551 and *Investigations*, 67.

33 *Investigations*, 66. See the intriguing development in Suits, *The Grasshopper*.

34 *Investigations*, 68.

35 *Mathematics*, p. 84, 46; p. 88, 48; p. 115, 46.

36 *Grammar*, 72, especially p. 117, and *Psychology* 1:563.

37 *Blue Book*, pp. 28–29. Here the expression "ideal language" is used instead of "language game," but the same method is clearly intended.

38   *Investigations*, 2.

39   *Brown Book*, p. 103.

40   *Psychology* 2:203–5 and *Zettel*, 98–99.

41   *Zettel*, 372, and also "Remarks on Frazer's *Golden Bough*."

42   *Psychology* 1:408–9.

43   Ibid., 1080.

44   *Investigations*, 130. See also Cavell, "Availability of Wittgenstein's Later Philosophy," and the daring and extensive discussion of Wittgenstein's relationship to systematization in modern linguistics in Baker and Hacker, *Language, Sense, and Nonsense*.

Chapter 5: Picturing

1   *Tractatus*, 4.22.

2   *Investigations*, 48.

3   Ibid., 60.

4   *Notebooks*, pp. 108–9, and *Tractatus*, 3.1432.

5   Sellars, defending a nominalistic reading of the *Tractatus*, has developed this point in detail in connection with his language *Jumblese*. See Sellars, "Naming and Saying."

6   Stenius, *Wittgenstein's Tractatus*, and Bergmann, "Glory and Misery of Wittgenstein." In the hands of Bergmann and some of his students, the names of individuals would be that of peculiar entities called *bare particulars*. It seems that, if the names of individuals are retained in elementary propositions as they are in ordinary language, the *Tractatus* becomes committed to a strange view of predicates and relations, and if the symbols for predicates and relations remain normal, the individuals become strange. All of these readings may result from bringing to Wittgenstein's texts alien views about the semantics of language.

7   Sellars, "Naming and Saying."

8   See the essays in Beard and Copi, *Essays on Wittgenstein's "Tractatus,"* where these representative positions are defended.

9   Wittgenstein says in the *Notebooks* that the *physical* representation of automobile accidents in Paris law courts by means of dolls, model cars, etc. gave him the fundamental insight into the picture theory of sentential truth (p. 7, entry of 29.9.14).

10   Shwayder, "Gegenstände and Other Matters," p. 388. Hertz's influence on

Wittgenstein, mentioned at *Tractatus*, 4.04, seems to be that Hertz thought one could get rid of mysterious forces in mechanics by describing them in terms of the movements of objects that were presently conjectural. This idea provides a nice figure for Wittgenstein's approach but should not be used to determine Wittgenstein's ontology.

11   See Allaire, "*Tractatus* 6.3751," and Austin, "Wittgenstein's Solutions," for a detailed discussion of the problem in the case of color.

12   *Tractatus*, 2.03. A chain just has links; it does not have anything to hold the links together. The names just fit together into an elementary proposition, a fact that we simply see when we speak the language. The names show that they fit together; any effort to state this fact would lead to nonsense.

13   *Tractatus*, 2.1. One can imagine cave paintings and other early human artifacts functioning to make assertions before an overt linguistic level was reached. Wittgenstein's fact ontology fits nicely the discrete two-dimensional form of written language. An interesting question is whether denser pictures are possible whose analogue properties cannot be coded into language and which cannot be broken up into discrete parts but yet can function as assertions. See the ground-breaking discussion in Goodman, *Languages of Art*. Wittgenstein's attention was concentrated on a fairly narrow set of philosophical examples when he developed the picture theory.

14   *Tractatus*, 2.17–2.2.

15   See Shwayder, "Gegenstände and Other Matters," for an incisive discussion.

16   *Tractatus*, 2.1513, notes that the pictorial relationship of a picture to reality turns it into a picture. The physical picture only pictures when this relationship can be seen. It seems to be made up of pictorial form, representational form, and logical form, as the subsequent remarks suggest, which taken together determine what is asserted of reality by the picture.

17   *Fact* is used in ordinary language in different ways, although ordinary language is in supposedly good working order. Wittgenstein here borders on abstract philosophical generality, as he later recognizes in his self-criticism.

18   Wittgenstein's German vocabulary does not translate smoothly into English, term for term, in this area. In this digression I wish to put some sensible bounds on what picturing can accomplish.

19   The general use of *representation (Darstellung)* is confirmed by *Tractatus*, 2.0231, which suggests that *green* in "the chair is green" represents a material property; *Tractatus*, 6.1203, which says that an accompanying diagram represents the truth function "p ⊃ q"; and in various other passages of the *Tractatus*.

20   *Notebooks*, p. 33, entry of 26.11.14.

21   On a phenomenological reading of the *Tractatus*, the feelers connect to objects of acquaintance, and only we can understand the language that we speak, because these feelers are private. It can then be argued that the Private-Language Argument in the *Investigations* is an attempt to refute this doctrine. This line of interpretation seems unsatisfactory when so much of Wittgenstein's work presupposes the existence of an ordinary language that we can mutually understand and use. If the solipsistic language discussed later in the *Tractatus* is phenomenological, it must be supposed that we all have access to the same phenomena, although we cannot state that fact in our language. For a defense of a phenomenological reading, see Hintikka, "Wittgensteinian Investigations," pp. 163–93. Some Jewish mystics have held that names are common to all languages, including divine languages. God gave the names to what he had created. When names fail to refer, language is nonsense.

22   *Tractatus*, 2.04–2.06, 2.063.

23   *Blue Book*, p. 37, and *Remarks*, 21.

24   *Zettel*, 32, 55.

25   *Grammar*, 62.

26   Ibid., 81.

27   Ibid., 83.

28   Ibid., 114.

29   Ibid., 98, 105, 113.

30   The general plan for psychological concepts is given in *Psychology* 2:63, 148. For the picturing of psychological states, see 1:282, 284, 385.

31   *Mathematics*, p. 117, 12.

32   *Investigations*, 352.

33   Ibid., p. 184.

34   *Notebooks*, pp. 35–36, entry of 6.12.14, and *Tractatus*, 6.342–6.343. On one occasion, he seems to have described science as a house built on a permanent foundation (*King/Lee Lectures*, p. 42).

35   Various writers have objected that we *do* learn from experience and that something must therefore be wrong with Wittgenstein's theory. The probability theory of the *Tractatus* is, however, consistent with Wittgenstein's views about the uncertainty of the future.

36   *Mathematics*, p. 96, 72.

37   Ibid., p. 114, 4.

38   *Mathematics* (rev.), p. 330, 28.

39   *Certainty*, 213.

Chapter 6: Mathematics

1   *Notebooks,* p. 40, entry of 14.2.15, and p. 98, lines 4–7.

2   *Tractatus,* 6.211.

3   *Notebooks,* p. 49, entry of 21.5.15, or *Tractatus,* 3.0321. Geometry is here clearly taken to be a priori, as noted at *Notebooks,* p. 48, entry of 16.5.15, or *Tractatus,* 3.032.

4   *Tractatus,* 6.021, 6.13, 6.21.

5   *Zettel,* 709–10, after which 706 may make some sense.

6   *Brown Book,* p. 79, and *Investigations,* 9.

7   *Remarks,* 162, see especially p. 192.

8   For an example of a low opinion of Wittgenstein's work by a qualified observer who was not otherwise hostile to Wittgenstein, see Kreisel, "Wittgenstein's *Remarks on Mathematics.*"

9   Naive set theory, for example, adopts the view that sophisticated logical inference does not effectively contribute to the development of the subject matter, at least not to the development required for mathematical practice. See Halmos, *Naive Set Theory,* pp. v–vi.

10   *Mathematics,* pp. 100–111, 78–88.

11   *Grammar,* pp. 290, 293.

12   Ibid., p. 319.

13   *Remarks,* 120–22. The equations of the *Tractatus* might have intimated the autonomy of mathematics if Wittgenstein had not been caught in the grip of a single horizon for assertion.

14   *Remarks,* pp. 144–45.

15   Ibid., 124, 129. An induction is like a scientific hypothesis in that it permits the generation of specific provable hypotheses.

16   Ibid., 142–43.

17   Ibid., 141, especially p. 161.

18   *Mathematics,* p. 15, 40. In this passage and in the subsequent discussion, Wittgenstein discusses the way in which training brings us to recognize the implications of proof structures. Inferences in proofs are usually not valid with respect to all of the conceivable logical possibilities. See also *Mathematics,* p. 13, 34–35, and pp. 19–21, 55–67.

19   Ibid., p. 21, 66, is a concentrated expression of this point.

20   Ibid., pp. 42–43, 137–38, 140–41.

21   Ibid., pp. 43–44, 142–52.

22   Ibid., pp. 43–45, 142–52.

23   Ibid., p. 47, 167.

24   Ibid., pp. 143–44, 18. One objection would be that formal systems are language games with perfectly controllable horizons of meaning and with common proof structures. Wittgenstein would reply that they are not appropriately interwoven with the rest of life insofar as they are purely formal.

25   Ibid.

26   See the intensive discussion in C. Wright, *Wittgenstein on the Foundations of Mathematics*, pp. 140–66.

27   *Mathematics*, p. 66, 3, and p. 74, 18.

28   Ibid., pp. 68–69, 7–8; pp. 71–72, 14–15; and pp. 76–77, 25.

29   Ibid., p. 96, 71.

30   The statement "2 + 2 ≠ 5" does not mean that "2 + 2 = 5" has not worked, a notion that would assimilate mathematics to factual assertion (see ibid., p. 114, 5). Mathematical assertions are overdetermined in their truth (see ibid., p. 115, 7).

31   Almost every commentary on the *Investigations* contains an extensive discussion of this issue, which, along with the so-called Private-Language Argument, has become a topic of central interest to philosophers reading the *Investigations*. See, for example, Kenny, *Wittgenstein*, pp. 170–77, and more extensively, Kripke, *Wittgenstein on Rules and Private Languages*, or C. Wright, *Wittgenstein on the Foundations of Mathematics*. Baker and Hacker, *Scepticism, Rules, and Language*, provides a discussion of these last two sources. To attribute skepticism about rules to Wittgenstein seems an error in the total context of his work. The rule-following discussions seem rather an attack on the usual philosophical explanations of how we follow rules, without in any way suggesting that we can legitimately doubt whether someone is following a rule in any particular situation.

32   See Baker and Hacker, *Wittgenstein*, pp. 89–98, 376–79, and 428–39. The notion that Wittgenstein passed through a stage in which he regarded languages as calculi is somewhat problematic, given the texts. Some language games are calculi, even in the later work. It is possible that Wittgenstein's pronouncements on calculi are all suppositional, however, discussing the consequences of rule following on this model and intending to establish the idea that the notion of a calculus with sharp rules following formalist philosophical intuitions is inapplicable to ordinary-language usage. Even in a calculus, incidentally, philosophical explanations of how we are able to follow rules are not acceptable to Wittgenstein.

33   *Investigations*, 240.

34   *Brown Book*, pp. 90, 113–25.

35 *Zettel*, 297–314.

36 *Psychology* 2:145, 401–2, 407. See also *Zettel*, 304.

37 *Investigations*, 85.

38 *Mathematics*, p. 3, 3.

39 See Kripke, *Wittgenstein on Rules and Private Language*, and C. Wright, *Wittgenstein on the Foundations of Mathematics*. Wittgenstein is defended from skepticism about rules in Baker and Hacker, *Scepticism, Rules, and Language*. There is some exchange between the two sides in the essays in Holtzman and Leich, *Wittgenstein*.

40 Philosophers have always been tempted to look for some form of language-transcending perception in order to legitimate the correctness of at least some forms of linguistic practice. Wittgenstein, having denied that language can be transcended, must rely on internal criticism and the success of existing practices, but he has all too little to say about change and improvement over time. Neither a simple objectivism nor a simple relativism can be charged against his full range of texts, and perhaps neither philosophical position can be coherently formulated within the compass of the ordinary linguistic practice that he accepts as coherent.

41 See Baker and Hacker, *Scepticism, Rules, and Language*, pp. 44–45, 71–73, 83.

Chapter 7: Seeing and Color

1 This phenomenon is illustrated in the history of optics. See, for example, any of the books on the history of optics by Vasco Ronchi (for example, *New Optics*). The problem becomes central for anyone who studies the mutual influence of colors in painting or any of the decorative arts.

2 "Some Remarks on Logical Form," especially pp. 35–37. See also Allaire, "*Tractatus* 6.3751," and Austin, "Wittgenstein's Solutions," for further discussion.

3 See Allaire, "*Tractatus* 6.3751," p. 192.

4 *Remarks*, 83–84. See also Austin, "Wittgenstein's Solutions," for a discussion. Carnap's analytic classic, *Der logische Aufbau der Welt*, can be regarded as an attempt to carry out this program in detail. The problems with the approach are explicated in Goodman's *The Structure of Appearance*, an attempt to rescue the program, using a logical system differing from the standard logic employed by Wittgenstein and Carnap. One might even think of the calculus of individuals as a grammar.

5 *Remarks*, 76.

6 *Blue Book*, p. 56.

7 Austin, "Wittgenstein's Solutions," pp. 146–49.

8 *Notebooks*, p. 81, entry of 16.8.16.

9 Ibid., pp. 50–51, entry of 24.5.15, and pp. 63–65, entry of 18.6.15.

10 *Tractatus*, 4.2211.

11 *Blue Book*, p. 31.

12 *Zettel*, 338, 357, 430.

13 *Grammar*, 82.

14 Ibid., pp. 208–9.

15 *Remarks*, 39. The German representation of color Wittgenstein refers to is not the same as the English representation often referred to, but they are functionally equivalent. See Wittgenstein's observations in ibid., 221.

16 Ibid., 38.

17 Wittgenstein does not see the sharp semantic break between ordinary language and scientific language often asserted by others. His position does not preclude two horizons for one-step hermeneutics—one in ordinary language and the other in scientific assertion—for the same acoustic sentence. The historical semantic development of language games can be ignored when they are played.

18 *Remarks*, 114, 218–20.

19 *Grammar*, 27.

20 *Remarks*, 218.

21 *Color*, p. 2, 5; p. 24, 57.

22 Ibid., p. 7, paragraphs 34, 36–38, 40.

23 Ibid., p. 46, 218.

24 Ibid., p. 26, 68.

25 Ibid., p. 12, 73.

26 Ibid., pp. 6–7, 28–32.

27 Ibid., p. 15, paragraphs 4, 7.

28 Ibid., p. 45, 211.

29 Ibid., p. 50, 255.

30 *Psychology* 1:644 or *Zettel*, 332.

31 *Investigations*, 381.

32 *Psychology* 2:197–98, 393.

33 *Investigations*, p. 187, and *Mathematics* (rev.), p. 329, 28.

34 *Mathematics*, pp. 30–31, 105.

35 *Investigations*, 610, and *Psychology* 1:552–553.

36 *Psychology* 1:804.

37 Perfume experts and other professionals may be able to improve on ordinary

performance in this area, but Wittgenstein's phenomenological remarks are reasonable enough for most of us.

38 *Tractatus*, 5.5423, 5.634.

39 *Brown Book*, pp. 141–43.

40 *Notebooks*, pp. 85–86, entry of 20.10.16, and p. 117.

41 *Brown Book*, pp. 162–63, 167–69.

42 *Zettel*, 221–22, 224.

43 Ibid., 223, and *Psychology* 1:1066.

44 *Psychology* 2:570, or *Zettel*, 225.

45 *Grammar*, 118.

46 *Psychology* 1:919–20.

47 Ibid., 991, and *Investigations*, p. 198.

48 *Investigations*, 536.

49 *Psychology* 2:219, 356.

50 *Grammar*, 130, and *Investigations*, p. 206.

51 *Grammar*, 126–27.

52 Whatever Wittgenstein's links to phenomenology, "bracketing" is not an operation that he thought could be successfully carried out.

53 *Culture and Value*, p. 23.

54 *Grammar*, 127.

55 *Remarks*, 214–15, and *Psychology* 1:1044–45.

56 *Psychology* 2:438–42.

57 *Investigations*, p. 198.

58 *Remarks*, 216.

59 *Psychology* 1:1–3, 8, 11.

60 Ibid. 2:472, and *Investigations*, pp. 212–14.

61 *Investigations*, pp. 193–95.

62 *Remarks*, 213.

63 *Psychology* 2:383.

64 *Investigations*, p. 54, paragraph (b) at bottom of page.

65 Ibid., p. 228.

66 Ibid., p. 180. See the discussion of *seeing as* in A. Wilson, "Picture Theory and the Duck-Rabbit."

67 *Psychology* 1:422, 427, and *Investigations*, p. 195.

68 *Investigations*, p. 195.

69 Ibid., pp. 196–97.

70 *Psychology* 2:373–74.

71   Ibid. 1:70.

72   Ibid. 2:492.

73   *Investigations*, pp. 193, 197–98.

74   *Psychology* 2:38.

75   Ibid., 496

76   *Brown Book*, pp. 141–42.

Chapter 8: Feeling

1   *Zettel*, 472, 483, 621, or *Psychology* 2:63. Wittgenstein's treatment of psychological topics gave rise to something called *philosophical psychology*, whose highwater mark is perhaps suitably represented by Kenny, *Action, Emotion, and Will*. See the criticisms of Kenny, however, in J.R.S. Wilson, *Emotion and Object*. I return in the last chapter to a consideration of the reason that development may have led to diminishing returns.

2   *Zettel*, 621 (or *Psychology* 2:63), and *Psychology* 1:458 (or *Investigations*, p. 174).

3   *Zettel*, 485, or *Psychology* 2:499.

4   *Remarks*, 64–65.

5   *Psychology* 2:659, and *Investigations*, 282–84.

6   *Zettel*, 545.

7   *Psychology* 1:313.

8   "Wittgenstein's Notes for Lectures on 'Private Experience' and 'Sense Data,' " p. 301.

9   *Investigations*, 404–5.

10   *Remarks*, 62–66, and *Psychology* 1:913.

11   *Psychology* 1:314.

12   *Zettel*, 552, and *Investigations*, 300.

13   *Zettel*, 498, or *Psychology* 1:440.

14   *Investigations*, p. 223.

15   *Zettel*, 540.

16   *Investigations*, 350–51.

17   Ibid., 391.

18   *Brown Book*, p. 103, and *Zettel*, 488.

19   *Psychology* 1:836.

20   *Zettel*, 504, or *Psychology* 1:959.

21   *Psychology* 1:127.

22 *Investigations*, p. 189.

23 "Wittgenstein's Notes for Lectures on 'Private Experience' and 'Sense Data' " pp. 303–4.

24 *Zettel*, 526, or *Psychology* 2:324.

25 *Investigations*, p. 174, and *Psychology* 1:324.

26 *Investigations*, p. 187.

27 *Psychology* 1:807.

28 Ibid., 137, 856, 896, 988; 2:129

29 *Zettel*, 549.

30 "Wittgenstein's Notes for Lectures on 'Private Experience' and 'Sense Data' " p. 278.

31 *Grammar*, 30.

32 "Wittgenstein's Notes for Lectures on 'Private Experience' and 'Sense Data' " pp. 317–18.

33 Wittgenstein's patterns of pleasure are not complicated enough to cover the notions available in the literature. From the standpoint of Lacan's economy of pleasure, for example, Wittgenstein remains in the realm of the signifier, providing not even a hint of the possibility of *jouissance*.

34 *Investigations*, p. 185.

35 Wittgenstein's phenomenology is restricted to what appears to consciousness, treating what may not be accessible to consciousness as a topic for scientific speculation. It is not clear that a division of labor can be worked out in this manner, with philosophy attending to grammar, and science to physiology. Although philosophy may adopt blinders with respect to physiology, the reverse is hardly plausible. If philosophy comes to clarify what we can say in various circumstances, it relinquishes all claims to explanation as to why we might say it. Clarity is achieved by a severe restriction of the relevant domain, and the restricted domain is probably highly unstable in the face of scientific discovery, even if some of ordinary language (not including scientific assertion) has been relatively stable in certain respects for centuries.

36 Images, in short, need not be pictures of reality. *Psychology* 2:80, and *Zettel*, 627.

37 *Psychology* 1:615, and *Zettel*, 341.

38 The drawings of M. C. Escher, frequently reproduced, show paradoxes of this kind. Local portions of the drawings may be consistent, but the complete drawings cannot be pictures of a consistent physical reality. See, for example, the reproductions and discussion in Ernst, *The Magic Mirror*, pp. 42–57.

39   *Zettel*, 275, or *Psychology* 1:826. The impossibility of picturing sufficiently abstract objects or infinite collections has a philosophical history, including a notable discussion in Berkeley's philosophy.

40   *Psychology* 1:172, 248, and *Investigations*, pp. 175–76.

41   *Psychology* 1:262, and *Investigations*, p. 177.

42   See *Investigations*, pp. 175–78, on the control over nonsense in images.

43   *Psychology* 1:359.

44   Ibid., 836.

45   Ibid., 760; 2:85.

46   Ibid. 1:885; 2:111 (or *Zettel*, 637).

47   *Psychology* 2:107.

48   Ibid., 69, 109.

49   *Zettel*, 621, or *Psychology* 2:63.

50   *Psychology* 2:543, and *Investigations*, p. 213.

51   *Psychology* 2:508, 513.

52   See *Psychology* 1:360, 726, 885; 2:449, and *Investigations*, 450, and p. 207. The language of imaging and imagining is involved with special language games, such as those connected with acting or giving impressions. Wittgenstein is objecting to the supposed *explanation* that these activities can be carried out only by forming a mental image and then copying it, where a mental image is meant to refer to an inner picture that we can "see" in some sense. Just as we may directly "see" something without forming an image of it in this sense, so we can mimic someone without first forming an inner image of what we are going to do. If we say that we have an image of so-and-so playing the trombone in such-and-such a way and then give an impression, the talk of images may serve only to explain what we are doing (that is, giving an impression), not to explain how we are doing it. The philosopher slides into pseudoexplanations by interpreting the relevant remarks on the model of scientific explanation and scientific assertion.

53   *Zettel*, 653–54.

54   *Investigations*, 649. Remembering how to do something, such as riding a bicycle or getting a desired color by mixing other colors, is an example of a nonverbal memory, since it cannot be described in detail. On the whole, Wittgenstein concentrates on verbal memory.

55   *Psychology* 1:159.

56   Ibid., 47.

57   Ibid. 2:596, or *Zettel*, 666.

58   *Psychology* 1:837.

59 *Investigations*, 342.

60 *Psychology* 1:716. In ordinary usage, we can perfectly well ask what people remember—say, of an event. Wittgenstein is here cautioning against the philosopher's question and the hypostatization of an inner process that follows in its wake.

61 *Remarks*, 49–50.

62 *Psychology* 1:378.

63 *Zettel*, 396–98, and *Psychology* 1:371. See also Malcolm, *Dreaming*, for an extended discussion.

64 *Psychology* 1:363. This claim, of course, could be subject to modification by scientific research. Observations of the eye movements of sleeping persons could conceivably reveal patterns common to various dreamers that are correlated with specific dream content, but this research has not as yet reached a point where Wittgenstein's dream phenomenology can be directly challenged. My point here is simply that it could be challenged.

65 Again, recent scientific research suggests that dreaming is quite normal but that our ability to recall our dreams is variable, depending on such factors as when we are awakened. The mere possibility of such discoveries is sufficient to indicate that our talk about dreams and the phenomenology of that talk could undergo a dramatic shift in the light of certain kinds of discoveries.

66 Wittgenstein's references to dream narratives in the now-published work are all to narratives that might be given in waking life or to daydreaming episodes. A peculiar feature of dream reports thus seems entirely overlooked, a mystery in that Wittgenstein himself, like many of us, seems to have been tormented by certain recurrent and pressing dreams. See the controversial discussion in Bartley, *Wittgenstein*.

Chapter 9: Psychology

1 *Psychology* 2:192, and *Zettel*, 129. Wittgenstein did not anticipate the development of computers nor the current reactions of some computer users to their interaction with computers.

2 *Psychology* 1:198.

3 Ibid., 165.

4 Ibid., 173, and *Zettel*, 1.

5 *Tractatus*, 5.541–5.542.

6 *Blue Book*, p. 30.

7 *Psychology* 1:671.

8   *Zettel*, 99. The language game in question can be interpreted in this way.

9   *Psychology* 2:12.

10 Ibid., 7–9.

11 Ibid., 217.

12 *Investigations*, 357–60.

13 Ibid., 470.

14 *Psychology* 1:184, 875.

15 Ibid. 2:253, and *Zettel*, 88.

16 *Psychology* 2:565. The difficulty one has in trying to express oneself in a foreign language that one is learning is well known to language students. Although it does not prove any connection between language and thought, we seem to formulate our thoughts in a language that we know and then attempt translation, or nothing occurs to us. We cannot seem to express our thoughts except in a linguistic medium. (I do not mean that we cannot think if we are not consciously formulating our thoughts.)

17 *Investigations*, 385.

18 The distinction between *knowing how* and *knowing that*, once central to analytical discussion of kinds of knowing, is not at issue here, since the variety projected by Wittgenstein is meant to be much more complex.

19 *Zettel*, 565. The phrase "picture of a mental process" here refers to the fact that the picture is hardened by grammar and determines the facts, rather than vice versa. Wittgenstein is one of the most naturalistic of modern philosophers, refusing a sharp separation between animal and human and allowing that human behavior, including behavior that is linguistically refined, has deep animal roots. The sharp separation is defended either theologically or philosophically, but always as a prejudice. At *Investigations*, 25, Wittgenstein refuses the notion that animals do not talk because they do not think, which is part of the philosophical defense. See also the intimations of these views in *Zettel*, 564, and the remarks in *Investigations*, p. 184.

20 *Grammar*, 10.

21 *Zettel*, 557.

22 *Color*, p. 63, 350, and *Psychology* 1:736 (or *Zettel*, 191).

23 *Investigations*, 78.

24 *Color*, p. 58, 311–12.

25 It is clear that, if Wittgenstein had developed his epistemology, what constituted knowing something would vary between the quarters of the City and, even at times, within the quarters. Standard analyses, such as the variations of the justified true belief analyses, give assertions of knowledge a uniform analysis, with some peculiar results. For a discussion, see Ackermann, "Context Dependent Knowledge."

26 *Certainty,* 593.

27 *Psychology* 2:285.

28 *Certainty,* 176.

29 *Psychology* 1:477, 480.

30 Knowledge and belief must be attained and possibly defended. Wittgenstein's analysis places both in contexts in which they have widely ramified consequences over time. In addition to direct expression, it is difficult to interpret remarks such as that at *Psychology* 1:748, unless this temporal spread is being referred to.

31 These statements are outright contradictions only if both occurrences of *know* or of *believe* are exactly the same, but Wittgenstein's acceptance of polysemy allows these expressions to play an occasional meaningful role in language use. It is useful to remember that Wittgenstein does not think that contradiction necessarily destroys the coherence of mathematical systems. See, for example, *Psychology* 2:418.

32 Ibid. 1:495.

33 *Investigations,* 574.

34 *Psychology* 2:344–45.

35 Ibid. 1:151; 2:303, and *Zettel* 408, 545.

36 *Psychology* 1:715. In common with most philosophers, Wittgenstein, in analyzing belief, does not accept the consequences of psychoanalytic theory to the effect that our beliefs (and even our knowledge) may often consist of elaborate rationalizations in the service of essentially irrational impulses.

37 Ibid. 2:282.

38 *Investigations,* pp. 190–92, 221, and *Psychology* 2:277.

39 *Certainty,* 204, 220–21.

40 Ibid., 102.

41 Ibid., 71–74.

42 Ibid., 88.

43 Ibid., 108.

44 *Investigations,* 575.

45 Ibid., p. 178.

46 *Certainty,* 478, 527.

47 Ibid., 160, 538.

48 Ibid., 473.

49 *Brown Book,* p. 105.

50 Wittgenstein's remarks on training seem uninformed when compared to the modern literature on language learning. If we do generate language according to innate structures until we reach agreement with the language we hear about us, rather than learning it by conditioning, as behaviorists had earlier argued, Wittgenstein's remarks

are still acceptable. His primary target is a philosophical account, and he is not attempting to provide a scientific explanation. The training remarks are an observation on our natural history, and their intention is merely to eliminate the supposed necessity of philosophical theories that assume that language can be explained to children.

51   *Investigations*, 32.

52   *Psychology* 1:588; 2:404.

53   *Certainty*, 496.

54   *Investigations*, p. 221.

55   Ibid., 627–32, p. 221.

56   *Certainty*, 552–53.

57   *Grammar*, 85, 87–89, 95.

58   *Psychology* 2:577.

59   Ibid., 180.

60   *Investigations*, 337, 571–72.

61   Ibid., 647.

62   *Psychology* 1:179, 1136.

63   *Investigations*, 2. The builder expects the building stones to be brought to him.

64   *Zettel*, 45.

65   *Investigations*, 576.

66   *Zettel*, 48.

67   *Grammar*, 98.

68   *Notebooks*, pp. 73–80 (various entry dates). Again in this connection, Wittgenstein is in the company of most philosophers, who ignore the implications of psychoanalytic theory and assume that our wills and the objects of willing are accessible to our introspection.

69   *Notebooks*, pp. 86–89, entry of 4.11.16. Biographical evidence suggests that the early Wittgenstein was heavily influenced in this respect by reading Schopenhauer.

70   *Investigations*, 614, 621–22.

71   Ibid., 628–29.

72   Ibid.

73   *Psychology* 1:776.

74   *King/Lee Lectures*, p. 40.

75   *Tractatus*, 5.63–5.641.

76   See Candlish, "The Real Private Language Argument."

77   *Psychology* 1:401–8.

78   *Zettel,* 426.

79   *Psychology* 1:395.

80   *Tractatus,* 5.641, and *Investigations,* p. 178.

81   *Psychology* 1:312, 985, and *Investigations,* p. 207. The beetle-in-the-box metaphor seems to express essentially the same idea at *Investigations,* 293.

82   *Investigations,* pp. 222–25, 228.

83   Ibid., 580.

84   *Psychology* 2:590.

85   Ibid. 1:287.

86   Ibid., 1133.

87   Ibid. 2:29.

Chapter 10: Philosophy

1   *Blue Book,* pp. 44–45. This image of a philosopher surveying and organizing human knowledge is taken from a surprisingly transcendental viewpoint.

2   *Investigations,* 10. At *Investigations,* 12, Wittgenstein makes the point by looking into the cabin of an old steam locomotive, where there is a dizzying variety of valves, cranks, etc. They are *used* quite differently, and the philosophical generalization that they are all controls is hardly revealing. The assertion to this effect in the training of engineers would be followed by a discussion of what each control does and how one operates it.

3   *Investigations,* 43.

4   Ibid., 41, 111.

5   *Brown Book,* p. 108.

6   The calculation here is simple. Let c be the earth's circumference, d the diameter of the earth, and d' the diameter of the circle formed by the lengthened rope when it is held everywhere equally from the earth's surface. If $c = \pi d$, then $c + 36'' = d'$. Regarding the earth as circular for simplicity, we may apply the familiar formula linking the circumference and the diameter of a circle. Substitution of πd for c and simplification yields $d' - d$ as approximately 11.46 inches. That is, the rope would everywhere be 5.73 inches from the earth's surface!

7   The anecdotes about his simple style of living are sufficiently available, but his architectural simplicity can be studied in the photographs in Leitner, *The Architecture of Ludwig Wittgenstein.*

8   *Certainty,* 132.

9 Kenny, "Wittgenstein and the Nature of Philosophy," pp. 21, 25.

10 *Zettel*, 455.

11 Kenny, "Wittgenstein and the Nature of Philosophy," pp. 17–19.

12 *Investigations*, 206.

13 Ibid., 128.

14 *Remarks*, 3, especially p. 53, lines 3–6. Wittgenstein has been read as holding, early and late, that he seeks the essence of language. See, for example, Bogen, *Wittgenstein's Philosophy of Language*, p. 3, and Llewelyn's insightful comment in his review of that book ("Wittgenstein Reinvestigated," p. 431). The pivotal point here is the text of *Investigations*, 92, which Llewelyn observes must be read under its important opening condition.

15 For a convenient survey of attempts to make Wittgenstein's notion of *criterion* precise, see Canfield, *Wittgenstein*. Criteria, incidentally, could be in question only in linguistically articulated language games, not in the areas of primitive behavior from which such language games can emerge. See Hintikka, "Wittgensteinian Investigations," p. 375.

16 See Morstein, "Erfahrung bei Ludwig Wittgenstein," p. 133.

17 *Tractatus*, 6.41–6.42, 6.422.

18 "A Lecture on Ethics," p. 5. The public uses of *good* and *beautiful* in a non-absolute sense could be replacements of primitive gestures of approval, bringing what can be asserted here into line with Wittgenstein's other psychological language terms.

19 Ibid., p. 11.

20 *Tractatus*, 6.41. As noted earlier, Wittgenstein's considerations on rule following have recently been adopted in one form to undermine various noncognitive and relativist positions in ethical theory. See McDowell, "Non-cognitivism and Rule-following," as well as other papers in the volume in which McDowell's paper appears, and Wiggins, "Truth, Invention, and Meaning." Although differing among themselves, the defenders of this line of argument want to conflate mathematics and ethics as offering various assertions that cannot be questioned within our form of life. For an argument against this conflation, see Lear, "Ethics, Mathematics, and Relativism." Lear repackages the old intuition that we do not observe significant cross-cultural variations in elementary mathematics, although we do in ethics, to attack variations of the line of argument just mentioned, although he goes on to suggest reasons against accepting relativism. In "Leaving the World Alone," p. 392, Lear supports the idea that there are no alternative conceptual schemes in Wittgenstein that would license relativism, following a line of argument somewhat independent of the usual literature. We do observe that ethical discourse in various

cultures differs, but these disputes are based only on Wittgensteinian ideas. Wittgenstein did not think that there were any nontrivial ethical language games. The two branches of traditional philosophical analysis of mathematics and ethics cannot be brought into this kind of comparison, if Wittgenstein is right.

21   *Remarks*, Foreword, p. 7.

22   *Culture and Value*, p. 28.

23   *Zettel*, 717.

24   *Culture and Value*, p. 53. Prayer *is* mentioned as a language game at *Investigations*, 23. The idea that Wittgenstein might have been a sort of unwitting Buddhist is traced out by amassing parallels in Gudmunsen, *Wittgenstein and Buddhism*.

25   As they have been in other areas, language-game notions have been extended into the philosophy of religion. See Hudson, *Wittgenstein and Religious Belief*, and Phillips, *The Concept of Prayer*.

26   G. Wright, "Wittgenstein on Certainty."

27   Ver Eecke, Translator's Introduction, pp. 1–25. Nyiri points out that, on the basis of *Zettel*, 371–72, the feeble-minded, who will not play many of our language games, will not live in Wittgenstein's City, ("Wittgenstein's Later Work," p. 66). Nyiri's work on Wittgenstein's conservatism is extremely suggestive, but see the criticism in Schulte, "Wittgenstein and Conservatism."

28   Ver Eecke, Translator's Introduction, p. 9. I would like to thank Ver Eecke for calling this point to my attention at the University of Massachusetts Lacan Conference, June 1985.

29   See Hester, *The Meaning of Poetic Metaphor*, for an analysis of poetic language, especially metaphor, in the light of Wittgenstein's theories of language. The extension beyond Wittgenstein's analysis of literal usage to involve imagery is noted on ibid., p. 213. An earlier attempt to use Wittgenstein's complexity of linguistic analysis can be found in Casey, *The Language of Criticism*. A quite recent attempt to use Wittgenstein to criticize the assumptions of deconstructive theory, among other topics, can be found in Guetti, "Wittgenstein and Literary Theory." Deconstructive critics can counter with their own deconstructive Wittgenstein. See Staten, *Wittgenstein and Derrida*. Different people have their own Wittgenstein and their own language games, and Wittgenstein is constantly used to license complexity and relativity. Wittgenstein's controlling intuitions are ignored in these extensions.

30   *Investigations*, 23. See also Funke, "Einheitssprache, Sprachspiel, und Sprachauslegung bei Wittgenstein," p. 218.

31   *Culture and Value*, p. 1.

32   *Investigations*, p. 226. See also *Certainty*, 239, which in context seems to

discuss what stands fast for certain people (*Certainty*, 235) and need not be interpreted as holding that these conflicting assertions can all be maintained in the total interweave of language and life.

33   As should by now be familiar, recent studies have undercut the old disputes about color objectivism and color relativism. See Berlin and Kay, *Basic Color Terms*. Wittgenstein's objectivism is not inconsistent with these investigations.

34   *Investigations*, p. 223.

35   Ibid., 19.

36   Ibid., 23, especially lines 8–10, and *Mathematics*, p. 96, 70. *Ambrose Lectures*, p. 88, suggests that so-called savages would use directional arrows in the same way that we do. See Baker, "Form of Life," for some interesting comments on the inexpressible aspects of forms of life.

37   *Investigations*, 241. "The common behavior of human beings" does not refer to a notion that all humans behave in the same way, which would be absurd, but to the idea that there are recognizably human ways of behaving. See Hintikka, "Wittgensteinian Investigations," p. 44. As shown in his "Remarks on Frazer's *Golden Bough*," Wittgenstein was sensitive to possible cross-cultural differences within the common human domain but believed that they could be overcome by understanding.

38   *Investigations*, p. 174.

39   *Psychology* 1:1039, and *Investigations*, p. 232.

40   The relevant issues in the philosophy of science are discussed in Ackermann, *Data, Instruments, and Theory*.

41   *Tractatus*, 4.1121.

42   *Psychology* 1:904, and *Zettel*, 608–9.

43   Bloor, *Wittgenstein*, pp. 6–21.

44   *Investigations*, 23.

45   Pitkin, *Wittgenstein and Justice*, p. 314; Danford, *Wittgenstein and Political Philosophy*. Such books relate Wittgenstein's ideas to political theory. As with earlier omissions in Wittgenstein's City, a viable social theory would have to be an *extension* of Wittgenstein's ideas. See, for example, the provocative explorations in Bloor, *Wittgenstein*. Experiments with people isolated from normal life, living in a cave or cell without direct knowledge of sunlight and without social interaction, show that they lose track of objective time periods and even lose the ability to express themselves coherently. Wittgenstein's social anchor simply provides an abstract external reference point for what would otherwise be internal chaos. As for linking Marx and Wittgenstein, see Benton, "Winch, Wittgenstein, and Marxism"; Rossi-Landi, "Towards a Marxian Use of Wittgenstein"; and Rubinstein, *Marx and Wittgenstein*. As

Benton and Cook (see his "Hegel, Marx and Wittgenstein") note, conflations such as Rubinstein's must overlook quite essential differences between Marx and Wittgenstein. Wittgenstein has no concept of social class or of differences between people (although people's language usage can vary) and no concept of a *collective mistaken practice* (as opposed to religious or philosophical nonsensical word play). There is no evidence that Wittgenstein thought that clarifying language would have social implications.

46   Hanson, *Patterns of Discovery*, is an interesting and sympathetic attempt to extend Wittgensteinian insights into the philosophy of science. On the function of argument in science, which is not conceived merely as an expression of emotional attachment to one's own views, see Ackermann, *Data, Instruments, and Theory*, pp. 36–40, 62–68.

BIBLIOGRAPHY

Works by Wittgenstein

Works by Wittgenstein are cited in the footnotes by title, often a shortened title, and numbers for pages and paragraphs. Numbers by themselves always refer to paragraphs in the work cited.

Ambrose Lectures (see *Wittgenstein's Lectures: Cambridge, 1932–1935*).

The Blue and Brown Books. 2d ed. New York: Harper and Brothers, 1960. "The Blue Book," pp. 1–74; "The Brown Book," pp. 75–185.

Certainty (see *On Certainty*).

Color (see *Remarks on Colour*).

Culture and Value. Edited by G. H. von Wright. Chicago: University of Chicago Press, 1980.

Grammar (see *Philosophical Grammar*).

Investigations (see *Philosophical Investigations*).

King/Lee Lectures (see *Wittgenstein's Lectures: Cambridge, 1930–1932*).

"A Lecture on Ethics." Edited by Rush Rhees. *Philosophical Review* 74 (1965): 3–12.

Mathematics (see *Remarks on the Foundations of Mathematics*).

Notebooks: 1914–1916. Edited by G. H. von Wright and G. E. M. Anscombe. Oxford: Basil Blackwell, 1969.

On Certainty. Edited by G. E. M. Anscombe and G. H. von Wright. New York: Harper Editions, 1969.

Philosophical Grammar. Edited by Rush Rhees. Berkeley: University of California Press, 1974.

Philosophical Investigations. 3d ed. New York: Macmillan, 1969.

Philosophical Remarks. Edited by Rush Rhees. New York: Barnes and Noble, 1975.

Psychology (see *Remarks on the Philosophy of Psychology*).

Remarks (see *Philosophical Remarks*).

Remarks on Colour. Edited by G. E. M. Anscombe. Berkeley: University of California Press, 1977.

"Remarks on Frazer's *Golden Bough."* In *Wittgenstein: Sources and Perspectives,* edited by C. G. Luckhardt, pp. 61–81. Ithaca: Cornell University Press, 1979.

Remarks on the Foundations of Mathematics. Edited by G. H. von Wright, Rush Rhees, and G. E. M. Anscombe. Cambridge: MIT Press, 1967. Rev. ed., 1978.

Remarks on the Philosophy of Psychology. 2 vols. Edited by G. E. M. Anscombe and G. H. von Wright. Chicago: University of Chicago Press, 1980.

"Some Remarks on Logical Form." *Aristotelian Society,* supp. vol. 9 (1929): 162–71. Reprinted in *Essays on Wittgenstein's "Tractatus,"* edited by Robert Beard and Irving Copi, pp. 31–37. New York: Macmillan, 1966.

Tractatus Logico-Philosophicus. Edited by D. F. Pears and B. F. McGuinness. New York: Humanities Press, 1972.

Wittgenstein's Lectures: Cambridge, 1930–1932. From the notes of John King and Desmond Lee. Edited by Desmond Lee. Chicago: University of Chicago Press, 1980.

Wittgenstein's Lectures: Cambridge, 1932–1935. From the notes of Alice Ambrose and Margaret Macdonald. Edited by Alice Ambrose. Chicago: University of Chicago Press, 1979.

"Wittenstein's Notes for Lectures on 'Private Experience' and 'Sense Data.' " Edited by Rush Rhees. *Philosophical Review* 77 (1968): 271–320.

Wörterbuch für Volksschulen. Edited by Adolf Hübner, Elisabeth Leinfellner, and Werner Leinfellner. Vienna: Hölder-Pichler-Tempsky, 1977.

Zettel. Edited by G. E. M. Anscombe and G. H. von Wright. Oxford: Basil Blackwell, 1967.

Other Works Cited in Text

Ackermann, Inge; Ackermann, Robert; and Hendricks, Betty. "Wittgenstein's Fairy Tale." *Analysis* 38 (1978): 12–13.

Ackermann, Robert. "Context Dependent Knowledge." *Philosophy and Phenomenological Research* 42 (1981–82): 425–33.

———*Data, Instruments, and Theory.* Princeton: Princeton University Press, 1985.

Allaire, Edwin B. "Tractatus 6.3751." In *Essays on Wittgenstein's "Tractatus,"* edited by Robert Beard and Irving Copi, pp. 189–93. New York: Macmillan, 1966. Originally published in *Analysis* 19 (1959): 100–105.

Austin, James. "Wittgenstein's Solutions to the Color Exclusion Problem." *Philosophy and Phenomenological Research* 41 (1980–81): 142–49.

Bachmaier, Peter. *Wittgenstein und Kant: Versuch zum Begriff dem Transzendentalen.* Frankfurt am Main: Lang, 1978

Baker, Gordon P., and Hacker, Peter M. S. *Language, Sense, and Nonsense: A Critical Investigation into Modern Theories of Language.* Oxford: Basil Blackwell, 1984.

———. *Scepticism, Rules, and Language.* Oxford: Basil Blackwell, 1984.

———. *Wittgenstein: Understanding and Meaning,* vol. 1. Chicago: University of Chicago Press, 1980.

Baker, Lynne Rudder. "On the Very Idea of a Form of Life." *Inquiry* 27 (1984): 277–89.

Bartley, William Warren. *Wittgenstein.* Philadelphia: Lippincott, 1973.

Beard, Robert W., and Copi, Irving M., eds. *Essays on Wittgenstein's "Tractatus."* New York: Macmillan, 1966.

Benton, Ted. "Winch, Wittgenstein, and Marxism." *Radical Philosophy, no. 13* (Spring 1976): 1–6.

Bergmann, Gustav. "The Glory and Misery of Ludwig Wittgenstein." Chapter in *Logic and Reality,* pp. 225–41. Madison: University of Wisconsin Press, 1964.

Berlin, Brent, and Kay, Paul. *Basic Color Terms.* Berkeley: University of California Press, 1969.

Bloor, David. *Wittgenstein: A Social Theory of Knowledge.* New York: Columbia University Press, 1983.

Bogen, James. *Wittgenstein's Philosophy of Language: Some Aspects of Its Development.* London: Routledge and Kegan Paul, 1972.

Candlish, Stewart. "The Real Private Language Argument." *Philosophy* 55 (1980): 85–94.

Canfield, John V. *Wittgenstein: Language and the World.* Amherst: University of Massachusetts Press, 1981.

Carnap, Rudolf. *Der logische Aufbau der Welt.* Berlin, 1928. Revised edition, Hamburg: Meiner, 1961. Translated as *The Logical Structure of the World.* Berkeley: University of California Press, 1967.

Casey, John. *The Language of Criticism.* London: Methuen, 1966.

Cavell, Stanley. "The Availability of Wittgenstein's Later Philosophy." Chapter in *Must We Mean What We Say?* pp. 44–72. New York: Scribner's Sons, 1969.

Cook, Daniel J. "Hegel, Marx, and Wittgenstein." *Philosophy and Social Criticism* 10, no. 2 (1984): 49–74.

Danford, John W. *Wittgenstein and Political Philosophy.* Chicago: University of Chicago Press, 1978.

Daniels, Charles B., and Davidson, John. "Ontology and Method in Wittgenstein's *Tractatus.*" *Nous* 7 (1973): 233–47.

Drury, M. O. *The Danger of Words.* New York: Humanities Press, 1973.

Dummett, Michael. "Frege and Wittgenstein." In *Perspectives on the Philosophy of Wittgenstein,* edited by Irving Block, pp. 31–42. Cambridge: MIT Press, 1981.

Ernst, Bruno. *The Magic Mirror of M. C. Escher.* New York: Random House, 1976.

Fogelin, Robert J. *Wittgenstein.* London: Routledge and Kegan Paul, 1976.

Fromm, Susanne. *Wittgensteins Erkenntnislspiele contra Kants Erkenntnislehre.* Freiburg: Alber, 1979.

Funke, Gerhard. "Einheitssprache, Sprachspiel, und Sprachauslegung bei Wittgenstein." *Zeitschrift für philosophische Forschung* 22 (1968): 1–30, 216–47.

Gier, Nicholas. *Wittgenstein and Phenomenology.* Albany: State University of New York Press, 1981.

Goodman, Nelson. *Languages of Art.* Indianapolis: Bobbs-Merrill, 1968.

———. *The Structure of Appearance.* 2d ed. Indianapolis: Bobbs-Merrill, 1966.

Gudmunsen, Chris. *Wittgenstein and Buddhism.* London: Macmillan, 1977.

Guetti, James. "Wittgenstein and Literary Theory." *Raritan* 4, no. 2 (1984–85): 67–84; no. 3: 66–84.

Hacker, Peter M. S. "Laying the Ghost of the *Tractatus.*" *Review of Metaphysics* 29 (1975): 96–116.

———. "The Rise and Fall of the Picture Theory." In *Perspectives on the Philosophy of Wittgenstein,* edited by Irving Block, pp. 85–109. Cambridge: MIT Press, 1981.

Haller, Rudolf. "Die gemeinsame menschliche Handlungsweise." *Zeitschrift für philosophische Forschung* 23 (1969): 521–33.

Halmos, Paul R. *Naive Set Theory.* Princeton: Van Nostrand, 1960.

Hanson, Norwood R. *Patterns of Discovery.* Cambridge: Cambridge University Press, 1958.

Hester, Marcus B. *The Meaning of Poetic Metaphor.* The Hague: Mouton, 1967.

Hintikka, Merrill B. "Wittgensteinian Investigations: Toward a Unified Interpretation of Ludwig Wittgenstein's Philosophy." Ph.D. diss., Stanford University, 1982.

Holtzman, Steven H., and Leich, Christopher M., ed. *Wittgenstein: To Follow a Rule.* London: Routledge and Kegan Paul, 1981.

Hudson, William Donald. *Wittgenstein and Religious Belief.* London: Macmillan, 1975.

Ishiguro, Hidé. "Wittgenstein and the Theory of Types." In *Perspectives on the Phi-*

losophy of Wittgenstein, edited by Irving Block, pp. 43–59. Cambridge: MIT Press, 1981.

Kenny, Anthony. *Action, Emotion, and Will.* London: Routledge and Kegan Paul, 1963.

———. "The Ghost of the *Tractatus.*" Chapter in *The Legacy of Wittgenstein*, pp. 10–23. Oxford: Basil Blackwell, 1984.

———. *Wittgenstein.* Cambridge: Harvard University Press, 1973.

———. "Wittgenstein on the Nature of Philosophy." In *Wittgenstein and His Times*, edited by Brian McGuinness, pp. 1–26. Chicago: University of Chicago Press, 1982.

Koenne, Werner. "Rekursive Techniken und der Tractat." In *Österreichische Philosophen und ihr Einfluss auf die analytische Philosophie der Gegenwart*, edited by J. C. Marek, J. Zelger, H. Gauthaler, and R. Born. *Conceptus* (Sonderband) 11 (1977): 289–303.

Kreisel, Georg. "Wittgenstein's *Remarks on the Foundations of Mathematics.*" *British Journal for the Philosophy of Science* 9 (1958–59): 135–58.

Kripke, Saul A. *Wittgenstein on Rules and Private Language.* Cambridge: Harvard University Press, 1982.

Lear, Jonathan. "Ethics, Mathematics, and Relativism." *Mind* 92 (1983): 38–60.

———. "Leaving the World Alone." *Journal of Philosophy* 79 (1982): 382–403.

Leinfellner, Elisabeth; Haller, Rudolf; Hübner, Adolf; Leinfellner, Werner; and Weingartner, Paul, eds. *Language, Logic, and Philosophy.* Proceedings of the Fourth International Wittgenstein Symposium. Vienna: Hölder-Pichler-Tempsky, 1980.

Leitner, Bernhard. *The Architecture of Ludwig Wittgenstein.* Halifax: Press of the Nova Scotia College of Art and Design, 1973.

Llewelyn, John E. "Wittgenstein Reinvestigated." *Inquiry* 16 (1973): 431–45.

McDowell, John. "Non-cognitivism and Rule-following." In *Wittgenstein: To Follow a Rule*, edited by Steven Holtzman and Christopher Leich, pp. 141–62. London: Routledge and Kegan Paul, 1981.

Malcolm, Norman. *Dreaming.* London: Routledge and Kegan Paul, 1959.

———. "Wittgenstein: The Relation of Language to Instinctive Behaviour." *Philosophical Investigations* 5 (1982): 3–22.

Marshack, Alexander. "Implications of the Paleolithic Symbolic Evidence for the Origin of Language." *American Scientist* 64 (1976): 136–45.

Morstein, Petra V. "Erfahrung bei Ludwig Wittgenstein." *Archiv für Philosophie* 12 (1963–64): 133–51.

Nedo, Michael, and Ranchetti, Michele, eds. *Ludwig Wittgenstein: Sein Leben in Bildern und Texten.* Frankfurt am Main: Suhrkamp, 1983.

Nyíri, J. C. "Wittgenstein's Later Work in Relation to Conservatism." In *Wittgenstein and His Times*, edited by Brian McGuinness, pp. 44–68. Chicago: University of Chicago Press, 1982.

Phillips, Dewi Zephanian. *The Concept of Prayer.* London: Routledge and Kegan Paul, 1965.

Pitkin, Hanna Fenichel. *Wittgenstein and Justice.* Berkeley: University of California Press, 1972.

Rhees, Rush. "Wittgenstein on Language and Ritual." In *Wittgenstein and His Times*, edited by Brian McGuinness, pp. 69–107. Chicago: University of Chicago Press, 1982.

Ronchi, Vasco. *New Optics.* Florence: Olschki, 1971.

Rossi-Landi, Ferruccio. "Towards a Marxian Use of Wittgenstein." In *Austrian Philosophy Studies and Texts*, edited by J. C. Nyíri, pp. 113–49. Munich: Philosophia, 1981.

Rubinstein, David. *Marx and Wittgenstein: Social Praxis and Social Explanation.* London: Routledge and Kegan Paul, 1981.

Schulte, Joachim. "Wittgenstein and Conservatism." *Ratio* 25 (1983): 69–80.

Sellars, Wilfrid. "Naming and Saying." Chapter in *Science, Perception, and Reality*, pp. 225–46. New York: Humanities Press, 1963.

Shwayder, D. S. "Gegenstände and Other Matters: Observations Occasioned by a New Commentary on the *Tractatus.*" *Inquiry* 7 (1964): 387–413.

Spiegelberg, Herbert. "The Puzzle of Wittgenstein's Phänomenologie (1929–?)." *American Philosophical Quarterly* 5 (1968): 244–56.

Staten, Henry. *Wittgenstein and Derrida.* Lincoln: University of Nebraska Press, 1984.

Stenius, Erik. "The Picture Theory and Wittgenstein's Later Attitude to It." In *Perspectives on the Philosophy of Wittgenstein*, edited by Irving Block, pp. 110–39. Cambridge: MIT Press, 1981.

———. *Wittgenstein's "Tractatus": A Critical Exposition of Its Main Lines of Thought.* Oxford: Basil Blackwell, 1960.

Suits, Bernard. *The Grasshopper.* Toronto: University of Toronto Press, 1978.

Thiele, Susanne. *Die Verwicklungen im Denken Wittgensteins.* Freiburg: Alber, 1983.

Ver Eecke, Wilfrid. Translator's Introduction to *Schizophrenia*, by Alphonse De Waelhens, pp. 1–25. Pittsburgh: Duquesne University Press, 1972.

Wiggins, David. "Truth, Invention, and the Meaning of Life." *Proceedings of the British Academy* 67 (1976): 331–78.

Wilson, Arnold. "The Picture Theory and the Duck-Rabbit." In *Wittgenstein, The Vienna Circle and Critical Rationalism*, edited by Hal Berghel, Adolf Hübner Eckehard Köhlei, pp. 149-151. Vienna: Hölder-Pichler-Tempsky, 1979.

Wilson, J. R. S. *Emotion and Object.* Cambridge: Cambridge University Press, 1972.

Winch, Peter. "Im Anfang war die Tat." In *Perspectives on the Philosophy of Wittgenstein*, edited by Irving Block, pp. 159–78. Cambridge: MIT Press, 1981.

———. "Introduction: The Unity of Wittgenstein's Philosophy." In *Studies in the Philosophy of Wittgenstein*, edited by Peter Winch, pp. 1–19. London: Routledge and Kegan Paul, 1969.

———. "Understanding a Primitive Society." *American Philosophical Quarterly* (1964): 307–24.

Wright, Crispin. *Wittgenstein on the Foundations of Mathematics.* Cambridge: Harvard University Press, 1980.

Wright, Georg Hendrik von. "Wittgenstein on Certainty." Chapter in *Wittgenstein*, pp. 163–82. Minneapolis: University of Minnesota Press, 1983.

INDEX